D1426416

C334547570

It Takes Two

BY THE SAME AUTHOR

Bloody Brilliant Women

It Takes Two

A History of the Couples Who Dared to be Different

CATHY NEWMAN

WILLIAM
COLLINS

William Collins
An imprint of HarperCollins*Publishers*
1 London Bridge Street
London SE1 9GF

WilliamCollinsBooks.com

First published in Great Britain in 2020 by William Collins

1

ISBN 978-0-00-836333-8 (hardback)
ISBN 978-0-00-836334-5 (trade paperback)

Typeset in Adobe Caslon Pro by Palimpsest Book Production Ltd,
Falkirk, Stirlingshire

Printed and bound in Great Britain by CPI Group (UK) Ltd, Croydon CR0 4YY

MIX
Paper from
responsible sources
FSC® C007454

This book is produced from independently certified FSC™ paper
to ensure responsible forest management.

For more information visit: www.harpercollins.co.uk/green

It takes two in my life too: love, respect and gratitude to John and our dynamic duo Scarlett and Molly.

Contents

Introduction

One of the pleasures of promoting my last book, *Bloody Brilliant Women*, was doing the rounds of literary festivals and bookshops and getting the chance to meet readers. I'd never written a book before, so I had no idea what to expect. It was a wonderful feeling – and, I must admit, a relief – when the reception turned out to be so warm, generous and enthusiastic.

The book was a kind of alternative history of modern Britain: at its heart the forgotten heroines who played such a crucial part in our shared past. But something which surprised me when I chatted to readers at these events was the level of interest shown in stories about collaboration between couples – not just married or otherwise romantically linked couples, but other kinds of partnerships to do with, say, business, politics and scientific research. I hadn't realised until it was pointed out to me how many I'd included.

People seemed to enjoy reading about characters such as Louisa Garrett Anderson and Flora Murray, the doctors who formed the Women's Hospital Corps shortly after the outbreak of the First World War. They also liked Edith Lomax and her assistant Elsie Harrison, the two highest ranking women in MI5 during the same period. Very much thought of as a pair, this duo handled all personnel matters for the hundreds of women who worked for them, storing, classifying and retrieving secret documents in MI5's hallowed registry.

Moving further into the century, the Second World War gave us the mixed-gender pairing of Elsie Widdowson and Dr Robert McCance, Imperial College research partners whose vital work on food nutrition informed the wartime government's rationing programme. Then there were the architects Jane Drew and Edwin Maxwell Fry, who married in 1942 and worked together on projects such as the Rodent House at London Zoo, as well as housing and public buildings in Britain's colonial territories: after the partition of India in 1947 they were invited by Prime Minister Pandit Nehru to design Chandigarh, the new capital of Punjab.

One of my personal favourite couples from *Bloody Brilliant Women* is Jennie Lee, Minister of the Arts under Harold Wilson between 1964 and 1970, and her husband Aneurin 'Nye' Bevan, who helped to establish the National Health Service as minister of health in Clement Attlee's postwar Labour government. Lee's lasting legacy is the Open University, the 'university of the air' that used TV and radio as its teaching platforms. But really that had its roots in her relationship with Nye. Both were working-class autodidacts. Nye had helped to pay for his sisters to attend college. As a result, Lee explained, 'we knew, we both of us, from our backgrounds, that there were people in the mining villages who left school at fourteen or fifteen who had first-class intellects'.[1]

All of this set me thinking about the 'power of two' – the unique, contained bond that can form between two people and generate a particular kind of catalysing spark. There is something about a duo . . . a reason why Arthur Conan Doyle wrote about Holmes and Watson and not Holmes,

Watson and Mrs Hudson (no disrespect to their house-keeper); why we are fascinated by so-called 'odd couples' but not odd trios; why we love watching double acts and obsess over the antics of Hollywood couples; and why so many great achievements seem to have been the work of dual partner-ships, from Lennon and McCartney, to Marie and Pierre Curie, French and Saunders. But what is that something?

Perhaps one of the reasons I'm so drawn to duos like this is that I am not a natural collaborator. As a child, I ploughed my own furrow and was, I suspect, rather similar to Briony, the heroine of Ian McEwan's novel *Atonement*: 'one of those children possessed by a desire to have the world just so', as McEwan puts it.[2] Briony not only writes the play she puts on at the start, but designs the posters, programmes and tickets – and constructs the sales booth. Way to go, Briony!

Well, up to a point. In my professional life I've had to learn to be collegiate. Television – and to a lesser extent newspapers – relies on teamwork to get the programme to air or the paper to press.

Of course, nobody loves wishy-washy groupthink. But equally, while journalistic myth often glorifies the lone-wolf reporter, the biggest political scoop of the last fifty years – uncovering the Watergate scandal – was the achievement of two journalists working in tandem. Bob Woodward and Carl Bernstein at the *Washington Post* subsequently inspired one of the best-known cinematic pairings when Dustin Hoffman and Robert Redford played them in *All the President's Men*.

When I first joined *Channel 4 News* fifteen years ago, I realised there was a special magic about the relationship between correspondent and producer. In a good pairing, both halves of the couple know almost instinctively how to approach a story, who is doing what, and how to go from a standing start to three or four minutes of film by the end of the day.

In fact, duos are the linchpins of countless live TV shows: Ant and Dec, Phillip and Holly, Mel and Sue, Phil and Kirstie, Dick and Dom, Piers and Susanna, Richard and Judy. Many news programmes, including *Channel 4 News*, follow the convention.

It's nearly a decade since I started presenting the programme and I most often share the studio with veteran anchor Jon Snow. I have boundless respect for someone who has witnessed all the big moments in recent history – from the fall of the Berlin Wall to the release of Nelson Mandela. I've learnt an enormous amount from him about the presenter's craft. So on the rare occasions when I'm the solo anchor, the programme feels as if it's missing something, the studio rather cavernous, the business altogether lonelier. Even in TV, where big egos abound, it takes two, after all.

———————

The technical term for a basic unit of two individuals is a dyad. In the dry language of social network theorists, a dyad is 'an unordered pair of actors and the arcs that exist between the two actors in the pair'.[3] What matters is the nature of these 'arcs'. We could be talking about a strictly professional relationship. Or a romantic or sexual relationship. Or an intense friendship. Or what theorists call a multiplex, where the bond consists of two or more of those elements.

Dyads tend to work best horizontally rather than vertically. Things get awkward when the relationship becomes hierarchical – when one person, for whatever reason, moves into position above the other.

When this happens, it is not necessarily immediately obvious. To give another example from the world of television, back in 2016 there was much discussion in the media about whether it was correct for the *BBC Breakfast* presenter Louise Minchin to sit to the right of her co-anchor Dan Walker. In TV, the unwritten rule is that the 'main' presenter sits on the left. And patriarchy being what it is, this presenter is usually a man.

I sympathise with the feminist argument against it but, as I said at the time, I'm willing to bet that most viewers tune into *BBC Breakfast*, ITV's *News at Ten* or *Channel 4 News* without giving a second thought to presenter placement. What matters more is whether one half of the duo seems to have the upper hand or reduces the other half to a 'silent partner'. Generally, couples who have chemistry and seem to get on (Holly Willoughby and Phillip Schofield, say) do best; though it is possible to have chemistry and seem *not* to get on, as in the case of Piers Morgan and Susanna Reid on *Good Morning Britain*, who make a virtue of winding each other up (and, as far as I am aware, get on perfectly well offscreen).

Some of the most intriguing thinking about the power of two was done by the German philosopher Georg Simmel. Born in Berlin in 1858, Simmel was the youngest of seven children. He studied philosophy and history at the University of Berlin, but his range of interests was vast, taking in psychology, economics and the discipline we now call sociology, of which he is regarded as a founding father.

Simmel was intrigued by social geometry, especially the role of dyads and other small groups in shaping behaviour. He was curious as to why the number of individuals in a group affects the behaviour of that group; why, the bigger a group gets, the more isolated its individual members feel.

In his best-known book, *The Metropolis and Mental Life* (1903), Simmel considers the profound way the 'overwhelming fullness' of fast, modern, big-city life affects individuals so that 'the personality . . . cannot maintain itself under its impact'.[4] The more meaningful relationships, established over a long period, that characterise rural life have no place in a city. Instead, urban dwellers form attachments to money rather than to other humans.

For Simmel, a dyad contains the germ of other more complex forms, but is also important in itself. Dyads are different from, say, triads (groups of three) because they have greater unity, co-responsibility and interdependence. As a result, 'a common fate or enterprise, an agreement or secret between two persons, ties each of them in a very different manner than if even only three have a part in it'.[5]

By comprising only two people, dyadic groups preserve the individuality of their members and encourage complicity between them. But they are also fragile. Either party can end the relationship voluntarily by withdrawing from it, or involuntarily by dying. Awareness of this colours the interaction so that a dyad 'feels itself both endangered and irreplaceable'.[6] In a triad, the dynamic is different because if one person withdraws, the group lives on.

As Simmel explains, the decisive characteristic of the dyad is that each member must 'actually accomplish something'. In the case of failure, only the other person remains. And this is important. 'Precisely the fact that each of the two knows that he can depend only upon the other and on nobody else,' says Simmel, 'gives the dyad a special consecration – as seen in marriage and friendship, but also in more external associations, including political ones, that consist of two groups . . . The dyad element is much more frequently confronted with All or Nothing than is the member of the larger group.'[7]

In a dyad, neither member shares the other's attention with anyone else. Triads are trickier because when three people are involved there is a possibility of a dyad forming within the triad. And this is a problem because it threatens the remaining individual's independence and causes her or him to become subordinate. Nobody wants three people in a marriage.

This explains why, within a group of three or more, it's sometimes the relationship between two particular individuals that is the important one.

The quest to develop penicillin into a workable drug after it had been discovered years before by Alexander Fleming involved a whole team of people. At the core of this team was a triad of brilliant research scientists: Norman Heatley, Howard Florey and Ernst Chain. But at the core of this triad was a dyad.

Heatley was no-nonsense and humble, happy to stress the role of luck not just in his having secured a job at Oxford University's Dunn School of Pathology in the first place, but in the successes that followed. Shy, solitary Florey – an Australian – and the gregarious Chain – a half-Russian, half-German Jew from Berlin – were much thornier personalities. Chain had only ended up working on the penicillin project because the biochemist Florey originally wanted on his team was not available. A talented musician, Chain left Berlin aged twenty-six when Hitler came to power on 30 January 1933, and had been working in Cambridge, studying how snake venoms cause fatal paralysis, when Florey came calling. Short and with (for the time) uncommonly long, flowing hair, Chain was an excitable character – famous for pacing the room and gesticulating wildly: totally the opposite of the reserved, taciturn Florey.

Chain 'brought to science an artistic temperament, true inspiration, and originality – an emotional approach that gave joy in achievement and despair in supposed failure',[8] writes Florey's biographer Gwyn Macfarlane. It was Chain who, while researching the action of an enzyme called lysozyme, came across Alexander Fleming's old paper on penicillin in the *British Journal of Experimental Pathology* and thought it warranted further investigation; Chain who was unafraid of asking Oxford's cash-strapped authorities for the equipment he needed.

The friendship that formed between Florey and Chain was, on the face of it, a surprising one. For one thing, Florey was known to be anti-Semitic. For another, he distrusted flights of fancy and displays of emotion; his idea of praise was to tell someone: 'We don't seem to be going backwards.' He was quite withdrawn and could be ruthless and brutal.

Yet Florey had great sympathy for the underdog. And Chain was very much his charge: his first protégé, ten years his junior; a man who knew things Florey did not.

Every day, the pair would walk together through Oxford's University Parks, chatting mostly about their research, for Florey hated small talk. But it was a closer friendship than any the Australian had previously permitted himself. In an odd way, the two men's personalities were as complementary as their talents. As Macfarlane says: 'Chain's intuitive brilliance and originality balanced Florey's equally intuitive sense of direction and his genius for picking his way by simple, methodical experiments through a maze of attractive side issues.'[9]

Funnily enough, it was Heatley with whom Chain clashed

over such matters as whose name went first on a paper. Chain identified 'a certain pettiness and lack of generosity'[10] in Heatley's character, while Heatley accused Chain of 'servility towards those in higher places'.[11] Chain and Florey argued so fiercely that the walls of Florey's office shook, but it never stopped them working together when that was what mattered.

They saved their falling out for after penicillin had been tried, tested and found to be miraculous. By the end of the 1940s they were communicating only in writing – Chain claiming he had received insufficient credit for leading the Dunn School team down the route that ultimately led to penicillin's mass production.

———————

Perhaps it is significant that Chain was a musician. Crucial to being a great musician is learning how to play with others. Even concert pianists must learn to play with an orchestra. But it isn't easy.

A sense of when to lead and when to submit to being led seems to be a key quality in successful couples. Some possess it intuitively. Others have to learn it.

Gerald Moore was one of Britain's best-known piano accompanists. In the course of a long and illustrious career he played alongside giants such as the cellist Pablo Casals and the soprano Elisabeth Schwarzkopf. His job, he was always aware, was to restrain himself so that he did not overwhelm the soloist – though not so much that he made himself inconspicuous, because that wouldn't do either. He said that he learned a lot from the tenor John Coates, for whom the accompanist was a partner sharing equally with him the mood of the composer. 'Joy, sadness, passion, exultation, serenity, rage,' wrote Moore, 'must be experienced by each of them. How can the singer project an emotion to the listener if the accompanist holds back self-effacingly from the scene? . . . The accompanist should be a source of inspiration.'[12]

As with everything else in life, it is about striking a balance. And Moore admitted that being the half of the duo who was obliged to hang back and keep a low profile occasionally riled him. 'Nobody notices the accompanist at all,' he wrote. 'He looks so slender and shy and so modest that people think he's there just to do what he's told, to follow the singer through thick and thin. Well, there's a great deal more to it than that.'[13]

Indeed there is.

Something Simmel would have found fascinating, if unsurprising, is the extent to which the tech field is domi- nated by dyads. Google, Apple, Hewlett-Packard, Microsoft – all were founded by duos. All, to some degree, were the fruits of nerdy friendships between essentially unsociable people – risk-taking outsiders who relished being, in Simmel's words, 'confronted with All or Nothing'.

These companies' creation myths repay scrutiny, not least because of the questions they raise. Does success change the dyad's status from horizontal to vertical? Is it desirable for the soloist/accompanist dynamic to remain stable, or does that impede progress? Do you need that volatility to be truly successful?

Microsoft founders Bill Gates and Paul Allen were child- hood friends at Lakeside private school in Seattle, where they shared a passion for computers and would often skip lessons to hang out in the school's computer room. At the age of fifteen, Gates hacked into a major corporation's computer network and was banned from using computers for a year.[14] In 1973, he left Seattle to attend Harvard University as a pre-law student, but spent most of his spare time in its computer department. Allen moved to Boston too, where he worked as a programmer. He encouraged Gates to leave Harvard so they could collaborate. Both men were, says Allen in his memoir, *Idea Man*, restless and ready to try something new.

Allen had read an article in a magazine about the Altair 8800 microcomputer which he showed to Gates. Gates contacted its manufacturer, suggesting he and Allen write a version of the new BASIC programming language for it. It took them eight weeks, after which the pair jointly formed Microsoft on 4 April 1975.

The impetus behind Microsoft came from its dyadic origins, the 'special consecration' Simmel talks about. But the relationship between Gates and Allen couldn't endure because it quickly stopped being horizontal and became hierarchical.

Allen had always assumed his partnership with Gates would be a 50–50 proposition. In his book he casts himself as the thinker, the seer-like visionary asking the big questions: 'Where is the leading edge of discovery headed? What should exist but doesn't yet? How can I create something to help meet the need, and who might be enlisted to join the crusade?'[15]

Gates obviously appreciated his friend's worth, but did not agree that Allen was an equal partner. He argued that he had worked harder – and unsalaried, unlike Allen – on the initial BASIC project. He proposed a 60–40 split in ownership, which ended up being 64–36.

Gates was – is – the son of a lawyer. He knew how to push for what he wanted and had greater entrepreneurial flair. Awareness of Gates's exceptional abilities left Allen wondering about the weight of his contribution and how it deserved to be rewarded. What was 'the value of my Big Idea – the mating of a high-level language with a micro-processor – or my persistence in bringing Bill to see it? What were my development tools worth to the "property" of the partnership? Or my stewardship of our product line, or my day-to-day brainstorming with our programmers?'[16]

It was Allen who had come up with the name Microsoft; Allen who had overseen the big deal with IBM that was so crucial to Microsoft's initial success. Everyone worked hard at Microsoft in the early days. But Gates was fiercely driven and aspired to be more 'hardcore' – a favourite adjective of his – than everyone else, often working through the night and coming in the next day grumpy and with bloodshot eyes.

As Gates's power grew, it became Allen's job to have the rows with him that nobody else could have. 'As longtime partners,' he wrote, 'our dynamic was unique. Bill couldn't intimidate me intellectually. He knew I was on top of tech-nical issues . . . And unlike the programmers, I could challenge Bill on broader strategic points . . . On principle, I refused to yield if I didn't agree. And so we'd go at it for hours at a stretch, until I became nearly as loud and wound up as Bill.'[17]

The high-stress environment that Gates relished did not, in the end, suit Allen: 'My sinking morale sapped my enthu-siasm for my work, which in turn could precipitate Bill's next attack.'[18] By the time Allen left Microsoft in early 1983, having been diagnosed with Hodgkin's lymphoma the year before, he and his old friend were barely communicating.

A similar drama played out at Apple. Steve Wozniak was twenty-five and working at Hewlett-Packard designing calculators when the company turned down his revolutionary idea for a home computer with its own built-in keyboard and video display. So Wozniak set up Apple with his twenty-one-year-old friend Steve Jobs, who had dropped out of college to work at the video game company Atari.

Wozniak was the engineering brains in the duo. Unlike Jobs, he had no real desire to run a company: 'I'd decided long ago that I would never become someone authoritative,' he told Walter Isaacson, Jobs's biographer.[19] Jobs had to cry, scream, have tantrums and repeatedly call Wozniak's family before he agreed to co-found the company.

But the dyad could not withstand Wozniak's wish to keep a low profile and have nothing to do with Apple's management. By the time he left Apple in 1985, Wozniak was working as a mid-level engineer on the Apple II, a product he had helped to invent but felt Jobs did not value, despite the fact that it accounted for 70 per cent of Apple's sales at the end of 1984.

Jobs, on the other hand, wanted world domination. He too resigned from Apple in 1985, but returned in 1997 to turn it into the world's most valuable company. Jobs was a narcissistic perfectionist. On a corporate level, he believed in what he called 'deep collaboration' – all the company departments working together. But in order to achieve this, to galvanise Apple so that every employee shared his lofty vision of the company as 'making tools for the mind that advance humankind' (his mission statement),[20] he had to be individualistic and autocratic.

Wozniak has said that from the earliest days of their friendship, Steve Jobs would talk about historical figures who had made a mark on humanity, like William Shakespeare and Leonardo da Vinci. 'He wanted to be one of them, and he felt he had the motivation,' Wozniak revealed, then twisted the knife: 'Sometimes motivation, wanting something, is a lot more important than having the real skill.'[21] That Jobs, who encouraged the cult of personality that formed around him with his trademark minimal wardrobe and gnomic pronouncements, saw himself in these terms is no surprise.

Nothing, however, short-circuits the power of two more than the countervailing theory of the Lone Genius.

Nearly two centuries after Thomas Carlyle promoted his 'great man' theory of history in *On Heroes, Hero-worship and the Heroic in History* (1840) – broadly, the idea that individuals, and male ones at that, are the drivers of historical change – many still prefer to see history as a roll call of charismatic leaders, from Joan of Arc to Henry VIII, Napoleon to Hitler, Stalin to Churchill.

'They were the leaders of men, these great ones,' Carlyle writes. 'All things that we see standing accomplished in the world are properly the outer material result, the practical realisation and embodiment, of Thoughts that dwelt in the Great Men sent into the world: the soul of the whole world's history, it may justly be considered, were the history of these . . . He is the living light-fountain, which it is good and pleasant to be near.'[22] Of course, as the historian Frank McDonough has pointed out, the cult of personality is central to all recorded history: 'The Greek and Roman Empires linked their greatest periods with great leaders. Most European monarchs claimed to rule by divine right. Individual greatness was integral to the Renaissance and the Industrial Revolution.'[23]

Surely, though, most of us accept nowadays that it is possible to have two or more Carlylean 'light fountains'?

That two of the things put next to each other might actually generate *even more light*?

The idea that industrial or technical inventions are the result of one brilliant person's efforts has long been discredited. A funny piece in the *Quarterly Journal of Economics* from February 1926 – 'Industrial Invention: Heroic, or Systematic?' – makes the point subtly in a story about car tycoon Henry Ford: '[Rival automobile inventor] Charles B. King, pedalling a bicycle, followed Ford's car and picked up the bolts and parts which fell off on its trial trip.'[24]

The myth that individuals can rise above society to shape the course of history remains pervasive. For one thing, the dictatorships of Hitler and Stalin happened frighteningly recently. For another, in the last decade we have seen, on both the left and the right, a resurgence in populist politics fuelled by economic insecurity and worries about immigration. This has led to a new generation of political 'strongmen': Donald Trump in the US, Vladimir Putin in Russia, Viktor Orbán in Hungary, Rodrigo Duterte in the Philippines, Jair Bolsonaro in Brazil.

These leaders see themselves as transcending the usual constitutional checks and balances, if not the political process itself. As I write this, Putin is finding creative ways to stay on as president despite his term coming to a constitutional end. In Turkey, President Erdoğan may well govern until 2029 thanks to new powers he has awarded himself. These characters want to rule not as mortals but as undeposable kings.

Yet there are limits to individual power. One of the early architects of what became Marxism, the Russian thinker Georgi Plekhanov, took on Carlyle in his book *On the Role of the Individual in History* (1898).

Plekhanov conceded that individuals could influence the

fate of society and that this influence could be considerable. But how far a single person's influence stretched depended on the way a society was organised: 'The character of an individual is a "factor" in social development only where, when and to the extent that social relations permit it to be such.'[25]

In other words, social and economic forces beyond that individual's direct control – a hungry, dissatisfied peasantry, say – will limit and maybe even end power. A leader can be swept along by events that catch them by surprise and push them in a direction they would otherwise have had no intention of going. Were it not for Covid-19, Prime Minister Boris Johnson would surely never have countenanced his chancellor Rishi Sunak's multi-billion-pound state bailouts.

A better example might be Russia at the start of the First World War. Weak, stubborn and disorganised, Tsar Nicholas II was obsessed with the idea of being a military leader and made the disastrous decision to take direct command of the Russian armies when, in Trotsky's words, he was 'not fit to run a village post office'. From then on every military failure – and there were many – was directly associated with Nicholas personally. Meanwhile, the growing influence of Rasputin over the tsarina in Nicholas's absence did irreparable damage to the royal family's image so that, by the spring of 1917, the Romanovs had surrendered charge of Russia to Kerensky and the provisional government. By the end of 1917, the Bolsheviks had taken power in Russia's major cities.

While we are on the subject, Marxism is just one phenomenon we lazily attribute to a single person when it was actually the creation of two – Karl Marx and Friedrich Engels. Engels co-authored *The Communist Manifesto* with

Marx and supported him financially so that he could research and write *Das Kapital.*

Ditto evolutionary theory. So closely linked with Charles Darwin is its formulation that few people are aware of the contribution of Alfred Russel Wallace, another British naturalist, who had been thinking and writing along similar lines at exactly the same time. Wallace hit upon his version of the theory – that the fittest animals survive and reproduce, passing advantageous characteristics on to their offspring – in 1858 while he was ill with malaria and confined to his hut on the island of Ternate, in what is now Indonesia. 'Every day, during the cold and succeeding hot fits, I had to lie down during which time I had nothing to do but to think over any subjects then particularly interesting me,' he wrote later.[26] Wallace immediately shared one of these thoughts with his friend and older mentor, Charles Darwin.

When he received Wallace's letter, Darwin was momentarily taken aback – 'smashed', actually, was the word he used. He had been working on this same theory for twenty years and now risked being leapfrogged by a younger rival, albeit one he admired hugely. His friends Joseph Hooker and Charles Lyell came to the rescue. They arranged for both men's works to be read at the Linnean Society in Piccadilly – a way of preserving Darwin's claim. 'Wallace's letter gave Darwin a good kick up the backside,' says the geneticist Steve Jones. 'He had prevaricated for 20 years and would have done so for another 20 if he hadn't realised someone else was on the trail.'[27] Darwin quickly got to work writing up his mass of research as *On the Origin of Species by Means of Natural Selection* (1859).

This highly readable tome cemented Darwin and Darwinism in the public imagination, to the exclusion of any collaborators. But Wallace did not seem to mind. He knew Darwin was the better scientist, the person whose research had been needed to verify his hunch. Some modern scholars allege that Darwin is guilty of intellectual theft. His biographer, Janet Browne, insists this is not so: 'No two authors thrown together in such a fashion tried harder than Darwin and Wallace to treat each other fairly. Wallace greatly admired *On the Origin of Species*. In turn, Darwin regarded Wallace as the one man who truly understood the idea of evolution by natural selection.'[28] Browne points out that Darwin persuaded the British government to award Wallace a pension for services to science; also that Wallace dedicated his book *The Malay Archipelago* to Darwin, 'as a token of personal esteem and friendship', and called a collection of essays *Darwinism*. Indeed, she says, even before the term 'Darwinism' had become popular, Wallace observed that the theory was coming to be called 'Darwinianism' and wrote to Darwin in 1868: 'I hope you do not dislike the word, for we really must use it.'[29]

Darwin and Wallace did not have close contact at the point when their theory took off. Neither was present at the reading of their joint paper at the Linnean Society. Even so, as a couple they still managed to achieve something of immeasurable importance, not just to science but to religion and humankind's sense of its relationship to the world – something neither would, arguably, have achieved on their own.

———

Sometimes, to appreciate people fully, we need to see them through the prism of the person closest to them.

The writer Virginia Woolf and her artist sister Vanessa

Bell had an intense sense of themselves as a duo, of what Virginia called 'a very close conspiracy'.[30] To grasp their importance as individual artists, we need to understand their closeness and interdependency, what their biographer Jane Dunn describes as the 'essential reciprocity' in their natures.[31]

Virginia and Vanessa were bonded young and in adversity – by the experience of having the needy, hypochondriacal, emotionally bullying Leslie Stephen as a father; and by the sexual abuse they both (though especially Virginia) suffered at the hands of their stepbrother, George Duckworth. And then there were the deaths: so many of them – of their mother, Julia Stephen, when they were teenagers; of their half-sister Stella, who had taken over the running of the household and whose place, going through the accounts with her bellicose father, Vanessa was forced to take; and of Thoby, their adored brother, from typhoid diagnosed too late.

Together Vanessa and Virginia endured the male-dominated, high Victorian stuffiness of the family home at 22 Hyde Park Gate – a symbol of everything they would go on to reject. 'We had an alliance that was so knit together that everything . . . was seen from the same angle; and took its shape from our own vantage point,' wrote Virginia, who was two and a half years younger than Vanessa. 'Very soon after Stella's death we saw life as a struggle to get some kind of standing place for ourselves.'[32]

This standing place was different for each of them, appropriately given their opposing temperaments. Virginia wrote, dazzlingly. She had always had a way with words, been a beguiling, witty conversationalist; while Vanessa struggled to be articulate in company, often retreating into herself and declaring: 'I feel the only refuge is to become quite abstracted.' Vanessa would find herself through painting and motherhood and extravagant sexuality; through creating a court for herself at her country house, Charleston.

They wrote to each other nearly every day. And they cemented their roles in conscious opposition to each other, an 'artificial polarisation' (as Dunn puts it) 'which had protected them since childhood from the extremes of sisterly rivalry and had cast Vanessa as the sexual, maternal woman and Virginia as the intellectual and sterile one'.[33]

People were fascinated by the sisters as a joint phenomenon: Leonard Woolf, later Virginia's husband, initially fell in love with both of them at first sight. Clive Bell, too – Vanessa's husband: he had a serious flirtation with Virginia shortly after the birth of his and Vanessa's first child, Julian, in 1908 which caused a rift between the sisters. Virginia's love letters to him make Vanessa complicit in their affair, so intensely that it is as if she is Vanessa (or Vanessa's lover): 'Kiss her,' she instructs him, 'most passionately, in all my private places – neck, arms, eyeball, and tell her – what new thing is there to tell her? How fond I am of her husband?'[34]

Things changed between them after Vanessa married Clive Bell. For a period, when she suffered the first of her nervous breakdowns in 1904, Virginia rejected Vanessa, angered by her blithe ascension into the world of family and domesticity. The other polarisation the sisters encouraged was the identification of Virginia with mental instability – 'Oh you know very well the Goat's mad,'[35] they would say, jokingly – and Vanessa with sanity and rootedness.

You could say that Vanessa and Virginia were each other's muses. That they inspired each other. 'I always feel I'm writing more for you than anybody,' Virginia told Vanessa,[36] while Vanessa admired Virginia's impressionistic approach to character and narrative. I wonder if this had its roots in the intense mutual loyalty they felt towards each other, the sort of loyalty you often see in siblings who have had tricky or non-existent relationships with their parents.

Bonds forged in childhood are especially strong – an idea I'll be exploring in more detail a little later on, when talking about Charles and Mary Lamb.

Duos are often invoked in this way to explain the mystery of artistic creation – or, as in Virginia and Vanessa's case, the formation of a creative personality.

Most people know the story of Lewis Carroll and Alice Liddell – of 'Alice's Adventures Under Ground' (as the original title had it) spun to entertain Carroll's friends' daughter Alice and her sisters Edith and Lorina as they journeyed along Oxford's Isis river in a rowing boat on 4 July 1862. When, in 1932 at the age of eighty, Liddell went to America to collect an honorary PhD from Columbia University, she met Peter Llewelyn Davies who as a boy had inspired J. M. Barrie to write *Peter Pan*. For him, being a muse turned out to be too close a conspiracy: he threw himself under a tube train at Sloane Square station in 1960, having grown to hate the association with Peter.

This follows a pattern of tragic muse relationships, starting with Dante and his lost love Beatrice. But it is worth reiterating that this kind of coupledom is not always exploitative and disastrous. We are all inspired by and seek to please those who are closest to us. As long as the right balance is struck, nobody need come to harm. John Lennon and Yoko Ono made a success of it, as did Gala and Salvador Dalí. A successful poet, Gala acted as Salvador's agent and publicist as well as his model and muse. In the early 1930s, Dalí took to signing his paintings with her name as well as his own, in recognition of the fact that it is 'mostly with your blood, Gala, that I paint my pictures'.[37]

A good metaphor for the multifaceted nature of partnerships is the *pas de deux* in ballet – often the most intense, mythologised sequences. We think of these dances for two people as being expressions of love. But a lot of the time they are not; or at least, that is not the whole story. *Swan Lake*, for instance, has two *pas de deux*. There's the 'Love Duet', danced between Prince Siegfried and his beloved Odette, the Swan Queen. But the other, the 'Black Swan' *pas de deux* from the third act is much darker, much more angular and complicated. It is danced between the prince and the disguised Odile, who tricks the prince into thinking she is his betrothed, thereby destroying his future with the Swan Queen.

One of the twentieth century's most productive artistic collaborations was between the choreographer George Balanchine and the composer Igor Stravinsky. Their plotless, twenty-two-minute 1957 ballet *Agon* is significant politically as well as musically. At its premiere, Balanchine used the African American dancer Arthur Mitchell and the white ballerina Diana Adams to dance the *pas de deux*. He was making a daring civil rights point, but also mirroring Stravinsky's first ever use of an idiom based on a twelve-tone technique in which every note in the chromatic scale – in other words, the black as well as the white notes – is equally important.

The title *Agon* derives from the Greek word for debate and conflict, with overtones of athletic contest. The whole point is that the relationship between the dancers never resolves into a single thing – it is always kept in a state of galvanised suspension. As the dance critic Alastair Macaulay has written: 'The combination of formality and intimacy has a charge both erotic and strenuous. To us watching, the dancers' relationship keeps changing. Are they lovers? Sovereign and vassal? Muse and poet? Sculpture and sculptor?'[38]

Coupledom is not about blissful, frictionless togetherness. Earlier, I mentioned Bob Woodward and Carl Bernstein, journalist legends with whom I was obsessed when I was a rookie reporter. (I was thrilled in 2000 to get a chance to work at the *Washington Post* and follow in their hallowed footsteps.) But the story of their partnership is more *agonised* than we perhaps remember.

Bernstein almost was not involved in reporting Watergate at all, as he was close to being fired for being lazy. ('Stories he didn't particularly like, he waltzed around a lot, procrastinated, dawdled, found small crevices that somehow became big problems,' said his editor at the time, Tom Wilkinson.[39]) Bernstein did not like Woodward, considering him a 'prima donna, and an ass-kisser, a navy guy, green lawns of Yale, tennis courts' and admitting, 'I didn't really think a lot of most of Woodward's stories.'[40] And Woodward mistrusted Bernstein because he was a college drop-out who wrote about rock music. But hey – something went right. Because in the end, as the academic Vera John-Steiner says, 'collaboration thrives on diversity of perspectives and on constructive dialogues between individuals negotiating their differences'.[41] Or to put it more simply, Woodward and Bernstein worked out how to work together.

These are testing times. As I write this, within the confines of lockdown, it is hard to tell what the post-Covid future is going to look like. We can say with some certainty that the virus will change the way we work, shop and socialise. But how many of those changes become permanent features of our lives is hard to guess.

One thing is certain, though. Working together productively towards a shared goal has never been more important. At the peak of the crisis, the majority of scientific research ground to a halt as scientists combined efforts to find a vaccine or an effective treatment. Formalities such as who takes credit were set aside. Studies were made available and viral genome sequences identified and shared as rapidly as possible.[42]

This blueprint is the one to which we should aspire – not the one used by those countries who treated Covid-19 as a purely national concern. Former prime minister Theresa May was right to warn that the global response 'risks exacerbating the shift towards nationalism and absolutism in global politics'. We might well end up with a world 'in which a few "strong men" square up to each other'.[43] Although it sometimes feels as if we are inhabiting that one already.

———————

Over the pages that follow I explore and celebrate coupledom in all its guises by telling stories about duos whose achievements particularly captivate me. In each case, each half of the couple has brought a different resource to the partnership. It might be the type of personality that thrives on opposition and tension. It might be bravery, or respect, or love, or generosity, or simply a willingness to tolerate fracture as well as fusion. All kinds of qualities are needed to sustain a shared endeavour.

I have approached the subject thematically. Coupledom is a jewel with many facets; this struck me as the best way to show them all off. So the first chapter looks at Commitment, focusing on the extraordinary mutual dedication of runaway slaves William and Ellen Craft; the quirky, self-sufficient world-building of the Ladies of Llangollen; and spies such as Peter and Helen Kroger, whose coupledom was cemented by a shared ideology.

Communication between couples is vital. The late Kate Figes talks about 'the courage of honest communication' in her brilliant book *Couples: How We Make Love Last.* 'It is only when each [half of a couple] can articulate their resentments and face their fears that some sort of resolution can be found,' she says.[44] She is talking about romantic partnerships, but I think this holds true for all varieties. As I show in Chapter 2, good communication bequeathed the world the scientific discoveries of Henry Cavendish and the music of Frederick Delius. Both required a specialised kind of help from a uniquely tolerant adjutant.

Competitiveness is important too. Chapter 3 examines rivalries – some healthy, others less so – in the worlds of art, sport and music and partnerships, and finds the missing link between Francis Bacon and Lucian Freud and cyclists Laura Trott and Jason Kenny.

Tension, the subject of Chapter 4, may not be healthy, but it was at the root of the relationship between the writer Edward Bulwer Lytton and his wife Rosina, and between on–off lovers and professional narcissists Cecil Beaton and Greta Garbo.

Sometimes what makes a duo work is down to the purest chance. Chapter 5 examines the role of Serendipity in the sometimes-fleeting pairings of characters as vivid and eccentric as Groucho Marx and T. S. Eliot; playwright Samuel Beckett and wrestler André the Giant; and legends of British film-making, Michael Powell and Emeric Pressburger.

Were this a book solely about romantic couples then I would have made Love the subject of Chapter 1. But it isn't, so I haven't. Instead, in Chapter 6, I show how different types of love have animated different types of partnerships, from writer siblings Charles and Mary Lamb to Indian transgender path-blasters Aarav Appukuttan and Sukanyeah Krishna.

Finally, in Chapter 7, I square up to Power Couples, from Hollywood big beasts to tech titans. Are Jay-Z and Beyoncé wise to make their marriage the subject of their art? And how the hell did the movie *Cleopatra* ever get made when its stars, Richard Burton and Elizabeth Taylor, were so busy throwing their weight around?

I've tried not to be dogmatic in my habits of selection or appraisal; although, that said, I have tried to make it as much of a smorgasbord as possible. A book about Straight White Male couples would be duller and more predictable than I hope this one is.

I owe a massive debt to the many people who suggested couples for inclusion in *It Takes Two*. I thank them in the Acknowledgements, but given this book's subject it would be remiss not to thank my husband John upfront. My domestic collaborator for nearly thirty years, he was also my professional partner on this book, doing masses of research and helping me wrestle the manuscript into shape. Working with him has taught me a huge amount about trust and cooperation.

1

Commitment

The village of Ockham sits twenty-five miles south-west of London in the Surrey countryside, not far from where I grew up in Godalming. It is a friendly, unassuming place, most famous until recently for being the birthplace of the fourteenth-century monk-philosopher William of Ockham (sometimes written 'Occam'). His gift to humankind was the problem-solving principle, Occam's Razor, which holds that the simplest explanation is far more likely to be correct than a complex one.

Between 1845 and 1873, Ockham was the home of one Dr Stephen Lushington, a leading figure in the British anti-slavery movement. He was a former judge and privy councillor who presided over a wealth of reforming legislation, including a law banning the transfer of slaves between British colonies. Lushington had, in the twilight of his career, become a teacher at the rural branch of the progressive Ockham Schools, founded by the mathematician – and daughter of Lord Byron – Ada Lovelace. Lushington and his family lived at Ada's manor house, Ockham Park, where, according to a neighbour, he 'collected around him the cleverest folk of the day' and enlisted the help of his own daughters in running the school.[1]

Fast forward to Ockham in September 2018 and an event to celebrate the unveiling of new signs at the entrance to the village. A tall, stocky, seventy-year-old man with a jaunty cravat tucked into his blue open-necked shirt is standing in the middle of a field holding up one of the green signs with the help of local historian Garry Walton. The sign bears the legend 'Historic Ockham Village'; then, underneath, 'Refuge of Fugitive American Slaves William & Ellen Craft'. The man is Christopher Clark, great-great-grandson of the Crafts, to whom the sign is a tribute. At the ceremony Christopher gives a moving speech: 'I like to think that if people are thought of and spoken about, they still in some respects live among us,' he says. 'I would like to thank everybody responsible for the signs . . . but most of all I would like to thank William and Ellen for what they strove for and what they achieved.'[2]

What the Crafts strove for and how they achieved it – how, in other words, they ended up in Ockham in 1851 – is one of the most incredible stories ever told. Fittingly, they told it themselves in the book they published in 1860, *Running a Thousand Miles for Freedom; Or, The Escape of William and Ellen Craft from Slavery*.

If anything, their tale is even more incredible than that of the celebrated runaway slave, Henry 'Box' Brown from Virginia, who in 1849 arranged to have himself posted in a three-foot-long wooden crate to Philadelphia in the free state of Pennsylvania. He moved to Britain where he married an English woman and became, appropriately enough, a magician.

Brown was obliged to conceal himself. But Ellen and

William Craft did everything brazenly, in plain sight. The disguise Ellen adopted allowed her – though not William – to stay at the best hotels, travel first class on trains and dine at the captain's table on ships. It was an incredible performance on Ellen's part, even if the stress of it – the couple were nearly caught on several occasions – left her not only physically sick but suffering from what we would now recognise as post-traumatic stress disorder (PTSD).

The idea, however, was William's. And they would not have been able to pull off the whole crazy scheme if they had not been so close as a couple. They were totally trusting, capable of intuiting down to the subtlest raised eyebrow what the other was thinking and going through. Separation was unthinkable to them. At the same time, they knew that if one of them was caught then the other would have to struggle on alone, with everything that that implied.

At the centre of it all was an absolute steadfast conviction that slavery was wrong – that if all men were indeed created equal, none had the right to hold others as chattels and deprive them of their rights. In the Southern states of America, wrote the Crafts, there is 'a greater want of humanity and high principle amongst the whites, than among any other civilised people in the world'.[3]

Ellen and William were originally from Macon, Georgia. Like his mother, brother and sister, William had been auctioned off by his original master at sixteen to settle gambling debts. Owned thereafter by a local bank clerk, he still worked at the furniture store to which he had been apprenticed as a cabinetmaker, but while he was allowed to be paid – and hence able to save money for his and Ellen's escape – he received only a fraction of the wages due to him.

William was dark-skinned: his ethnicity was not and never would be in doubt. Ellen, on the other hand, was far paler. This was because she was a so-called 'quadroon', the daughter of a mixed-race slave named Maria, who had been raped by her planter master Major James Smith. So similar to her 'legitimate' half-siblings did she look that she was often mistaken for their white sister. Although Ellen was relatively well treated for a slave – inasmuch as she was not flogged or sexually assaulted – her whiteness angered the mistress of the house and in 1837 she gifted Ellen, aged eleven, to her daughter, Eliza Cromwell Smith, to get her out of the way. When Eliza subsequently married and moved to Macon, she took Ellen with her.

How exactly William and Ellen met, became a couple and married, it's hard to say. But William knew the household that Ellen worked for because he was part-owned by her master. When plotting their escape, the pair ran through a variety of theoretical plans in their heads, dismissing each as impossible to execute for one reason or another. The basic problem was how to flee the area quickly enough when it was unlawful for slaves to take any public transport without their masters' consent. Slave-hunters with their bloodhounds would track them down in no time. William and Ellen would have been separated for life and either put to 'the meanest and most laborious drudgery',[4] or tortured to death as a warning to other slaves.

The key to William's plan was that slaveholders could take their slaves to any state, including 'free states' where slavery did not exist. White women in the South did not usually travel with their servants. But what if Ellen, with her fair complexion, pretended to be his master – a white *man*?

William and Ellen were 'favourite slaves' so managed to obtain passes from their masters over Christmas (even if their illiteracy meant they were unable to read what they were permitted to do). This gave them a few days to get away before anyone noticed they were missing. William had managed to save some money from his job. He went to different parts of town at odd times, buying supplies and clothes – including parts of Ellen's 'white man's' costume – which he took back to the cottage where his wife worked. Being a favourite, she had a room to herself containing a lockable chest of drawers.

Once on the run, the difficulty for Ellen was preserving the continuity of her performance as a man; making it seamless and plausible while also avoiding male company, where she would run the risk of exposure. She could not, for example, drink and smoke with other men. She had to be careful in conversation, lest she unwittingly said something that gave her away. The courage it took to enact the plan hardly bears thinking about. There were so many ways it could (and nearly did) go wrong. But William's presence made it marginally easier for Ellen than other female slave escapees who dressed as men, such as Clarissa Davis of Virginia, who successfully reached Philadelphia in 1854, having hidden in a chicken coop for ten weeks to evade bounty hunters.

Before they set out, William cut Ellen's hair to neck length. As neither she nor William could read or write, Ellen put her right arm in a sling to deter port authorities or hotel receptionists from asking her to sign documents or registries. To flesh out her identity as an invalid, Ellen asked William to wrap bandages around her face to hide her smooth, beardless skin. She wore the right kind of clothes,

clothes that identified her as a man who would own slaves: men's trousers which she had sewed; a jacket; a cravat; a pair of green spectacles; and a top hat.

Throughout the slave states, as the Crafts wrote in their book, 'every coloured person's complexion is prima facie evidence of his being a slave; and the lowest villain in the country, should he be a white man, has the legal power to arrest, and question, in the most inquisitorial and insulting manner, any coloured person, male or female, that he may find at large'.[5] They each took a different route to the railway station. William got into the 'negro car' while Ellen bought a ticket for herself and one for William to the port of Savannah, 200 miles away. Ellen had to do all the talking, including the purchasing of tickets and hotel rooms. They were nearly caught at the outset when William spotted his boss questioning the ticket seller and peering through the train windows, obviously suspecting that his slave had done a runner. William shrank back in his seat. The boss searched the first-class carriage but did not notice Ellen in her disguise. Before he had a chance to reach William's car, the bell rang and the train left the station.

It got worse, however. Ellen had been staring out of the window, but then turned and realised the man sitting beside her was an old friend of her master and mistress who had known Ellen since childhood and had only recently attended a dinner party at the house where she lived. Her panic at the thought that he had almost certainly discovered her identity and was there to capture her only faded when he greeted her with a: 'It is a very fine morning, sir.' Ellen then feigned deafness and eventually the man gave up trying to talk to her.

In Savannah, William and Ellen boarded a steamer for

Charleston, South Carolina. William prepared flannels and opodeldoc – a treatment for his master's supposed rheumatism consisting of soap, camphor and wormwood in alcohol – which he warmed on the stove in the gentlemen's saloon. Then, while Ellen slept, William paced the deck – there was nowhere for black passengers to sleep – eventually finding some cotton bags by the funnel where he sat until morning. This was obviously noticed by the captain, for at breakfast the next day he singled out William, turning to Ellen and saying: 'You have a very attentive boy, sir; but you had better watch him like a hawk when you get to the North. He seems all very well here, but he may act quite differently there . . .'[6] At the same meal, a slaver tried to persuade Ellen to sell William to him. 'I think not, sir,' she said. 'I have great confidence in his fidelity.' At this the slaver became so enraged that he slammed his fist on the table – so hard that his neighbour's coffee spilled.[7]

The level of threat is unimaginable – the slaves are surrounded by violent, racist Yankees. How on earth did they cope? They are constantly having to parry questions about slavery and abolitionism, staying in character all the while. Say too much and you give yourself away. Say too little and you arouse suspicion for being antisocial.

Ellen and William finally arrived in Philadelphia – in the free state of Pennsylvania – on Christmas Day. Ellen's first reaction, understandably, was to burst into tears. She was exhausted: so weak and faint she could barely stand. In Philadelphia they were given assistance by the underground abolitionist network. A local Quaker man, Barkley Ivens, invited them to stay at his home beside the Delaware river, 'the first act of great and disinterested kindness we had ever received from a white person'.[8] Ellen could not relax and was convinced they were about to be double-crossed; but no. Still, it was not safe to stay in Pennsylvania. The Fugitive Slave Act of 1850 made it illegal to assist slaves on the run, even in free states. So three weeks later they moved to Boston where William found a job as a cabinetmaker and furniture broker and Ellen as a seamstress.

For a time, all went well. Then, later that year, two slave-hunters from Macon arrived to capture them. The pair were obliged to flee again, this time to England. Their owner had even written to the US president, Millard Fillmore, to ask him to intervene in the matter. He ruled that the Crafts should be returned, even if that involved using military force.

Ellen and William sailed for Liverpool via Canada. She became ill on the voyage, nearly died and took several weeks to recover after they arrived. But once they were in England the abolitionist network – including Harriet Martineau and Ada Lovelace – ensured they were looked after and received an education. Afterwards Ellen wrote that since escaping from slavery she had 'gotten so much better in every respect . . . I had much rather starve in England, a free woman, than be a slave for the best man that ever breathed upon the American continent.'[9]

In one sense it's absurd to say that the Crafts were 'fortunate'. How could they be described as such, after all they went through? But it is not totally nonsensical. Through a combination of luck and judgement, this astonishing couple were able to forge an unbreakable commitment to each other, despite the many obstacles in their path. That commitment also gave them far more power and autonomy than many slaves could hope for.

Consider that most slaves were not entitled to marry legally in any American colony or state (even the Northern states where slavery ended in 1830); also that enslaved families could be separated and individual members sold off one by one at any point. If a white master wanted to have sex with a female slave, that was perfectly permissible. Quite often, in what were termed 'abroad marriages', an enslaved man might have a different owner to the mother of his children; might even live a significant distance away on a different plantation, in which case he would only be able to see his family when his owner allowed it. In this context of forcible dislocation, coupledom was a precious commodity: a safe space, to use a modern term, where slaves were able to be themselves and form trusting, secure relationships.

Perhaps we have, ever so slightly, lost the sense that coupledom can have a radical edge. A feeling prevails in the modern world that few things are more boring than content couples, particularly if they're 'smug marrieds' forever berating, with a sigh, others' inability to 'settle down' or demonstrate 'maturity' in love. To sceptics, romantic coupledom is fairy-tale schmaltz – conformist, prescriptive, suffocating. Not so long ago, they point out, marriages were business arrangements between families. Whether or not a husband and wife liked each other was beside the point. Like the novels that fed demand for it, romantic love was an eighteenth-century invention.

You can certainly make the case that domesticity, or at least the 'minutiae of daily living', is a passion killer, as Laura Kipnis does in her book *Against Love: A Polemic*: 'Taking out the garbage, tone of voice, a forgotten errand – these are the rocky shoals upon which intimacy so often founders.'[10]

Kipnis maintains that individuals can only endure sharing living space for extended periods by compromising and adapting. But there is a problem with this: our 'post-Romantic ideals of unconstrained individuality', which require both parties to rid themselves of those qualities that might prove troublesome while retaining enough individuality to feel their autonomy is not being sacrificed.[11]

One of the most fascinating examples of committed coupledom dates from precisely the point when these kinds of issues were being debated by artists and philosophers. The Romantic period, broadly 1750 to 1850, celebrated the idea of the individual as heroic and solitary. The couple we are about to meet possessed a sort of 'double singleness' – to use the phrase Charles Lamb coined to describe his relationship with his sister Mary, of which more later. Both halves combined to present a unified front which was stylised and performative but also emotionally sincere.

This tale also starts with an escape. On the evening of Monday, 30 March 1778, a twenty-three-year-old Anglo-Irish woman called Sarah Ponsonby climbed out of the parlour window of her guardians' mansion in Woodstock, Kilkenny. She was wearing men's clothing and carrying both a pistol and her small dog, Frisk. A trusted workman friend escorted her to a barn on the family estate where Lady Eleanor Butler, a spinster sixteen years Sarah's senior, was waiting for her. She too had changed into men's clothes, before saddling up her horse and riding away from Butler Castle, the family pile up the road.

This first getaway attempt was thwarted, however. 'I cant Paint our distress,' wrote the wife (and Sarah's cousin) of her guardian Sir William Fownes, Lady Betty, to a friend. 'My Dr Sally leapt out of a Window last Night and is gon off. We learn Miss Butler of the Castle is wt her. I can say no more. Help me if you can.'[12]

Eleanor and Sarah had been planning this for a while. Eleanor's mother wanted her to enter a convent as she was no longer marriageable because of her age. Sarah, an orphan, was facing the unwanted attentions (attempted rape, followed by repeated declarations of love) of her guardian, Sir William Fownes – her late father's cousin – who hoped Sarah might provide him with a male heir. (Lady Betty had only given him a daughter.)

Their friendship had begun over a decade earlier when Sarah was only thirteen. Aged twenty-nine, Eleanor was charged with looking after Sarah, who had been placed at Miss Parke's school near Kilkenny Castle in 1768. It began as bookish – the pair's favourite novels were Samuel Richardson's *Clarissa* and Sarah Scott's *Millenium Hall* – but had matured via the sending of turbid letters into a grand passion for each other and the sort of life they could enjoy together. ('Poor Soul if she had not been so fond of her pen so much would not have happened,' observed Lady Betty.) Only by leaving Ireland could they escape the shadow of their families' ambitions and live as they pleased, which is to say without being criticised; for Eleanor this was for being 'masculine' and 'satirical'.

The first stop on their journey was Waterford, where they planned to catch a boat to England. But they missed the boat and were discovered sheltering in a barn. Sarah caught a cold which turned into a serious fever. Her narrow evasion of death only confirmed for her and Eleanor the rightness of their course of action. They insisted to anyone who would listen that they would only be happy together and that there were no men involved. Eventually, after a second escape attempt, their families acquiesced. They were permitted to go with something approaching a blessing, accompanied by one of Eleanor's maids, Mary Carryl.

On a tour of Wales, the ladies settled in Llangollen and found a five-roomed stone cottage. They christened it Plas Newydd and set about transforming it, despite their lack of funds (a running theme). It was perfect for their needs in the sense that they had the freedom to reconstruct it to their sombrely Gothic specifications. They added a library (famously well stocked) and a dairy and a glasshouse in which they grew peaches and melons. Everywhere there were ornate wooden carvings, while the windows were filled with stained glass covered in celestial motifs. In the garden there was even a 'ruined' archway.

Their stated goal was 'retirement' – not what we think of it: they were not old, plainly. Rather, they sought what their biographer Elizabeth Mavor calls a 'dignified withdrawal from the press and vulgarity of the world to a life of virtue and rustic simplicity'.[13] 'Rustic' in this context meant an idealised version of rural life. And if things were not rustic enough, they could be made so. 'Sat in the rustic seat,' Eleanor wrote in her journal, 'disliked the appearance of the Stones over which the Water falls, thought it appeared too formal. Sent our workman to it with a spade and Mattock.'

As for 'simplicity': they still had a gardener, a footman and several maids, despite having an annual income of under £300, which is why they were constantly asking for a government pension (which they eventually received) and borrowing money from friends and relatives, including Eleanor's estranged brother. So stressful did Eleanor find dealing with her brother that a letter from him would often trigger one of her migraines. These she detailed – together with minute accounts of other aspects of their lives – in meticulous journals from which we can piece together what the ladies called 'the system'. Their lives were strictly ordered, every day broken down into chunks. The goal was improvement, of their minds (though not their bodies) and of the house and garden. They read a huge amount and took pride in their library. 'My B[eloved] has a Book of (I think) very well chosen Extracts from all the Books she has read since we had a home,' Sarah wrote to a friend.[14] These contained recipes, notes about plants and the names of local tradesmen. They liked each day to be similar to the one before.

Their personalities complemented each other. Eleanor dominated and could be forceful. She was given, says Mavor, to 'discharging gardeners like cannon balls'[15] and whipped boys she suspected of stealing strawberries (tipping them apologetically when she realised she had accused them unjustly). Sarah could be taciturn and, in the account book it was her job to keep, indulgent and emollient. They often fell out with people. 'Miss Davies, Mrs Barrett and we meet no more,' Eleanor noted. 'The Barretts having manifested themselves ungrateful, unworthy, treacherous and in every respect the reverse of what we so long thought them.'[16]

The paradox of the Ladies of Llangollen is that they, like Greta Garbo, became famous for wanting to be alone – so famous that their visitors book reads like a roll call of the late eighteenth-century great and good, from William Wordsworth to Josiah Wedgwood, the Duke of Wellington and Lady Caroline Lamb. Their idea of perfect contentment was walking a short local route they called the Home Circuit, then sitting in front of a blazing fire and reading aloud to each other. Occasionally visitors stayed with them, but this was discouraged; if possible people were shunted along the road to a local pub, the Hand.

They dined well and plentifully, even if they gave up hog's puddings after Eleanor decided they were 'too savoury, too rich for our abstemious Stomachs'. 'Abstemious'! It's hardly the right word. In one letter Eleanor tempts someone by describing what she would typically be served if she came to stay: 'New laid Eggs from our Jersey Hens Who are in the Most beautiful Second Mourning you ever beheld . . . Dinner Shall be boil'd chickens from our own Coop. Asparagus out of our garden. Ham of our own Saving and Mutton from our own Village . . . Supper Shall consist of Goosberry Fool, Cranberry Tarts roast Fowel and Sallad.'[17]

Within five years of taking their 'retirement' the ladies' celebrity was so great that Queen Charlotte asked to see plans of their cottage and garden. It seems likely they never reached her, as the ladies were in the habit of dousing all their letters (and everything else, including linen) in a musky scent which the Queen was known to dislike.

Still, how had this celebrity come to pass? The answer is that the ladies were compulsive writers of letters and diaries and journal entries. They idealised their life in their letters to their friends and relatives and these were discussed in salons where influential people met to discuss the matters of the day. Their Francophilia was, in the run-up to the French revolution, extremely fashionable. They seemed to be living the Romantic dream – the eighteenth-century equivalent of Instagram perfection. Elizabeth Mavor describes the scene beautifully: 'The public rooms of the Gothick cottage burbled and scratched and rustled with readings, writings, illuminations and purse settings. In the domestic offices six species of fruit were being expertly converted into wines; bread baked, meat salted, sheets stitched; while outside in the dairy, fowl yard and potager, there were regular milkings and churnings, wringings of turkey necks, generous dungings and vigorous rakings of gravel paths.'[18]

The other element in the ladies' system was the almost dandyish invention of themselves as living works of art. They powdered their hair and wore black riding habits and men's top hats. This was their way of setting themselves apart and of showing their impatience with gender protocols. On the whole, the ladies seem to have been liked locally: John Gibson Lockhart, Sir Walter Scott's son-in-law, wrote that they were the 'guardian angels' of Llangollen, 'worshipped by man, woman and child about them'.[19] Others weren't so sure. Lady Louisa Stuart wrote that they clearly belonged to the 'Genus Mountebankum'. She felt that the ladies had a schtick: 'You may think me severe on these poor ladies, but if I were to count up to you the persons of my acquaintance who have at several times visited them, and been each the very individual they had all their lives particularly longed to see, and for whose favourite relation, or friend, or patron, or chef de parti, they had ever had the most peculiar partiality, or admiration, or veneration (as the word chanced to suit), you would not wonder.'[20]

The couple's suspicion of strangers might perhaps be bound up with their sexuality. They were almost certainly lesbians, even when you make allowances for shifting cultural norms. But is it appropriate to label them? They referred to each other as 'my Beloved' (though this had less weight than it does today) and they shared a bed. Some contemporary observers seem to have prized their chastity as a supreme virtue: one called them the two most celebrated virgins in

Europe. Elizabeth Mavor prefers 'romantic friendship' and insists it is anachronistic to read the relationship as erotic, as if we have lost the ability to construe such a friendship in any other way: 'Much that we would now associate solely with a sexual attachment was contained in romantic friendship: tenderness, loyalty, sensibility, shared beds, coquetry, even passion.'[21] This is a fair point. However, it seems likely they used the cover of an intense platonic friendship to live as lesbians when the world averted its gaze.

Sometimes, of course, the world peered right in, to their acute displeasure. When, in June 1791, the *General Evening Post* published an article full of innuendo about them not having married and accusing the ladies of having eloped in order to indulge their unnatural passions, Eleanor was so outraged that she cancelled their subscription. 'Miss Butler is tall and masculine,' the article read, 'she wears always a riding habit, hangs her hat with the air of a sportsman in the hall, and appears in all respects as a young man, if we except the petticoats which she still retains. Miss Ponsonby, on the contrary, is polite and effeminate, fair and beautiful.' The implication is that Sarah may have been 'corrupted'. The ladies contacted Edmund Burke to ask if he thought there was any profit in bringing a libel action against the paper. He sympathised but thought it unwise.

And yet they seem, as Mavor says, 'to have been aware of the eccentric impression they were creating'.[22] It was this that made them a draw to visitors such as Thomas De Quincey, Robert Southey and Wordsworth. At the same time their priority was the creation and tending of a private world of private enthusiasms, from fossils to ghosts, Egyptology, Pompeii and a lady rumoured to be able to lay eggs.

As the ladies aged their money worries receded. In 1819

the house became theirs. 'The system' changed to allow for physical infirmity and digestive comfort. Their evening meal was brought forward to four or five o'clock. They were still improving the interior, finding uses for the oak furniture that admirers kept sending them. Eleanor had operations to remove cataracts, but she never recovered her full sight. Sarah had dropsy but hoped Eleanor would die before her as she worried how her friend would cope on her own. As Eleanor faded, Sarah read her the novels of Sir Walter Scott. Eleanor did indeed die first, on 2 June 1829, aged ninety; Sarah followed two years later on 9 December 1831, aged seventy-six.

For contemporary chroniclers, one of the most intriguing things about the ladies' enmeshed lives was what it proved about the possibility of long-term friendship for women. In this period many followed the sixteenth-century French philosopher Michel de Montaigne, who believed the best and closest friendships were only possible between men. After his best friend Etienne de la Boétie died in 1563, Montaigne famously wrote: 'If someone were to ask me why I loved him, I feel that it could not be expressed, except by answering "Because it was him; because it was me."'

Friendship, Montaigne suggests, is an instinctive, ineffable force and one of the highest human goods. Loyalty to your best friend should come before loyalty to lovers, God, family – everything. But, predictably, Montaigne claims it is all very different for women, who, he writes, 'are in truth not normally capable of responding to such familiarity and mutual confidence as sustain that holy bond of friendship, nor do their souls seem firm enough to withstand the clasp of a knot so lasting and so tightly drawn'.[23]

Absolute rubbish, responded Mary Pilkington in her 1804

Memoirs of Celebrated Female Characters, one of the first books to bestow upon Eleanor and Sarah the 'national treasure' status they still possess almost two centuries after their deaths. The pair had, at the point when Pilkington was writing, been close friends for over twenty years. Therefore, as she writes, 'those who have asserted that females are incapable of a permanent attachment, must now certainly acknowledge that their opinion was ill-founded . . . Why should that sex, allowed to possess a superior degree of sensibility, be disqualified from feeling a passion, which is calculated to dignify the human mind?'[24]

Pilkington cleaves to Elizabeth Mavor's 'romantic friendship' theory. But as the nineteenth century ground on, the boundaries between passionate female friendships and lesbian relationships became increasingly blurred. After the 1886 publication of Henry James's novel *The Bostonians*, which features one such couple, the term 'Boston marriages' began to be used to describe long-term cohabiting women. In some cases, passionate friendships between women were just that – heady and romanticised, according to the fashion of the day. In others, friendships that looked to the outside world like passionate friendships were really passionate *lesbian* relationships. This ambiguity made it easy for women in such relationships to mask the true nature of their activities. It also made it easy for those who preferred not to confront reality to be genteelly obtuse about what was actually going on, leaving us with what the feminist critic Lisa Moore calls a 'flattened notion' of competing constructions of female sexuality in late eighteenth-century and early nineteenth-century England.[25]

You could argue that, having been cast out of their birth families, the ladies' ultimate goal was to create an idealised family unit consisting of themselves and their servants. Managing the house and its gardens therefore became a sort of family business. As its founders, they showed a high level of what workplace theorists call 'organisational commitment' to the task of building their brand. This was, of course, because it came with a side order of *emotional* commitment.

I'm always surprised when I read the statistic that only 30 per cent of family businesses survive the transition from first- to second-generation ownership.[26] Such a high failure rate is partly to do with poor succession planning. Too few leaders of family businesses succeed in passing on to their offspring the level of commitment to a company that they presumably had when they founded it. Communication fails, relationships founder and the ensuing tensions end up overwhelming everyone. As the psychotherapist and family business consultant Tom Davidow told the *Financial Times*, a family member might: 'decide, "It's not worth telling my brother that what he does bothers me" because if they have to talk about that issue it's going to open up all these other issues".'[27]

The annals of corporate history are littered with families – frequently married couples, sometimes their children, sometimes siblings – who messed up their businesses in this way. The Canadian food processing giant McCain was founded and run by Wallace and Harrison McCain, brothers from New Brunswick. They had once been exceptionally close. They shared the same bedroom as children and, in the first flush of success in the late 1950s, lived next door to each other in identical white houses across the river from their first frozen-chip plant. By the 2000s, however, they were no longer on speaking terms because of a dispute over whose child was going to take over the company.

Likewise, the succession of Sumner Redstone for the controlling interest in the media conglomerate Viacom has been compared to the *Game of Thrones* saga, culminating as it did in Redstone writing an open letter to *Forbes* magazine denouncing his daughter, Shari, for ignoring 'the cardinal rules of good governance that the boards of the two public companies, Viacom and CBS, should select my successor'.[28]

What seems to work better is when succession involves the passing on of tangible skills. Giles Martin, son of the late Beatles producer George, is an acclaimed producer in his own right and has, since his father's death in 2016, been the chief custodian of the band's music, presiding over a wealth of remixes and high-profile reissues. He learned his craft from his father, who brought him along to mixing sessions for the Beatles' *Anthology* albums in the early 1990s as a second pair of ears: Martin Snr was, by then, losing his hearing. Giles Martin is trusted by the surviving Beatles and their families because, as he puts it, he innovates while ensuring that standards are kept; remains committed to what we might call the Beatles' core sonic values, while understanding that the modern marketplace requires them to apply to a wider variety of media than vinyl records and CDs.

In the early 2000s, Giles was instrumental in constructing, from the Beatles' master tapes, the soundtrack to the award-winning Cirque du Soleil show *Love*. Sometimes his father would join him, as Giles told the *Guardian*: 'I would sit and chop things up and create stuff and think about the show, he would come in on Thursday, and I'd play him bits and we'd talk about it, and just have a nice time together . . .

Very few people have the chance of going through their dad's dirty laundry for two years.'[29]

I want to consider another father–son couple who, like the Martins, were bonded rather than broken by their commitment to a particular way of doing things. The duo in question are glass-blowers Leopold and Rudolf Blaschka. From their workshop in Dresden, they created exceptionally detailed and lifelike models of sea-dwelling invertebrates, based on the latest scientific illustrations and, later, live creatures they kept in aquaria. They also produced equally detailed models of plants and flowers. 'The savant finds the rendering of the minutest details of vegetable organism almost inconceivably accurate,' marvelled *Popular Science* in May 1897. 'Not even the daintiest productions of the Venetian and Bohemian glass workers have prepared us for the delicacy and pliability which we find here.'

Leopold was born in 1822 into a glassmaking family in the Czech village of Böhmisch Aicha. His family speciality was prosthetic glass eyes. As a child, he showed artistic promise and was deemed to be the only one among three brothers gifted enough to apprentice with his father. He was still a relatively young man when his father died, just two years after Leopold lost his wife to cholera. Grief-stricken, he set out on a year-long journey to the United States, intending to devote himself to his passion for natural history. When his ship, the brig *Pauline*, was becalmed for two weeks in the Azores, Leopold became obsessed with watching bioluminescent jellyfish darting around under the water. 'Hopefully we look over the darkness of the sea which is as smooth as a mirror,' he wrote in his diary. 'In various places there emerges all around a flashlike bundle of light-beams, like thousands of sparks, that form true bundles of fire and of other bright lighting spots, as if they are surrounded by mirrored stars . . . It is as if they wanted to lure the enchanted observer into the realm of fairies.'[30] Wouldn't it be amazing, he wondered, if you could recreate these creatures using glass?

On returning from his trip in 1854, Leopold married a second time, to a woman called Carolina Riegel. Rudolf, the couple's only child, was born a few years later. At the age of twenty-three, Rudolf began assisting his father professionally. 'He was the only apprentice whom the elder man initiated into the mysteries of his art,' noted *Popular Science*.

The Blaschkas' models proved exceptionally popular. Dresden's Botanical Gardens and Natural History Museum commissioned the pair to make glass flowers as well as sea creatures. The Blaschkas also began to offer a mail-order service. Before long, other museums and universities came calling, intrigued by the possibility of using the models as teaching tools; for as well as being three-dimensional, glass models of invertebrates retained their colour and form, unlike samples preserved in alcohol, which disintegrated into a squishy mess because of the lack of bone structure.

So it was that the Blaschkas turned out thousands of jellyfish, octopus and squid, every eye and polyp and tentacle rendered perfectly. It is estimated that over the course of thirty years they averaged one model per day.

The secret of the duo's excellence was their unique working dynamic, a natural symbiotic rhythm that owed as much to an instinctive, familial intimacy and deep-rooted mutual respect as anything else. Their process involved creating detailed illustrations before actually making the models using traditional flameworking techniques – over a wooden table using a foot-pumped bellows. The models were created from blown glass, shaped with tongs and tweezers. Written like that, it sounds straightforward. But the fact is that even today expert glassworkers struggle to explain exactly how the Blaschkas made the models, wrongfooted by the fact that, for one thing, they were not exclusively made of glass but also paper and enamel, wire and different kinds of resin.

During quiet periods Rudolf would make field trips to America – increasingly the main market for their work – to study the natural world and collect samples. These were scientific models, after all, so accuracy was all-important. In her book *A Sea of Glass*, the marine biologist Drew Harvell notes cannily that 'some part of the deeper motivation to create these masterpieces must have resided in the relation-ship between father and son'.[31] It was a mutual obsession which turned into a duopoly. In the absence of any appren-tices, the pair's dedication to perfecting their technique was so intense it was as to be unfathomable. 'Many people think that we have some secret apparatus by which we can squeeze glass suddenly into these forms, but it is not so,' Leopold wrote in 1889 to the Blaschkas' patron Mary Lee Ware, who paid for what became known as the Ware Collection of glass flowers at Harvard. 'We have tact. My son Rudolf has more than I have, because he is my son, and tact increases in every generation.'[32]

In July 1895, while Rudolf was away on a field trip, his father died unexpectedly. Rudolf described his reaction three months later in a heartbreaking letter to the botanist Walter Deane:

In America I could not suppress a strange apprehension, a presentiment of some mischief menacing me and which oppressed my mind, especially during the last days in North

Carolina, with a strange power. But when I received the sad news the blow came though I was prepared and floored me terribly. I shall never forget my sad returning across the ocean with my grief and additional anxiety about my good mother's health. Fortunately, my mother got well and I could collect myself and find comfort in my work and the study of nature again. At first my studio appeared to me very lonely, but my father's spirit seems to be always with me. I see him in my thoughts sitting with me and hear his voice – how could I ever forget him? We have been working together for almost 25 years and the people in the city called us 'the inseparable' – now the unmerciful death has though separated us. I am however used, and have early been induced by my father, to be self-dependent in my work and as I am familiar by the long practice with everything in my art there is no trouble with me about the continuation of the flower-work for Harvard University. I trust you shall not find any difference of my work from the former models made by us both. The only circumstance is the quantity. So much as two active artists have produced can impossibly be done by one alone . . .[33]

By the end of the following year Rudolf was exhausted from doing all the work himself. He apologised to Deane for his lack of contact, but 'I was working so continuously all year that I could not spare even an hour for corresponding . . .' In 1897 *Popular Science* pondered the question of whether 'there is no one besides Rudolf Blaschka who can make these models, or who can at least assist him in making them'. The answer was no. Tact may increase in every generation, but there was to be no next generation of glassmaking Blaschkas. In 1911 Rudolf married, but they had no children and, because he had never trained an apprentice, there was no one to carry on the business.

The Blaschkas' success was the result of something singular in their natures, a complicity so intense that it became a kind of concealment. Between them, father and son created a space – the hot, smoke-fuggy interior of their workshop – which the outside world could not see. It was a space in which they could create artefacts so exquisite they might have been dropped from the heavens.

What is it that bonds couples, be they mothers and daughters, fathers and sons, business partners or 'romantic friends'? Perhaps one is drawn in by the other, who may be the dominant partner. Perhaps there are areas – covert, shadowy areas – where the whole point is that you are two people keeping a secret or playing a role: I'm talking, of course, about espionage.

Most traditional spy narratives focus on individuals, mostly fictional men such as James Bond, but occasionally real-life women like the famous 'honey trap' specialist Mata Hari, a Dutch exotic dancer who was convicted of spying for the Germans during the First World War. Hari was accused of obtaining her intelligence by seducing prominent French politicians and officers. Bond does his fair share of seduction in the line of duty but is a classic loner oddball, and a sadist to boot. It is hard to imagine him settling down with anyone (even though he does, briefly, at the end of *On Her Majesty's Secret Service* and in 2015's *Spectre*).

Yet spousal spies are a perennial obsession of Hollywood,

whether it is *Homeland*'s Carrie Mathison and her double-agent lover, Brody, or Brad Pitt and Angelina Jolie playing two assassins hired to kill each other in *Mr and Mrs Smith*. In *The Americans*, about Russian sleeper agents in suburbia, a glamorous couple kill together and use sex to lure their targets.

People who spy sustain clandestine double lives – hard enough to do on your own, you might think. But does being in a couple help? Spies are often depicted as narcissists or psychopaths. And psychopaths, says Dr Ursula Wilder in a CIA report on 'The Psychology of Espionage', rarely learn from mistakes and have difficulty seeing beyond the present. They cannot plan long-term and are, Wilder observes, 'deeply antagonistic to sharing decision-making with others'.[34] This is tricky if you are one half of a spy couple.

Some spy pairings seem to have had amazingly healthy relationships and been capable of the most elastic adaptability. Others, not so much. If you're part of a duo, you're more dependent – and dependency, says Wilder, 'makes a person particularly susceptible to manipulation and control'.[35]

So how do spy couples make it work? In Britain, the Krogers are the best known. They were key players in the so-called 'Portland spy ring' scandal – Soviet spies who operated in England during the late 1950s and early 1960s, until they were rumbled by the British security services.

Antiquarian book-dealer Peter Kroger and his wife Helen were sociable denizens of suburban Ruislip. Peter worked from home, buying and selling rare books, which he posted to dealers across the world. In reality, many of these books contained microdot reductions of information Peter and his wife were being given to pass on to the Russians. The pair had the necessary technology to do this, plus a keying device to encrypt the radio transmissions they made to the USSR and attenuate them so that they could not be detected.

One of Helen's main roles was to charm (and watch for signs of suspicion in) other residents of the street, especially the Search family, whose house overlooked the Krogers' bungalow. Now a writer and broadcaster, Gay Search, then aged fifteen, remembers that Helen popped over nearly every day to chat with her mother and, sometimes, take photos of Gay and her brother Phil with her expensive-looking camera. Every weekday, that is – the couple never seemed to be around at weekends.

On 5 November 1960, Special Branch approached the Searches and revealed why. Weekends were when the Krogers met their contact – Russian spy Gordon Lonsdale, real name Konon Molody, the head of a spy ring based at the Admiralty Underwater Weapons Establishment at Portland in Dorset. Two corrupt civil servants who worked there, Harry Houghton and Ethel Gee, supplied secret information to Lonsdale, who took it to the Krogers, whose real names were Morris and Lona Cohen. 'Helen' photographed this material using the same expensive camera she used to photograph Gay and Phil Search.

Excitingly for Gay and Phil, Special Branch used Gay's bedroom as a lookout. This led to some near misses when Helen paid her visits and the British agents would have to hide in the downstairs bathroom. Gay's mother bore the brunt of all this – she would have to pretend to be Helen's friend, just as Helen was pretending to be hers. In early 1961, the Krogers were arrested and their bungalow was taken apart to reveal the radio transmitter and camera equipment, plus lighters with secret compartments and what disgraced civil servant Houghton in his account of the case called 'the whole James Bond collection'.[36] It tells you a lot about the psychology of the Krogers that Helen told Gay – who visited her in prison shortly before the Krogers were swapped for some British spies and returned to Moscow – that she would never forgive her mother for 'betraying' her by allowing her house to be used as an observation post.

You can see the same shamelessness at play in the story of Donald Healthfield and Tracey Foley. In June 2010, shortly after returning from an evening out to celebrate their son Tim's twentieth birthday, Heathfield and Foley's worst nightmare was realised. Their house in Cambridge, Massachusetts, was raided by armed FBI officers who promptly arrested them, bundled them off in separate black cars and began an intensive, forensic search of the property. Tim and his brother Alex, who had always believed their parents to be a political consultant (Donald) and a real estate agent (Tracey), were told the pair had been arrested on suspicion of being 'unlawful agents of a foreign government'. Which, it transpired, they were.

The ring they were part of had been busted in an FBI operation called 'Ghost Stories'. Heathfield and Foley were not Canadians, although their names were: they belonged to long-dead Canadian children whose identities the spies had stolen and adopted. Their real names were Andrei Bezrukov and Elena Vavilova and they were Russian nationals who had been recruited as a couple by the KGB. After intensive training in spycraft, such as communicating in code and evading detection, they were sent abroad in the late 1980s as what the CIA calls 'illegals' – deep-cover secret agents. Taking root in the new soil of Canada, they worked on acquiring the identities of ordinary Western citizens. As 'Tracey Foley', Elena gave birth to Tim in a Toronto hospital in June 1990. Alex followed in 1994, after which the family was sent, presumably on SVR (the new KGB) orders, to Paris so that 'Donald' could study for an MBA. Their next stop was not a return to Canada but a new life in Boston: 'Donald' had got a place at Harvard University's Kennedy School of Government. During their time in Europe, the old Soviet Union had continued its long process of dis-integration under Boris Yeltsin. Their relocation to Boston coincided with the arrival of Vladimir Putin, their new boss, who was keen to reactivate agents who had been left dis-combobulated by developments in their home country.

What is amazing is how well Andrei and Elena kept up the pretence of being ordinary parents with ordinary jobs. Sure, Andrei travelled frequently, especially once he got a job at a business development consultancy called Global Partners, but Elena was a classic 'soccer mom', apparently devoting herself to her sons until they were old enough not to need her, at which point she went into real estate. Tim has described his and his brother's childhood as 'absolutely normal': 'I never had anything close to a suspicion regarding my parents,' he told the *Guardian*. 'It seemed all my friends' parents led much more exciting and successful lives.'[37] In an interview she gave in 2019 under her real identity, to promote a novel she wrote based on her experiences, Elena confirmed that sustaining this atmosphere of dullness was the whole point: 'If one day you come and do something like James Bond, then that's it and you're done, you can't sustain a longer life and work doing that. People think it's always on the edge, but actually most of it is very routine and very boring.'[38]

While no one was paying attention, the couple were communicating with the SVR using digital steganography – posting images online that contained messages hidden in the pixels. Their son Tim thinks his parents would never have told him or his brother about their true identities. They were professionals, committed both to the deception and *also to each other* at the deepest possible level. Only they, as a couple, knew the truth, which was terrifying if you stopped to think about it. None of their friendships was real because they themselves were not real; even more troubling is that they had had children in the certain knowledge that they would never be able to tell them who they really were and what they were doing.

Rather than prison, the couple's fate was to be exchanged as part of an official spy swap with Russia. (A Russian spy for the British intelligence services, Sergei Skripal – later to become world famous when he was poisoned in Salisbury with the nerve agent Novichok in 2018 – was part of the swap.)

Handling spies is often about exploiting the vulnerable – using sophisticated techniques to manipulate the personality flaws of damaged people who are happy to risk everything because they have nothing to lose. The 'Foleys' were different, however.

So too were Jason and Suzanne Matthews, their American equivalents, who worked for thirty-three years for the CIA's Operations Directorate trying to recruit intelligence sources. (Jason used his insider knowledge to write the successful thriller *Red Sparrow*, filmed with Jennifer Lawrence playing a Russian former ballerina forced to undergo espionage training.) The way they tell it, their coupledom was central to their success at 'turning' people because it put those people at ease.

'A tandem couple comes in really handy,' Jason admitted to the *Sunday Times*:

For instance, you've been working on Ivan for six months and you're not making any progress. So you invite Ivan over for dinner. Suzanne talks to Ludmilla – Mrs Ivan – in the kitchen, swapping recipes in English. And because Suzanne knows the game, she talks to Ludmilla about the future of her children, and what they can achieve, what America is like. And Ludmilla, back home with Ivan that night, says, 'You stay friends with that Jason guy because I like her and they're going to help us.' Then, one night, Ivan knocks on the door, tears streaming down his face: his five-year-old has leukaemia and he needs help. We had doctors on call, we could fly people anywhere.[39]

Being a tandem couple is the best sort of 'agency marriage' to have because you are both spies, rather than one person being 'inside' and the other being a 'civilian'. In that situation, it would be 'up to the inside spouse to decide to tell the civilian spouse what they're doing or why they're doing it. That often does not happen, for good reasons or bad, which contributes to the high divorce rate. It's a built-in excuse to fool around. With Suzanne and me, she knew when I had a meeting, when I was going to go out and what the story was. And, of course, it worked the other way, too.'[40]

The secret here is communication. Anyone who has ever been through relationship therapy knows that is not something couples *necessarily* excel at. For some, though, being able to communicate effectively is the glue that binds them – as I hope to show in the next chapter.

2

Communication

One day in the late eighteenth century, a lady was walking across Clapham Common in south London when a cow started following her.

This wasn't unusual in itself: cattle grazed freely on the common in those days. But this cow was behaving strangely – aggressively, even. It advanced swifter than the lady was able to escape from it. Fearing it meant to trample her, she cried out; at which point a man emerged from one of the grand houses bordering the common. Under the circumstances, the woman would have been too distracted to notice much about this fast-approaching figure. Yet the man demanded to be noticed because he looked rather, well, peculiar.

He was wearing clothes so old-fashioned they were practically fancy dress: a faded violet suit with a high collar which hung loosely over a shirt with frilly cuffs. On his head perched a periwig and, atop that, a three-cornered hat of the type worn by military personnel in the early part of the century. He wasn't even *walking*, really – it was more like shuffling. The woman called out to him but he didn't reply (though he may have done one of his trademark nervous squeaks). He also seemed to be deliberately avoiding her gaze, as if her physical presence in front of him was not a fact he was prepared to concede. Still, actions speak louder than words, and the man gallantly interposed himself between the mad cow and the woman, allowing her to get away across the common to safety.

Assuming the woman was local, it is likely that she would have had some idea of the man's identity, even if she only knew him as 'the Wizard of Clapham Common'. Because that was the name by which Henry Cavendish was known to passing children, many of whom wondered what the 80-foot-high ship's mast in his garden was all about. (It was the mount for an aerial telescope.) Had the woman been invited in for a restorative sherry – which she would not have been, because she was a woman and Cavendish was deeply wary of women – she would have found the house unwelcoming. As most of it had been given over to science and experimentation, comfort was not a primary consideration. There were functional, sparsely furnished drawing rooms and bedrooms, but all the remaining spaces had been converted into laboratories, libraries or study areas. Scattered everywhere were gadgets of one form or another. All the rooms had green venetian blinds.

The woman would not have seen any of Cavendish's servants because he had arranged the house so that they were as good as invisible. This was because he hated running into people unexpectedly or having fluffy 'social' conversations. He had once been so terrified when he bumped into a maid on the stairs that he had a separate staircase built for the use of his staff, who included a maker of mathematical instruments.

Genius and eccentricity often go hand in hand – and

Henry Cavendish was one of the eighteenth century's pre-eminent geniuses. There were few areas of contemporary science (as it was not yet called; 'natural philosophy' was the preferred term) in which he did not take a consuming, questing interest – and in which he did not excel. He discovered the existence of hydrogen. He weighed the earth and estimated its density, arriving at a figure so accurate that it amazes modern scientists. By 'sparking' hydrogen and oxygen together, he demonstrated the composition of water, and showed that air was a mixture of nitrogen and oxygen and another substance (identified a whole century later as argon). He was the first person to realise that a fish (electric eels) could generate electricity. As the psychologist Oliver Sacks put it: 'Cavendish united extraordinary intuitive powers with great experimental ingenuity and consummate mathematical skill, in a manner perhaps unequalled since Newton.' What is telling, however, is that Sacks wrote this in a 2001 paper titled: 'Henry Cavendish: An early case of Asperger's syndrome?'[1]

Cavendish was consoled by rituals. He walked the same route every day, wore the same clothes and ate the same meal – a leg of mutton. Essentially solitary, he found crowded rooms stressful and often fled from social gatherings without saying goodbye. Word went around that you only got a reply from Cavendish if you did not address him to his face; and even then, you might not get any acknowledgement at all.

One of the only people whose company Cavendish was able to tolerate was his relative, Georgiana, Duchess of Devonshire: he was 'delighted with her', wrote her mother in a boastful letter, and 'calls upon her frequently'.[2] Like Cavendish, the duchess was a scientist – she had had her own laboratory built at Chatsworth, her country seat. Her particular interest was in so-called 'pneumatic chemistry', the science of air, especially its medical application: an area that also interested Cavendish. She alone was permitted to visit him unannounced, though her father discouraged the association on the grounds that Cavendish was 'not a gentleman – *he works*'.[3]

He did work, exceptionally hard – though he didn't have to, having been born into an aristocratic family. As well as Georgiana, one of his ancestors was Bess of Hardwicke, in whose vault in what is now Derby Cathedral he is buried. He was immensely wealthy and when he died he had more money deposited in the Bank of England than anyone else in Britain. James Watt, one of the inventors of the steam engine, wrote that Cavendish was 'worth above £100,000, and does not spend £1,000 a year. Rich men may do mean actions.'[4]

Henry's mother died when he was young, but the love and patience of his father, Lord Charles Cavendish, meant he was able to excel as a scientist, despite – or perhaps because of – what Sacks was surely right to identify as an autistic spectrum disorder (ASD). Lord Charles had abandoned his political career for one in science, becoming a member of the Royal Society in 1727 and rising to vice-president. As a child, Henry helped his father with his experiments, before going on to Cambridge University. After he left it was his father who introduced him to scientific society. He published his first paper – on 'factitious airs' – in 1766.

So far, so remarkable. The problem was that Cavendish was totally in his own world. He experimented because he liked experimenting, not because he was particularly ambitious. He didn't seek the approval of his peers because it didn't interest him. He was motivated by perfectionism, not ego. He was too shy to network. He published very little; only after perusing Cavendish's papers posthumously did people realise that he had discovered many scientific laws – for instance Ohm's law of electrical conductivity – years before those to whom they were attributed.

For what we know of Cavendish's achievements, we have another man – indeed, another scientist – to thank.

Charles Blagden was born in April 1748 in the small Gloucestershire village of Wotton-under-Edge. If he is remembered at all it is for the not-terribly-interesting Blagden's law: 'The depression of the freezing point of dilute solutions is proportional to the amount of the dissolved substance.' But he was sociable – good at networking and conversation; an avid consumer of scientific journals – as well as being fastidious and possessing an impressive memory. George Wilson, in his 1851 biography of Cavendish, says of Blagden: 'He was not a man of genius, his writings display no originality, nor has he any place among the discoverers of science. On the other hand, he appears to have preferred to occupy himself with the labours of those he might have rivalled. He appears before us as a somewhat formal and ungenial person, more an object of respect than of love to those who knew him.'[5]

Cavendish and Blagden first met through the Royal Society in the mid-1770s. Blagden was about to be posted to North America to work as an army surgeon (he had originally trained as a doctor) and Cavendish offered to help him with some research he intended to conduct there into the effects of the Gulf Stream. The pair hooked up again over breakfast in March 1782. Blagden was living in

Plymouth at the time, having settled there after leaving the army. Cavendish asked him to collect samples of the local air in bottles and bring them to him so that he could test them with his eudiometer – an instrument for measuring and analysing gases.

Bizarrely enough, it was a shared interest in extreme temperatures which formed the basis of a friendship, or at least the nearest Cavendish came to friendship. Blagden was fascinated by how much heat the human body could withstand and, in a specially constructed sauna, heated himself, several co-experimenters and a dog almost to roasting point in an attempt to find out.[6] Soon after their breakfast meeting, Cavendish gave him advice about a piece he was intending to publish in *Philosophical Transactions* about the effects of freezing mercury – or 'quicksilver' as it was known. Something must have clicked because the following year, after the death of his father, Lord Charles, Cavendish asked Blagden to become his assistant.

And so, between 1782 and 1789 when the relationship cooled, Blagden spent a lot of time at the Wizard of Clapham Common's mansion, playing Watson to Cavendish's Holmes, sublimating his private aimlessness into something helpful. He provided practical assistance of a holding-the-test-tube variety, but more importantly he made sure Cavendish's theories and the results of his experiments were disseminated in the appropriate organs. He also excelled at recording and organising data. In return, Cavendish acted as what Steve Silberman, in his brilliant book about neuro-diversity *NeuroTribes*, calls his 'human Google',[7] helping him with his own projects.

That Cavendish allowed Blagden so close suggests he found the younger man – seventeen years his junior –

unthreatening; also that Blagden was sensitive enough to know how to conduct himself around Cavendish. Blagden seems to have been popular. He became secretary of the Royal Society in 1784, winning the election by over a hundred votes and staying in the post until 1797. He was known to be frugal to the point of meanness, like Cavendish, with plain tastes. Dr Johnson found him a 'delightful fellow', though his biographer Boswell thought him pompous and pedantic – a view borne out by a satirical poem from the 1780s mocking Royal Society members which includes a telling couplet about Blagden:

> While o'er the bulk of these transacted deeds
> Prim Blagden pants, and damns them as he reads.[8]

This does not seem to have deterred admirers, however. 'Few men of science appear to have enjoyed the intimacy of so many eminent men as Blagden,' observed Frederick Getman in the science magazine *Osiris* in 1937.[9] Blagden knew the painter Sir Joshua Reynolds, Dr Johnson, the civil engineer John Smeaton – and, crucially, French scientists such as Georges Cuvier, Claude-Louis Berthollet and Antoine Lavoisier. Blagden eased Cavendish into society, taking him to clubs such as the Monday Club, which met on Mondays at the George & Vulture coffee house off Lombard Street. It was presumably Cavendish who, in return, introduced Blagden to Georgiana, Duchess of Devonshire. Blagden helped the duchess enlarge her mineral collection and was excited when she acquired a piece of 'elastic marble' from Italy.[10]

Until the outbreak of the French revolution in 1789, Blagden made annual tours of the Continent. As a confident traveller, he also encouraged Cavendish, an avowed home-body, to go on trips around England and Wales by carriage. Blagden went too, of course. They travelled to Oxford and to Wales, where they toured an ironworks, and to Birmingham, where they visited James Watt and observed his steam engine. After these trips turned out to be a success – not a given with Cavendish by any means – they made several more visits to the industrial north to watch copper-casting, lime-kilning and coal mining, taking with them a mobile chemistry kit so that they could conduct experiments on any samples they picked up. Along the way they would stop to take the temperature of any springs they came across and examine rocks. Cavendish was fascinated by process but completely uninterested in how anything looked, so the beauty of the scenery passed him by.

Blagden was well aware of Cavendish's unconventionality and would often find himself defending his friend's behaviour to others. 'Talk about Mr Cavendish, & explanation of character,' he recorded in his diary, though he admitted that Cavendish was 'sulky' and out of sorts (as he could also be). Blagden also shared Cavendish's taste for order and routine, one biographer noting that 'in his daily walk from his residence at Brompton to the rooms of the Royal Society, he invariably pursued the same path notwithstanding the fact that several different ways were at his disposal, and strangely enough the route chosen was the longest'.[11]

The association shored up Blagden's reputation, which was sealed in 1792 when King George III gave him a knighthood in recognition of his services to science. Blagden's intimacy with the great Cavendish became a qualification in itself, even if it attracted a certain amount of mean-spirited gossip – the rumour being that Blagden was in it for the money. Cavendish was certainly generous to him, leaving him £15,000 in his will – a huge sum at the time, though historians have struggled to substantiate the rumour that he was paid a £500 annuity.

An early biography of Cavendish says that both he and Blagden were 'reserved and undemonstrative persons'. Humphry Davy commented that the pair got on because they were both 'cold & selfish'. In fact, it seems likely that Blagden adjusted his behaviour when in Cavendish's company in order to put him (and keep him) at his ease. Discussing his own marriage prospects with friends, Blagden worried that any future wife would find Cavendish – his employer, at whose beck and call he was – boring and offensive, especially his inability to talk about anything except science.

After the pair's formal working relationship ended in 1789, some of the intimacy disappeared from their friend-ship, though they continued to correspond and to dine together when they could. When Cavendish died at Clapham in 1810, aged seventy-eight, Blagden confided to his diary that he felt 'much affected'.[12]

The sole chink in Cavendish's intellectual armour was his belief in the then-popular theory that combustible bodies contain a fire-like element called phlogiston, which is released when they burn. This is where the story of Cavendish and Blagden intertwines with the tale of another scientific couple, a married one this time: the glamorous Lavoisiers. For it was Antoine Lavoisier who disproved the phlogiston theory, with a little unwitting help from the hapless Blagden.

In June 1783 Blagden had visited Lavoisier in Paris and told him how Cavendish had created water by burning 'inflammable air'. Lavoisier, who had been working on his own theory of combustion, repeated the experiment and published his results in a paper entitled 'Réflexions sur le phlogistique', claiming he had discovered the result before Cavendish and had not known (in Blagden's words) 'that the experiment was made in consequence of what I had informed him of'.[13] Lavoisier moved the story forward not just by naming inflammable air 'hydrogen' but by showing more clearly than Cavendish that water was a compound of two gases, hydrogen and oxygen. The whole 'water controversy' became a massive deal and Blagden found himself caught in the middle.

But Lavoisier might never have made his critique of phlogiston had his wife, Marie-Anne, not translated for him Richard Kirwan's 'Essay on Phlogiston and the Constitution of Acids'. It was this essay that convinced him the theory was bogus. (An additional awkwardness was Blagden's rumoured weakness for Marie-Anne.) Thanks to her, the Lavoisier household became one of France's top scientific salons. But her talents went beyond the merely social and indeed beyond what would have been expected in scientific families, where it was common for everyone to muck in and help out with experiments. It is hard, contemplating this world of kitchen-sink chemistry, to gauge exactly how much Marie-Anne did, and possibly glib to invoke what we now call the 'Matilda Effect' (of which more later) – when men claim the credit for scientific discoveries made by women.

Still, there is no doubt that Marie-Anne Lavoisier was a remarkable woman. She was born Marie-Anne Pierrette Paulze on 20 January 1758 in the Loire region of France.

Her father, Jacques Paulze, a director of the French East India Company, became a member of the Ferme-Générale, a company which paid the monarchy for the right to collect certain taxes – and was much reviled by the general public as a result.

Antoine Lavoisier had worked with Marie-Anne's father at the Ferme-Générale, which is where he first met his wife-to-be. He married her on 16 December 1771. She was fourteen and straight out of the convent, where she had lived since her mother died in 1761; he was twenty-seven. Eighteenth-century bourgeois marriages were business deals. Marie-Anne was a desirable property and therefore much fought over, most ferociously by a fifty-year-old called Count d'Amerval. Lavoisier was lucky to win her, which he did after the intervention of Monsieur Paulze, who felt Lavoisier was a better bet.

The Ferme-Générale made the people who worked for it very rich. Lavoisier was worth 1.2 million livres (around £50 million) in 1786. He was appointed to the post of gunpowder administrator and the couple moved to a private apartment at the Arsenal in Paris, dividing their time between this residence and their vast estates in the Loire Valley and at Villefrancoeur. Here, Antoine and Marie-Anne used their wealth to build a state-of-the-art chemistry laboratory where, believe it or not, they spent some of the happiest times of their married life. Lavoisier had studied chemistry in his youth; now he had the money to indulge himself. So that she was better equipped to help him, Marie-Anne received lessons from her husband's colleagues and participated in the experiments.

The couple and their team would rise at 5 a.m. to spend three hours in the lab. The rest of the day would be devoted to other tasks, then another three hours in the evening were set aside for experimentation. Saturdays, wrote Marie-Anne, were 'a day of happiness' for her husband. 'A few enlightened friends, a few young people proud to be admitted to the honour of participating in his experiments, gathered in the laboratory in the early morning; it was there that we lunched, there that we held forth, there that we created that theory which has immortalised its author.'[14] Among these 'enlightened friends' would have been Charles Blagden, a regular visitor, though they also entertained Joseph Priestley, James Watt and Benjamin Franklin. Darlings of salon society, the Lavoisiers celebrated themselves as a couple by commissioning a large portrait by Marie-Anne's art teacher, Jacques-Louis David, which showed them together surrounded by lab equipment such as flasks and a hydrometer.

Given the social tumult then rocking France, however, it was never going to end well. Already marked as suspect for being a nobleman and for his work at the Ferme-Générale, Antoine had also made an enemy of the revolutionary leader Jean-Paul Marat, who declared: 'The Republic has no need of Savants.' On 8 February 1794, Antoine was arrested. Marie-Anne visited him regularly in prison to try and secure his release, citing his scientific breakthroughs and insisting that his involvement with the Ferme-Générale was ancient history, but to no avail. Following a show trial, in which he was 'found guilty of adding water to the people's tobacco', he was executed on the guillotine in the Place de la Concorde on 8 May 1794, along with his father-in-law.

Afterwards Marie-Anne was bitter and penniless, furious with former colleagues who had not come to her husband's defence. First, her money and possessions were confiscated, then she was arrested after 'seditious correspondence' was supposedly found in her house, though she was later released. Eventually she managed to recover her house and some possessions, including her husband's notebooks and scientific apparatus. She published his memoirs and wrote an angry preface for the first edition attacking his betrayers.

She did not want for marriage proposals after her husband's untimely end, but in 1804 she married Count Rumford, a former spy who dabbled at being a physicist. He was one of the founders of the Royal Institution and the Rumford professorship at Harvard. The marriage was not as easy as her previous one. For one thing, Rumford objected to her desire to retain her first husband's name. He also wanted to remodel her house and disliked the amount of time she spent entertaining. 'My Rumford would make me very happy could he but keep quiet,' wrote Marie-Anne – hardly a ringing endorsement.[15] In temperament he was more like Henry Cavendish, a loner who disliked socialising, and he was alienated by her gregariousness. They quarrelled violently and after two years together he moved out of the family home, although they remained married until 1809.

In the end it is not possible to say with any accuracy how involved in Antoine Lavoisier's work Marie-Anne was. She was a true multihyphenate: her husband's researcher, assistant, translator and collaborator; also his illustrator and then later, Antoine's editor and publisher. She probably wouldn't have had enough of the right sort of training to make significant discoveries. One of her main jobs was translating papers by the likes of Priestley and Cavendish into French so that her husband could read them. So she was a communication aid – an amanuensis. And as one of the most intriguing and successful stories of creative collaboration shows, that is one of the most important roles anyone can play.

———————

Frederick Delius was an English Romantic composer, born in Bradford, Yorkshire. His work – lush, melodic, defiantly idiosyncratic – takes in choral works, violin sonatas and beautiful orchestral pieces such as 'On Hearing the First Cuckoo in Spring' (1912). It evokes landscape, especially the English landscape, with charged efficiency. You can see why so many people think of Delius as a quintessentially English composer.

In reality, though, he spent very little of his life in England. In the 1880s, after a stint working for his father's textile firm, he went to Florida to run an orange plantation, before moving to Paris, where he lived a wild life and contracted the syphilis that would debilitate him so painfully in his final years. Towards the end of the century he settled in Grez-sur-Loing, a tiny hamlet on the edge of the forest of Fontainebleau, with the painter Jelka Rosen, whom he married in 1903. They lived there until their deaths nearly thirty years later.

By the late 1920s, Delius's syphilis had entered its tertiary stage and he was in a bad state – blind and confined to a wheelchair. Ironically, this twilight period became the most celebrated of the composer's life. A widely seen dramatisation of it by Ken Russell, *Song of Summer*, made for the BBC's arts strand *Omnibus* in 1968, fixed him in the public imagination as an old grump. (Kate Bush's 1980 song 'Delius' was inspired by the programme, Bush having been much affected by watching it as a child.)

What made it so extraordinary were the events set in train one day in May 1928, when a young, self-taught composer called Eric Fenby, also a Yorkshireman, heard some of Delius's music on the radio while he was playing chess with a friend. Enraptured by it in a way he could not articulate, he became determined to find out more about the composer. When he discovered Delius's plight, he was shocked: not by his illness per se – though it would have been shocking to a devout, upright Christian such as Fenby – but by what his illness denied him: the ability to write more music. 'To be a genius,' he noted, 'as this man plainly was, and have something beautiful in you and not be able to rid yourself of it because you could no longer see your score paper and no longer hold your pen.'[16]

Fenby developed an obsession with the idea of helping Delius. Without telling anyone and with no expectation of receiving a reply, he wrote to him offering his services for three or four years. On 29 August 1928 a letter plopped onto his doormat: 'My dear young friend, Your sympathetic and appreciative letter gave me the greatest pleasure . . .' It warned him, however, to visit the house as soon as possible and 'see if you like it' before making a decision. This was wise advice.

Fenby arrived at Grez-sur-Loing on 10 October 1928, unaware that he would spend much of the next six years there. Jelka met him at the train station in nearby Bourron in an old Ford with yellow curtains at the windows.

His first meeting with Delius was inauspicious. The composer was gaunt, deathly pale, with a great screen stretched around him as protection against draughts, and a checked rug on his lap. He was plainly in a huge amount of pain. His suffering was horrible to witness and one of the reasons why he was so moody. 'We talked about Yorkshire, the wolds and moors, Filey Bridge, Festival cricket at Scarborough,' Fenby recalled. All was friendly until the talk turned to music, when a contemptuous smile appeared on the composer's face and he declared: 'English music. I've never heard of any' – and the rest of the meal passed in silence.[17] Fenby realised that if he was going to survive there he must not express any opinions of his own.

Silence usually reigned at mealtimes as Delius could not bear the sound of conversation or the rattle of cutlery. With everyone he was rude, imperious and demanding – including Jelka, who devoted her days to looking after him. He was no better with his other staff – a team of nurses from Germany, a cook and a housekeeper.

Life in the house was rigidly ritualised. Delius rose at six in the morning in order to be washed and exercised. Then he was read to until 8 a.m. A servant then brought up breakfast and took over reading until 10 a.m. Then there was a household conference to decide if Delius was sufficiently well to be taken into the garden. If the weather was good enough, he was dressed and put in a wheelchair and wheeled to a sheltered spot where letters and a newspaper were read to him. Lunch was at noon. Delius would only eat soup if salt had been added during cooking, never afterwards. In the evening Delius was helped into a bath chair and pushed up the road accompanied by a helper carrying a lantern and, if necessary, an umbrella.

Fenby's first attempt to work with Delius was not a success. The old man threw his head back and hollered out a tune: '*Ter-te-ter, Ter-te-ter . . .*' At the end he asked Fenby: 'Have you got that? Now sing it!' – apparently unaware that what he had been singing had no tune or coherent pitch.

Fenby asked what key Delius had in mind and was told 'A minor'. Fenby then asked him to call out the names of the notes as well as singing. This Delius grudgingly agreed to do and so the piece took shape.

'I had not thought that it would be like this, and the sting of my emotion pierced me to the heart,' Fenby admitted. 'My pen flopped about in my fingers, and in my confusion I found myself holding it upside down. My fingers were inky, and the tears that I had been fighting to keep back now blurred my spectacles, and I could not see.'[18] As Fenby left the room, the session over, he overheard Delius say to Jelka: 'That boy is no good. He is too slow. He cannot even take down a simple melody.'

Against the odds, however, things got better. A routine evolved, and a better working method. On the days when he felt like composing, Delius's armchair was placed next to the piano in the music room. Then each pair of double doors was opened along the corridors and Jelka sent ahead for the final inspection. If she gave her consent, at 4 p.m. the male nurse would heave Delius up over his shoulder and carry him, hanging limply, up the steep, polished stairs from the living room and through his bedroom into the music room. Adjustments to cushions and feet and the room's temperature were made. And then the composition would begin.

Yet as Fenby wrote later: 'Never was music written so laboriously.'[19] Delius could only work for a maximum of one and a half hours a day. It wasn't unusual for this effort to tire him out for the whole of the next day too. 'Thus it took him days to dictate in full score what in his prime would have been accomplished in an hour.'[20]

Initially tense, the sessions became more relaxed as Fenby's technique improved and as he acquired the courage to stand up to Delius when he thought something wasn't right. This won him the composer's trust, as Delius came to realise that Fenby was criticising him from a place of respect and, often, coming up with constructive criticism.

At the start of work on a project, they would play through any fragments that might exist. Sometimes Delius used old sketches as the basis for new pieces. Then the composer's bearing would change intimidatingly. He became, Fenby wrote, an 'upright, excitable, gesticulating fighter as he felt himself deeper and deeper into the music with more and more frenzied intensity, calling out the notes, their values in time, the pitch, the phrase-lengths whilst I struggled at the keyboard to reproduce them and jot them down in manuscript'.[21]

Sometimes Delius had only the vaguest sense of what he wanted until that rough idea had been played to him at the piano. Even then he was never able to retain more than a few bars at a time.

With Fenby's help, Delius completed by dictation two works for Thomas Beecham's Delius Festival in 1929 – *A Late Lark* for tenor and orchestra; and *Cynara*, for baritone and orchestra. When these pieces were well received, Fenby agreed to help Delius with some more ambitious works, including a third sonata for violin and piano and a tone poem for orchestra – 'A Song of Summer'. Again, progress was slow and the sessions arduous: '[Delius] was so ill when he began to dictate the sonata that I almost despaired of the day-to-day threading of effort and thought essential to the making of a coherent whole,' Fenby remembered.[22]

It was an inspired match. One of the reasons Fenby was able to get so much out of Delius is that he worked hard to empathise with Delius's difficulties – and keep on empathising, no matter how hard his composer-boss sometimes was to work for. A recurring frustration for Fenby was Delius's refusal ever to talk about music. He hated any intellectual discussion of compositional technique. In general he had a contempt for erudition and for most musicians, who he felt did not play his music sensitively enough.

Then there were the religious differences: Fenby was a committed Christian, Delius an atheist whose cold, hard philosophy of life derived from Nietzsche's *Thus Spake Zarathustra*. Delius and his wife were old and living in the past whereas Fenby was a 'raw young man who had barely begun to live'.[23] They wanted to listen to no music but Delius's. One day Fenby bought a miniature score of a Sibelius symphony. When he told Delius, the old man told him to throw it away, go out into the woods and listen to the music of nature instead.

I touched earlier, in the Introduction, on the subject of muse relationships. It could be said of both Fenby and Marie-Anne Lavoisier that they were their partners' muses.

On the face of it there is a fine line between a muse – a personified source of inspiration – and a facilitator in the form of, say, an amanuensis like Fenby or a literary copyist. The original nine muses in Greek mythology were the daughters of Zeus and Mnemosyne: Calliope (responsible for lyric poetry), Clio (history), Euterpe (flutes and lyric poetry), Thalia (comedy and pastoral poetry), Melpomene (tragedy), Terpsichore (dance), Erato (love poetry), Polyhymnia (sacred poetry) and Urania (astronomy). That all the muses were women has, over the years, lent the concept unsavoury 'erotic' overtones. (Why are most muse-inspired artists men?) A muse is – select your own cliché – a difficult mistress, as beguiling as she is fickle and elusive; or a femme fatale with the power to withhold inspiration in a manner which casts the whole business of artistic creation as a sado-masochistic game.

Fenby's predicament suggests the situation is more nuanced than this: not just that a muse can be male as well as female, but that both creator and inspirer can benefit from the arrangement. Fenby went on to be a successful composer in his own right – he wrote the music for Alfred Hitchcock's 1939 film *Jamaica Inn* – though his intensely self-critical nature led him to destroy a lot of his work unheard. Another example would be the American ballerina Suzanne Farrell and the choreographer George Balanchine who, as the writer Francine Prose observes, collaborated to produce work neither would have managed alone. This, she notes, is where the sexism creeps in: 'Farrell was inevitably described as Balanchine's muse, and no one seems to have proposed that the reverse was also true.'[24]

Towards the end of the eighteenth century in Britain, for a woman to be a muse was seen as a great and noble thing. Women were beginning to enter the public literary sphere and to be celebrated for it. Indeed, the role of female muses was hotly debated. Was it simply to inspire men, or to champion burgeoning female creativity? Foremost among these muses were the so-called 'bluestocking' hostesses, such as Elizabeth Montagu and Hannah More: well-connected and often wealthy women, who created courts around them-selves in the form of salons where famous writers and artists met to discuss literary matters of the day. The nine most prominent feature in Richard Samuel's 1778 painting *The Nine Living Muses of Great Britain*. Oddly idealised so that it is almost impossible to tell them apart, they wear classical-style robes adorned with emblems linking them to the muses of antiquity.

One muse who is not included in Samuel's painting, probably because she hadn't published anything significant at the point when it was painted, is a tiny, vivacious Welsh woman called Hester Thrale. Late to the bluestocking party, she befriended the Queen Bee-like Montagu while also subtly setting herself apart from them. Her wit, as she saw it, was of a different texture: 'Mrs Montagu's Bouquet is all out of the Hothouse – mine out of the Woods & Fields & many a Weed there is in it.'[25] In other words, her wit was informal, wry, conversational.

In her writing Hester's tone of voice comes through clearly, like a digital radio broadcast from across the centuries, adding to the sense of her as a modern woman historically misplaced. As the scholar Felicity A. Nussbaum puts it: 'She broke with bluestocking patterns to voice an active sensibility that valued erotic desire, unfettered nature, improvisation and a plebeian cosmopolitanism.'[26] Astonishingly, she did all this while being almost permanently pregnant – she had twelve children, only four of whom lived into adulthood.

Thrale's friendship with the critic, essayist and compiler of one of the earliest and most influential dictionaries, Dr Samuel Johnson, is the subject of Beryl Bainbridge's brilliant 2001 novel *According to Queeney* – Queeney being the nickname of Hester's precocious eldest daughter (her real name was also Hester), from whose point of view the story is mostly told. Should it bother us that Hester is better known now for this friendship than for anything she wrote? Or that so much of what she did write – later in her life, after the death of her first husband freed her to do so – was either about Johnson or plainly influenced by him? He remained *her* muse long after their friendship had ceased – long after his death, even. But she transformed Johnson's life at a point when it looked as if depression would swallow it whole and he would produce little further work of consequence.

Hester had been married off young after her father went bankrupt to Henry Thrale, a wealthy but low-born brewer with a reputation for wild promiscuity. Their main home was a three-storey mansion on Henry's hundred-acre Streatham Park estate, about eight miles south of London. It sounds grand, though Hester called it 'a little squeezed miserable Place'.[27] Clever and, by the standards of the time, well educated for a woman – she knew Latin, Italian, French and Spanish – she bore the limitations of the marriage with impressive stoicism and positivity. She bit her tongue rather than express an opinion or do something Henry had forbidden (such as choose the food she ate or go out riding) because the contempt he showed when she crossed him merely reminded her of how little power she had.

Henry was not a cruel man as such, but he had no interest in Hester. As she wrote: 'Confidence was no word in our vocabulary; and I tormented myself to guess who possessed that of Mr Thrale.'[28] (It was rumoured to be a young socialite called Sophy Streatfeild, whose 'trick' was to burst into tears to persuade men to take pity on her.) Not naturally suited to the role of obedient wife and hostess, Hester worked hard to fit in with fashionable society: 'By keeping genteel Company . . . and looking much at Paintings, learning to

Dance almost incessantly, and chusing Foreign Models, not English Misses as patterns of imitation, some Grace has been acquired.'[29] This is self-deprecating to a ludicrous degree. Hester was a formidable one-off – like the man who was to become her best friend, intellectual sparring partner and, possibly, lover.

The Thrales first met Dr Johnson in January 1765 at a salon hosted by Hester in their town house in Borough – their London residence, next to Henry's brewery. Hester was keen to set herself up as a literary hostess and securing Dr Johnson as a guest would have been a great coup. He was fifty-five and she twenty-three. He was famous, renowned for his essays and general wit as well as his dictionary. His wife, Tetty, had died ten years earlier, since which time a chaotic proxy family of waifs and strays had gathered around him, including the blind poet Anna Williams and a prostitute called Poll Carmichael, who Johnson had found collapsed in the street and brought back to his rooms so that she could recover her health.

Johnson's own health was a constant source of anxiety to him. This hypochondria was part of a broader spectrum of obsessional behaviours linked to what might today have been diagnosed as Tourette's syndrome. Johnson had a host of tics and mannerisms; he also twitched, mumbled and blurted out inappropriate words. He rocked from foot to foot and performed elaborate rituals whenever he was about to cross a threshold. Whenever he peeled an orange, he kept the peel in his pocket. If his behaviour was unusual, his looks were unprepossessing. He was pockmarked and scrofulous and paid little attention to personal hygiene. These quirks were tolerated because, when he was in an 'up' frame of mind, Johnson was such engaging, dynamic company. As

Hester wrote, his mind was 'great beyond the comprehension of common mortals'.[30]

Johnson soon became a regular visitor to Streatham Park. But in early 1776, while struggling to finish his edition of Shakespeare's plays, he suffered a complete mental collapse. His trips to Streatham stopped as he was unable to leave his rooms. Concerned, the Thrales went over to see him and found him in a state of acute distress, babbling so disturbingly that Henry 'involuntarily lifted up one hand to shut Johnson's mouth, from provocation at hearing a man so wildly proclaim what he could at last persuade no one to believe; and what, if true, would have been so very unfit to reveal'.[31] (Quite what this was no one knows, but it may relate to Johnson's fear that he was going mad and needed to be locked up. This 'restraint' fantasy was also one of his erotic obsessions.) The Thrales' solution was to invite him to live at Streatham Park semi-permanently, which he did for the next sixteen years.

At Streatham, Johnson was able to enjoy the therapeutic benefits of country life. He was cooked for, waited on and had his clothes washed regularly – a novelty for him. When he singed his wig reading by candlelight – a common occurrence – there was a servant on hand to get him a new one. Henry, with whom Johnson got on surprisingly well, built him a summer house in the grounds and a laboratory where Johnson and Hester conducted scientific experiments, until one day when an explosion nearly injured one of the Thrales' children and Henry ruled that the experiments must cease.

But explosions were commonplace whenever Johnson was around: in a verse she wrote to commemorate a portrait of him, Hester mentions Johnson's 'inflammable temper'. On the whole, though, Streatham seems to have relaxed and softened 'the good doctor'. He learned levity. As the novelist and diarist Fanny Burney – who was also adopted by the Thrales – noted: 'Dr Johnson has more fun, & comical humour, Laughable & nonsense about him, than almost any body I ever saw.'[32] Johnson especially enjoyed being around Hester's ever-growing brood of children and shared her grief when, one by one, eight of them died. In time, wrote Hester, he became a sort of lucky charm: 'I think you shall never run away so again,' she said to him after one period of absence. 'I lost a Child the last time you were at a distance.'[33]

Hester and Dr Johnson's friendship was intense and rumours quickly spread that it had, as we now say, benefits. There is no clear evidence of an affair, although it is thought Johnson may have confided in her about his secret sado-masochistic desire to be locked up and dominated. Among her possessions discovered after Hester's death was a padlock marked 'Dr Johnson's padlock', which Johnson experts believe may be a memento of some kind of sex game; or it may have been given to Hester by him with instructions that she should lock him up when he was having one of his depressive episodes.

Hester tolerated his 'oddness', while he delighted in her cleverness and wit. He encouraged her to fill notebooks with observations which she later turned into the massive compendium of autobiographical material that was published after her death as *Thraliana*. Urged on by friends, she also kept a record of his witty sayings, which she turned into *Anecdotes of the Late Samuel Johnson*, the first biography of Johnson – beating his self-appointed 'official' biographer Boswell to it. (Boswell disliked Hester, while she could be catty in response: 'Mr Boswell however is the man for

Johnsonia: he really knows ten Times more Anecdotes of his Life than I do who see so much more of him.' This was a fair point: Boswell spent only around six months with the writer over the course of two decades.)

The Thrales took Johnson with them on their travels, first to Wales, where Hester had been born, then to Paris. As well as benefiting from a soothing, restorative atmosphere, Johnson received practical help from Hester as he worked on one of his last great projects, the *Lives of the Poets* series, which, wrote Hester, 'he would scarce have lived, I think, and kept his faculties entire, to have written, had not incessant care been exerted at the time of his first coming to be our constant guest in the country; and several times after that, when he found himself particularly oppressed with diseases, incident to the most vivid and fervent imaginations'.[34] She worked as his copyist and corrected his proofs. His *Journey to the Western Islands of Scotland* – a record of a trip he took with Boswell in 1773 – began as a series of letters to Hester.

When Henry Thrale died – of apoplexy, brought on by overeating – it was assumed by many that Hester would marry Dr Johnson. In addition to the newspaper speculation, Boswell wrote a bad-taste poem on the subject of their supposedly incipient nuptials. In the immediate aftermath of Henry's death, Johnson and Hester saw a fair amount of each other as Johnson was joint executor of Henry's will and helped to sort the financial mess the brewer had left behind. For this Hester was grateful: 'If an Angel from Heaven had told me 20 Years ago, that the Man I knew by the Name of Dictionary Johnson should one Day become Partner with me in a great Trade & that we should jointly or separately sign Notes Draughts &c for 3 or 4 Thousand

Pounds of a Morning, how unlikely it would have seemed ever to happen!'[35]

But then things started to sour. Hester began to tire of the brewing business, which had never been her responsibility, and she wanted rid of Streatham Park, which she had never liked much anyway. She sought something new – and found it in the form of her children's music teacher, Gabriel Mario Piozzi, whom she married on 25 July 1784 when she was forty-three, triggering a lengthy period of estrangement from her children. Johnson knew nothing of the wedding until he received a formal letter notifying him. Upset and affronted, he went into a steep decline and died five months later, before he and Hester had had a chance to properly repair their friendship.

Paradoxically, the combination of Johnson's death and the social disgrace of her marriage to a lowly Italian Catholic – 'I see the English newspapers are full of gross Insolence towards me,' she noted[36] – freed Hester up to become a writer. *Anecdotes of the Late Samuel Johnson* was published in 1786, five years before Boswell's more famous biography, and was a huge success, selling out its print run in three days, even though some critics considered it a breach of his privacy. (Observed Fanny Burney: 'She has given all – every word – and thinks that, perhaps, a justice to Dr Johnson, which, in fact, is the greatest injury to his memory.'[37]) Hester followed it with a collection of their letters in 1788; a distinctly Johnsonian dictionary called *British Synonymy* designed for 'Foreign Friends as have made English Literature their peculiar Study'; and a radical, feminist-slanted history called *Retrospection*.

Her work clearly has value and falls into that vast category of unjustly overlooked writing by women. Still, we can ask: would it have been improved by Johnson's editorial scrutiny, as his later work was by hers?

––––––––––––

Even if they are not always healthy, muse relationships can at least be fair in terms of what is given and taken. Take, for example, the artistic and sexual relationship enjoyed by the writers Anaïs Nin and Henry Miller.

Fascinated by the erotic honesty of D. H. Lawrence, the subject of her 1932 book *D. H. Lawrence: An Unprofessional Study*, Nin was trapped in an affectionate but sexless marriage to an American banker called Hugh Guiler and living in Louveciennes, a suburb of Paris. Struggling writer Miller, a married New Yorker whom Nin met in Paris in 1930, was the closest thing she could find to Lawrence. He became her mentor, ally and lover, but also – like many of Nin's other lovers, including the psychoanalyst Otto Rank – the recipient of her husband's generous financial help. Guiler it was who paid for Miller's flat at 18 Villa Seurat in the 14th Arrondissement which became Villa Borghese in his autobiographical novel *Tropic of Cancer*.

The currency of Miller and Nin's relationship was lavish mutual praise. Miller called her often-explicit diaries – which she had kept since the age of eleven – one of the most beautiful things he had ever read, and raved about her Lawrence book. Nin, meanwhile, told Miller that he was the greatest writer on the earth. Nin helped Miller with *Tropic of Cancer* – technically and in terms of paying for it to be published – while he helped her with her prose-poem *House of Incest*.

Apart from the obvious fact of their sexual attraction to

each other, Nin believed she and Miller were, in a paradox-
ical way, bonded by being so different – being opposites, in
fact. This carried over into the role they each played as the
other's muse. Miller, Nin told one journalist, was an emissary
from 'a completely exotic world'. He was 'a man of the
people, and a man of Brooklyn; and I was fascinated by
that. And he was fascinated by the European world [that I
represented], which treated him very gently and allowed
him to work. There was a great distance . . . which increased
in time.'[38]

In 1939, on the eve of war, Nin and Miller left Paris,
Nin establishing herself in New York with her husband.
Their influence on one another began to wane, but neither
was in any doubt about how important their mutual support
had been. Nin saw herself as bringing a kind of feminine
Buddhist order to his masculine chaos: 'Woman sits in the
centre and brings the vaster peripheral into the centre . . .
I go out little to the periphery.'[39] Miller returned the compliment. 'You have been the teacher, not Rank, nor even
Nietzsche or Spengler,' he wrote. 'In you was the vivification,
the living example, the guide who conducted me through
the labyrinth of self to unravel the riddle of myself, to come
to the mysteries.'[40]

The frequent bumpiness of the journey from musedom
to apprenticeship to a more autonomous sense of artistic
identity is apparent in another notorious early twentieth-
century literary relationship – that between F. Scott and
Zelda Fitzgerald. Neither Henry Miller nor Anaïs Nin is
hugely fashionable nowadays, but broadly speaking Nin's
erotic confessionals have more contemporary resonance than
Miller's raucous, taboo-busting blend of fiction and autobiography. It is a different story with Zelda, who has always

languished in the shadow of her husband's reputation as a Great Novelist, not to mention her own as a twenty-four-hour party girl who jumped into fountains and rode on the roofs of taxis. How many people even remember that Zelda also wrote a novel – *Save Me the Waltz*, published in the autumn of 1932?

Both Scott and Zelda used their own lives, particularly their fraught marriage, as the basis for fiction. Scott even used Zelda's letters as material, prompting her to quip in a spoof review of *The Beautiful and Damned* written for the *New York Tribune* that Scott 'seems to believe that plagiarism begins at home'.[41] But when Zelda, in *Save Me the Waltz*, trespassed on personal territory that Scott had marked off for his own use in *Tender is the Night*, he made her remove the offending passages from the manuscript. Later, he remarked that she was a 'third-rate writer' and her novel 'unwise in every way'.[42] With friends like that . . .

One of the most notorious muse–artist relationships, which has been described by more than one biographer in vampiric terms, is that of the Pre-Raphaelite painter and poet Dante Gabriel Rossetti and Elizabeth Siddall (as she was before Rossetti persuaded her to drop the final 'l' from her surname, thinking it was more elegant).

Siddal has been called the first supermodel. She was tall and skinny with a long neck, a mass of coppery hair and an elegant posture that belied her lowly(ish) origins. She also painted – indeed, pursued her own painting career, with help from the art critic John Ruskin, who sponsored her, calling her a 'noble, glorious creature' with 'red gold hair, ethereal colouring, large limpid eyes, and . . . the look of someone in a medieval Florentine fresco'[43] – and wrote poetry. For the most part, however, she has been fixed in the public imagination as a symbol of inert, passive beauty – lent additional poignancy by her tragic early death.

At the root of Rossetti's obsession with Siddal was a queasy fascination with death and the ability of true beauty to transcend it. Considering how relatively well known Siddal is now, it's odd to think that, as the art historian Jan Marsh points out, 'in her lifetime, she had virtually no public identity, and in the twenty years following her death there were few published references to her'.[44] Only when Rossetti died in 1882 did she step out from beneath his shadow and begin to cast one of her own. For a long time, though, the fame that gathered around her was of a dark, gothic variety, thanks in no small part to Rossetti's extraordinary behaviour after her death.

In the middle of the night on 5 October 1869, Rossetti's friend Charles Howell, together with a doctor and a lawyer, lit a bonfire beside Siddal's grave in Highgate Cemetery and dug up her coffin in order to extract a manuscript that Rossetti had placed in it after her death seven years earlier. Rossetti had instructed Howell to exhume her corpse because he'd decided he wanted to publish the poems after all. Presumably to quell Rossetti's anxieties, Howell reassured Rossetti in a letter that the dead Siddal was still 'quite perfect' and her trademark red hair still abundant: it had grown posthumously until it filled the coffin.

The manuscript had suffered as we might expect. Soaked and worm-eaten, it was promptly sent away for disinfecting. Rossetti destroyed it as soon as he had copied from it the poems he needed. As for Siddal's body, Howell was obviously not telling the truth. It would have been as worm-eaten as the notebook.

Born in Hatton Garden, London, into a lower-middle-class family – her father made and sold cutlery – Siddal became an artist's model after the Pre-Raphaelite artist William Deverell depicted her as Viola in his painting *Twelfth Night*. Deverell had spotted her in 1849, working as a milliner's assistant in Cranbourn Alley off Leicester Square in central London. Years later, his fellow Pre-Raphaelite William Holman Hunt remembered the moment when Deverell broke the news of Lizzie's discovery:

Rossetti at that date had the habit of coming to me with a drawing folio, and sitting with it designing while I was painting at a further part of the room . . . Deverell broke in upon our peaceful labours. He had not been seated many minutes, talking in a somewhat absent manner, when he bounded up, marching, or rather dancing to and fro about the room, and, stopping emphatically, he whispered, 'You fellows can't tell what a stupendously beautiful creature I have found. By Jove! She's like a queen, magnificently tall, with a lovely figure, a stately neck, and a face of the most delicate and finished modelling: the flow of surface from the temples over the cheek is exactly like the carving of a Phidean goddess . . . I got my mother to persuade the miraculous creature to sit for me for my Viola in "Twelfth Night", and to-day I have been trying to paint her; but I have made a mess of my beginning. Tomorrow she's coming again; you two should come down and see her; she's really a wonder; for while her friends, of course, are quite humble, she behaves like a real lady, by clear commonsense, and without any affectation, knowing perfectly, too, how to keep people respectful at a distance.'[45]

Rossetti did not meet her on this occasion but a little later, in the winter of 1849–50, two years after he had co-founded the Pre-Raphaelite Brotherhood – a society of artists and critics seeking to overturn the restrictions placed on painting by the Royal Academy by returning to what they thought of as the values of the Renaissance.

This was the crux of Siddal's appeal to the group: her long, reddish hair and pale skin meant she corresponded to the Renaissance ideal of female beauty. In fact, she was one of several 'stunners' discovered by the Pre-Raphaelite Brotherhood – this really was what they called them – and was passed around between them, painted by John Millais, Holman Hunt and Ford Madox Brown, as well as Rossetti. Posing for Millais as the drowned Ophelia, Siddal was so desperate for money that she lay for days in a bath filled with water. (Sitting for an artist paid more than double what Siddal earned in the hat shop.) When the lamps heating the bath from underneath went out and the water temperature dropped, she did not complain – she knew she had to lie still – and as a result caught a dose of pneumonia so severe it nearly killed her.

Rossetti quickly became possessive. No sooner had she sat for him alone – Rossetti's first painting of Lizzie is thought to be the small watercolour *Rossovestita* – than painting her became a 'monomania' for him, as Madox Brown observed. Even his sister, the poet Christina Rossetti, noted in her poem 'In an Artist's Studio' his tendency to paint Lizzie 'not as she is, but as she fills his dream' and the way that 'every canvas means/ The same one meaning, neither more nor less'. Rossetti dressed Lizzie in clothes inspired by medieval costumes, drew her and taught her to draw. He was particularly obsessed with casting her as a reincarnation of Dante's muse Beatrice Portinari, whom the Italian poet met in childhood and celebrated in works such as *Vita Nuova* and the *Divine Comedy*. Rossetti's nickname for her was Guggums, or Gug.

In the nine years that they were together (though never engaged) their relationship became increasingly co-dependent. Both were moody and wilful, argumentative and prone to jealous outbursts. As Lucinda Hawksley puts it in her biography of Siddal: 'When they were in love and happy, they were deliriously so, not needing anyone else and perfectly content to stay cocooned in Rossetti's rooms for days at a time. When one – or both – of them was unhappy, ill, depressed or jealous, they made one another's lives hellish.'[46]

From the early 1850s onwards, Siddal suffered increasingly from laudanum addiction, euphemistically referred to in letters as 'ill health'. As her weight decreased and she became frailer and more listless, pressure was brought to bear on Rossetti by John Ruskin and other friends to marry her, which he finally did in 1860. By this time, Siddal's health was so poor many feared she would not make it to the church, and Rossetti was widely known to have transferred his affections to another Pre-Raphaelite favourite, the voluptuous Fanny Cornforth.

In 1862, following a miscarriage and depression – a hallucinating Siddal told visitors to her bedside to keep quiet lest their loud conversation wake the child she imagined to be sleeping in the empty cot beside her – she fatally overdosed on laudanum after suspecting that Rossetti had gone off to see Cornforth. Rossetti's response was to paint the eerie *Beata Beatrix*, in which his muse and lover seems to glow with an inner spiritual light as she experiences what could either be exquisite rapture or the moment of her own death.

What should we make of Rossetti and Siddal as a 'creative couple'? For Jan Marsh, Siddal's own artistic achievements are slight, her work 'appropriately derivative, a pale imitation of her husband's' in a manner that emphasises her status as a 'delicate Cinderella, discovered by a Prince and raised from menial obscurity to be a Pre-Raphaelite princess'.[47]

There is no doubt that much of Siddal's own work, both as an artist and a writer, is technically crude. Still, contemporary observers made much of her potential. Ruskin wrote to a friend (admittedly trying to appease her after Siddal's sulky 'artistic' temperament had offended her) that he had known five geniuses, 'Turner, Watts, Millais, Rossetti, and this girl', and justified his financial support of Siddal in a letter to the former shop girl: 'The plain hard fact is that I think you have genius; that I don't think there is much genius in the world; and I want to keep what there is, in it, heaven having, I suppose, enough for all its purposes.'[48]

In the past few years Siddal has been the subject of significant reappraisal, critics suggesting that, rather than being a passive muse, she produced work of genuine worth. She and Rossetti never collaborated, but what he taught her she put to good use, adding it to what she had known all along. (She was not totally uneducated: before she met Rossetti, she was already familiar with the work of Browning and Tennyson.)

In 2018, Dr Serena Trowbridge, senior lecturer in English Literature at Birmingham City University, compiled Siddal's mostly bleak poetry, including material never before published, in a fascinating book, *My Ladys Soul: The Poems of Elizabeth Eleanor Siddall*. 'I think her own work has always been overshadowed by paintings of her, and of course the work of women Pre-Raphaelites in all areas has always been seen as second to the men,' Trowbridge told the *Guardian*. 'I wonder if her poetry has not been taken seriously by scholars because it's always been read as autobiographical, so it's often seen as "evidence" rather than art.'[49]

An example of this is 'Fragment of a Ballad', which is often used by scholars to help answer the vexed question of whether Siddal and Rossetti had sex before they married. Lines like these have generally been taken to suggest they did, but that it was a bit awkward:

> And he came ready to take and bear
> The cross I had carried for many a year,
> But words came slowly one by one
> From frozen lips shut still and dumb.

The National Trust held in 2018 an exhibition of Siddal's artwork at Wightwick Manor in Wolverhampton. Called 'Beyond Ophelia: A Celebration of Lizzie Siddal, Artist and Poet', it examined her style and subject matter, but also what the trust called 'the prejudice she faced as a professional female artist in the patriarchal Victorian art world'. This is where things get tricky. Was Siddal really a 'professional' artist? Surely the truth is that she was a gifted but mostly untrained amateur who might never have attempted anything creative had she not fallen into Rossetti's dubious orbit.

The other undeniable, complementary truth is that Siddal was exploited and mistreated by a man who had considerable power over her and who was mostly interested in her as an idealised projection of his own fantasies. Perhaps, though, we ought to run a third truth cautiously up the flagpole: that when things were good between them – there's a lovely drawing of the pair that Rossetti made in September 1853, of Siddal sketching him as he reclines on some chairs – they genuinely were good.

Assuming Siddal had lived and developed her talent so that it matched or even exceeded Rossetti's, what would the implications have been for their relationship? As the next chapter shows, where couples are concerned it is often easier to be a muse than a rival.

3

Competitiveness

When nineteen-year-old Bob Dylan arrived on New York's folk scene, centred around Greenwich Village, in January 1961, he had only just cast off his birth identity of Robert Zimmerman. And although he was not what he would claim to be – a rootless runaway – there was enough of the 'hick' in him for him to be scared of meeting folk's reigning queen, Joan Baez.

Watching television back in his home town of Duluth, Minnesota, Dylan had caught Baez performing songs from her first album, which had just been released on the prestigious Vanguard folk label. He found he could not stop looking at her: he did not want to blink. With her shiny black hair and pleading eyes, Baez resembled a religious icon. And then there was her voice as she sang her haunting versions of traditional folk ballads. It 'drove out bad spirits',[1] Dylan wrote many years later in his autobiography, *Chronicles*. That she was the same age as him and had already sold a lot of records made Dylan feel useless and emphasised how much he still had to achieve. As for the possibility that the pair would ever meet, it seemed fantastical: 'She was far off and unattainable – Cleopatra living in an Italian palace.'[2]

But they both appeared to be moving in the same direction: 'She had the fire and I felt I had the same kind of fire.'[3]

Robert Zimmerman was born in 1941 into a middle-class family of Reform Jews. A few days before his fifth birthday, he stood up in front of his assembled family and announced: 'If everybody in this room will keep quiet, I will sing for my grandmother', before treating them to a rendition of 'Some Sunday Morning' that earned him a standing ovation. Over time, however, young Robert would grow more rebellious, rejecting his father's entreaties that he study hard to become a lawyer – instead embracing rock 'n' roll, then in its early stages.

By the time he arrived in New York, he had excised his parents from his life story altogether and reinvented himself as wandering hobo 'Bob Dylan'. As the critic Ian MacDonald puts it: 'He borrowed his vaudeville style from Jesse Fuller, studied the "folk-singer" from Woody Guthrie, took the downhome persona from Ramblin' Jack Elliott (himself a middle-class Brooklyner who posed as a musical cowboy).'[4] This slipperiness was part of a deliberate act. Dylan understood that, as he puts it in *Chronicles*, part of folk music is the trick of making people believe what they are hearing – that the characters and situations in the songs are real: 'I believed Dave Guard in the Kingston Trio . . . would kill or already did kill poor Laura Foster [in the murder ballad "Tom Dooley"].'[5] Paradoxically, he had to efface himself to make himself more convincing.

Joan Baez didn't have to resort to strategies such as this. She was able to convince simply by being herself. In some ways she was the opposite of Dylan – earnest and sincere, her heart worn on her sleeve.

The meeting Dylan had dreamed of took place in 1961

at the Greenwich Village club, Gerde's Folk City. Baez remembers her fan boy in unflattering terms in her memoir: as a soft boy-child dwarfed by his guitar, spitting out his blunt, jagged songs. But she felt strongly that he was exceptional and noted the way his songs touched people. They circled each other for nearly two years, Dylan being initially distracted by Joan's younger sister Mimi.

But in July 1963 Baez invited him to join her onstage at the Newport Folk Festival to sing one of his more straightforward protest songs, 'With God on Our Side'. This led to Dylan accompanying her on a tour of the East Coast the following month, where she brought him out to sing duets and gave him solo spots in which he could perform new songs – sometimes as many as half a dozen – and refine what Baez called his 'reverse showmanship': his ability to be charismatic while behaving as uncharismatically as possible. For this he was, shockingly but rather predictably, paid slightly more than Baez, despite his much lower status as a performer. 'I was getting audiences up to 10,000 at that point, and dragging my little vagabond out onto the stage was a grand experiment,' she wrote later, adding: 'The people who had not heard of Bob were often infuriated, and sometimes even booed him.'[6]

Over time, though, the response grew warmer. Audiences who had initially been hostile started to see the point of him and his rough-hewn, eccentrically played songs, apparently agreeing with Baez's assessment that 'Bobby Dylan says what a lot of people my age feel but cannot say.'[7]

Baez was only six months older than Dylan but felt like his mother. She bought him a black suit jacket and some cufflinks. They were falling in love, or so she thought. Gradually, her role expanded to include patroness: she set up her lover in her house in Carmel with a piano for his personal use. Dylan moved in in the autumn of 1963. His songwriting became more disciplined as he relaxed and submitted to the serene rural atmosphere: he swam in the secluded cove half an hour's walk from the house; Baez encouraged him to cut down on his smoking, brush his teeth and generally look after his health.

He was hard to reach, though. Aloof and unreadable, he seemed (wrote Baez) 'to function from the center of his own thoughts and images'.[8] As she reached back into the past, repurposing old folk ballads to give shape to her thoughts, her boyfriend seemed to be moving forward into new territory, producing songs at a tremendous rate, dropping words onto the page 'like so many golden nuggets shaken from somewhere up his sleeve'.[9]

Dylan had written political songs that chimed with the direction Baez thought he should be moving in as a folk singer – 'Blowin' In The Wind', 'Masters of War': songs that had, ironically, been influenced by the left-wing politics of his previous girlfriend, Suze Rotolo. But Baez wanted him to go further, to become more of an activist and spokesperson. In other words, she wanted Dylan to march for civil rights with Martin Luther King, as she had; and be prepared to go to jail, as she did, for staging a sit-in at a military induction centre to protest against the Vietnam war.

Dylan's reluctance to involve himself to this degree – he had the more trivial quarry of rock stardom in his sights – coincided both with a dip in Baez's commercial fortunes and with the snowballing success of his second album, *The Freewheelin' Bob Dylan*, which had been released at the end of May 1963. The relationship was suddenly inverted so that it was Dylan whom Baez called on to give *her* credibility by writing a poem for the sleevenotes of her album, *Joan Baez in Concert, Part 2*.

Still, their romance continued, though Dylan was drifting away from Baez. Under the influence of Allen Ginsberg, he embraced a new, opaque style rooted in Beat surrealism. His drinking and drug use increased, too, unbeknownst to Baez, whose world – not straight by any means, but one of respectable protest – started to seem slow and old-fashioned to him. One simple diagnosis is that fame and success went to Dylan's head.

In 1965 Dylan returned Baez's favour of two years earlier by inviting her along on his tour of Europe, promising her solo slots at his shows. Dylan's continual failure to honour this agreement and his callous treatment of Baez at this time was captured for posterity by the director D. A. Pennebaker, who was making what became the documentary *Don't Look Back*.

This film would fix Dylan in the public imagination as the epitome of cool – an impish, shades-wearing, journalist-chiding force of nature – while casting Baez as a sort of eternal also-ran, drippily trailing the boyfriend who was no longer interested in her. Baez was devastated, humiliated: as she put it, 'a wounded but still impetuous queen, long since dethroned but hanging on by the teeth to dreams of power'.[10] The atmosphere around Dylan changed. Thanks to all the drugs being consumed by him and his entourage, it became nasty and sarcastic and excluding. A relative innocent at the time, Baez says she wasn't aware of what was going on, which must have made her bullying treatment all the more upsetting.

One day on the UK leg of the tour, having not even been asked to his hotel room, Baez decided to visit Dylan unannounced and uninvited, hoping to talk to him and get to the heart of the problems between them. She took him a present – a blue Viyella shirt. She knocked on the door and it was answered by Sara Lowndes, the woman with whom Dylan had been two-timing Baez and who would soon become his wife. Her presence on the tour had been concealed from Baez by Dylan and the crew. Baez's account of what happened next is heartbreaking: 'She took the package from me with a patient and quizzical look on her lovely face, blinked her massive black eyes, thanked me softly, and shut the door.'[11]

It sounds about as final as an ending can get. But the careers of Dylan and Baez would remain entwined for some time. In the years that followed, Baez called Dylan out as a complicated, difficult person whose social conscience had withered into feckless nihilism ('I am afraid the message that comes through from Dylan . . . is: let's all go home and smoke pot, because there's nothing else to do'[12]) while continuing to champion his talent on her own albums. In 1968 Baez released *Any Day Now*, a collection of Dylan covers she had recorded with the same musicians Dylan had used a year earlier on his album *John Wesley Harding*. Two of her best – and best-known – self-penned songs, 'To Bobby' and 'Diamonds and Rust', are about Dylan. In 1975 she joined Dylan on his Rolling Thunder Revue tour of the US.

The uneasy symbiosis of their relationship is fascinating. Robert Shelton, Dylan's premier biographer, thinks it failed because 'they were still too preoccupied with defining themselves as individuals to have found a consistency as a couple'.[13] They seem to get on well enough these days. In a recent documentary about Baez, Dylan affectionately calls her 'Joanie' and praises her lavishly. Slightly disingenuously, he says he dumped her on the UK tour to stop her from being 'swept up in the madness my career had become', adding: 'I feel very bad about it. I was sorry to see our relationship end.'[14] For her part, Baez recognises that she was trying to force him into a mould that was not right for him.

———————

The question of whether competition stimulates achievement is one of those hardy psychological perennials. In 1898, Norman Triplett at Indiana University examined data from racing cyclists and found that they recorded faster times when competing against others than when they were racing alone against the clock. He called the phenomenon 'social facilitation' and attempted to duplicate the results under laboratory conditions using children and fishing reels. The children's task was to wind in a given amount of fishing line. Triplett found that many children worked faster in the presence of a partner doing the same task – an example of the 'co-action effect' whereby the mere presence of others carrying out the same task improves performance.

The co-action effect is why you might study more efficiently in a library, surrounded by others who are also studying, than on your own at home. On a one-to-one basis, it's why you get better results with a personal trainer when you exercise; why, as a professional athlete, you use a pacesetter. Competition is in our nature and, to some degree, the key to our success. So perhaps if you're in an intimate relationship with someone who also wants to excel at the things you do, healthy competition might do you both good.

The problems arise, as we shall see, when competition becomes extreme and destructive. Or when one half of a couple decides the best way to 'win' is to obstruct the other person.

This tussle for supremacy afflicted one celebrated literary couple: Martha Gellhorn and Ernest Hemingway. America's best-known female war correspondent, Gellhorn remained so furious about her ex-husband Hemingway's conduct that, later in life, she refused to discuss him with journalists who interviewed her, pointing out: 'I've been a writer for over 40 years. I was a writer before I met him and I was a writer after I left him. Why should I be merely a footnote in his life?'[15]

Gellhorn met Hemingway in December 1936 in a bar while holidaying with her mother and brother in the Florida Keys. He spent so long chatting her up that he forgot his wife and dinner guests were waiting at home and missed the meal. Gellhorn was twenty-six and had returned to the US after a six-year stint in Paris. She had just completed her book, *The Trouble I've Seen*, four novellas based on her recent experience of working for Roosevelt's Federal Emergency Relief Administration (FERA), for which she had visited textile mill towns in New England to interview the downtrodden poor whose lives had been devastated by the Depression. Hemingway was about to leave for Spain to report on and make a film about the Spanish civil war. Gellhorn secured a commission from the national magazine, *Collier's Weekly*, and went along with him.

Collier's was thrilled with her writing, which was clear and clean and forged a direct emotional connection with the reader by making heavy use of the first person and the present tense. It was the sort of unflowery style Hemingway had pioneered. But *she* was using it more effectively than *he* was, as in this famous account of the centre of Madrid being shelled by Franco's troops: 'A small piece of twisted steel, hot and very sharp, sprays off from the shell; it takes the little boy in the throat. The old woman stands there, holding the hand of the dead child, looking at him stupidly, not saying anything, and men run out toward her to carry the child. At their left, at the side of the square, is a huge, brilliant sign which says: GET OUT OF MADRID.'[16]

By the time Hemingway's divorce from his wife came through, he and Gellhorn had been together for five years. They married in Wyoming on 21 November 1940 (the wedding breakfast was moose). Soon after, *Collier's* despatched Gellhorn to China. Hemingway came too, but grudgingly: in her letters home Gellhorn nicknamed him 'UC' for 'Unwilling Companion'. She traversed the vast country covering the Sino–Japanese war, while Hemingway made a base for himself in the hotel bar in Hong Kong. On their return, they settled in Hemingway's villa in Cuba. But Hemingway, as jealous as he was concerned for her safety, disliked the frequent trips Gellhorn was having to make to Europe, America having entered the Second World War in December 1941. In a bid to save the marriage he accompanied her on her next trip, but the deal he struck with *Collier's* was way better than Gellhorn's. He was on a higher word rate and had a booked seat on a seaplane, while Martha made the crossing on a Norwegian freighter. Arriving at the Dorchester, where Hemingway was staying in regal style, Gellhorn found him being 'entertained' by a London-based journalist called Mary Welsh. Before long, Welsh would be Hemingway's next wife.

It is worth pausing to consider the extent of Gellhorn's achievements as a reporter. Lacking the necessary press credentials to witness the Normandy landings, she hid in a hospital ship bathroom, then pretended to be a stretcher bearer so that she could get to the action. (She was the only woman to land at Normandy on D-Day.) She was also one of the first journalists to report from Dachau after its liberation by US troops on 29 April 1945. Hemingway's attitude to his wife's journalistic triumphs is summed up by a letter he wrote to her when she left Cuba in 1943 to cover the Italian front: 'Are you a war correspondent, or wife in my bed?'[17] Never mind that it was she who had, figuratively speaking, bought the bed. The grand estate where they lived in Cuba had been spotted by Gelhorn in the classified ads section of a local paper and she had paid for it to be renovated with her own money.

Perhaps it is easier when professional rivals aren't romantically linked? When the connection is more diffuse – a shared milieu or historical moment? Or when those rivals are related in some way?

Sadly, the loyalty suggested by the phrase 'blood is thicker than water' often does not hold true. Rivalry between siblings can be especially intense, the repercussions running the gamut from mutual excommunication to outright violence. One of the earliest examples – Cain and Abel, the biblical brothers who fell out when God favoured Abel's sacrifice – ended in Abel's murder and, if you believe traditional interpretations, the release of evil into the world.

Of course, sibling rivalry *can* be extremely creatively productive. Tennis stars Serena and Venus Williams remain close despite playing each other on over thirty occasions in professional games. 'It was not really so much fun,' Venus remarked after watching Serena double-fault on match point at the 2000 Wimbledon semi-finals.[18] But the examples that spring most readily to mind, from the rock stars Noel and

Liam Gallagher to writers Margaret Drabble and Antonia 'A. S.' Byatt, seem to be riddled with jealousy and loathing. That many of these relationship breakdowns have played out in public is no help to any of the participants.

The Gallaghers – ex-Oasis – proved themselves to be pop's most combustible brothers since the Kinks's Ray and Dave Davies, fighting on stage and off, and using interviews as opportunities to throw petrol on the flames. 'I don't like Liam,' Noel Gallagher told *Q* magazine in 2009. 'He's rude, arrogant, intimidating and lazy. He's the angriest man you'll ever meet. He's like a man with a fork in a world of soup.' (Liam's surprisingly witty response, years later, was to post on Instagram a photo of himself eating soup with a fork.)

Margaret Drabble has been estranged from her elder sister, A. S. Byatt, for most of her life. She blames too much competition in their childhood, especially a battle for their father's affection. Antonia, or 'Sue' as she was known in the family, was born in 1936, Maggie three years later, by which time their father was away serving in the Second World War. 'When he came home at the end [of the war], she couldn't accept that I was there, too.'[19] Although the pair had two other siblings, 'Sue and I were forever in my mother's gaze', Drabble has said.[20] Both Sue and Maggie went to Newnham College, Cambridge to read English. Sue got a 2:1, Maggie a first. Sue had ambitions to be a novelist and began writing *The Shadow of the Sun*, her first novel; Maggie went into acting. But then Maggie 'just happened to write a novel when I was pregnant and had nothing to do'.[21]

This was *A Summer Bird-Cage*, published in 1963, a year before her elder sister's debut. Three years later, Byatt published the novel, *The Game*, about a pair of hostile, competitive sisters. Bar the occasional postcard, they have not been in touch since. 'It's irresoluble now,' Drabble told the *Daily Telegraph* in 2011. 'It's sad, but beyond repair, and I don't think about it much any more.'[22]

It feels almost intrusive to speculate that these tensions contributed to their mutual creative brilliance. But it surely must have done on some level.

A fact that contributes to rivalry between couples, siblings or otherwise, is that talents do not always develop in sync. Sometimes this is because they are not allowed to. Actress sisters Joan Fontaine and Olivia de Havilland fell out of step early. Fontaine, the younger child, was sickly and so not allowed to take part in the same activities as de Havilland. The family catchphrase was: 'Livvie can, Joan can't.' De Havilland became an actress first; when her sister was also offered a contract at Warner Brothers, their mother was livid. Warners was, Fontaine wrote in her 1978 autobiography *No Bed of Roses*, 'Olivia's studio, her domain. Its gates could not be opened to both of us. What's more, I must change my name – "de Havilland" was Olivia's, she was the firstborn, and I was not to disgrace *her* name.'[23]

When Fontaine became the first of the pair to win an Oscar – Best Actress for Alfred Hitchcock's *Suspicion* in 1942 – de Havilland, who had also been nominated that year for *Hold Back the Dawn* and was sitting with her at the ceremony, allegedly snapped, 'Get up there.' Joan burst into tears. 'Now what had I done!' she wrote later of the incident. 'All the animus we'd felt toward each other as children, the hair-pullings, the savage wrestling matches, the time Olivia fractured my collar bone, all came rushing back in kaleidoscopic imagery. My paralysis was total . . . I felt age four, being confronted by my older sister. Damn it!

I had incurred her wrath again.'[24] (For the record, in a 2016 interview to celebrate her 100th birthday, de Havilland had this to say on the subject of the feud between herself and the woman she called 'Dragon Lady': 'A feud implies continuing hostile conduct between two parties. I cannot think of a single instance wherein I initiated hostile behaviour. But I can think of many occasions where my reaction to deliberately inconsiderate behaviour was defensive.'[25])

Part of the problem in this case may be that they were so close in age: a mere fifteen months apart. Poor Olivia felt 'dethroned' (to use the Austrian psychologist Alfred Adler's expression) by her ambitious but – as she saw it – less favoured younger sister. For Adler, siblings are always 'striving for significance' within a family, and the extent to which they are competitive is determined significantly by their parents, who either encourage or discourage it. In the case of Olivia de Havilland and Joan Fontaine, it seems Mrs de Havilland did not discourage it sufficiently. At her funeral in 1975, her two daughters – who remain the only two siblings to have each won an Oscar for Best Actress – did not speak to each other.

––––––––––

Art would be nowhere without conflict. It might be between feeling and form, or between a modern technique and an established one. The goal is to make something authentically new, or at least different to what has come before.

Inevitably, sometimes that conflict becomes personal – bound up with a particular artist's approach or personality. In his brilliant book *The Art of Rivalry*, the art critic Sebastian Smee explores some of the tensions that animated four pairs of modern artists. Smee is particularly interested in what happens when an attraction develops between two artists with different temperaments before they have had a chance to develop a signature style. As time goes on, a familiar narrative starts to assert itself. One artist makes headway, the other lags behind. One is comfortable courting risk, the other overthinks and stalls. Then the risk-taking artist starts to worry that she is not thinking enough and looks to the other artist for guidance. It is all part of finding a voice, a creative identity, or what Smee calls 'the solitude, the singularity, of greatness'.[26] But it can generate an unpleasant amount of static.

The painters Francis Bacon and Lucian Freud were friends when, in 1952, Freud painted Bacon in all his shadowy, looming intensity. 'I saw a lot of him at that time and we were very friendly, so it was natural for me to paint him,' Freud remembered in 2011.[27] In the paperback-sized portrait, painted on copper, Bacon's hooded eyes are downcast, his mouth lifts at the edge as if he is considering smiling but has thought better of it, and a strand of hair dangles over his shiny forehead. While it isn't exactly flattering, it's a veritable hagiography compared to the kind of unsparing paintings with which Freud made his name. Its most remarkable quality is its atmosphere of suppressed tension. The art critic Robert Hughes said it had 'the silent intensity of a grenade in the millisecond before it goes off'.[28]

Lucian Freud was born in Berlin in 1922, the son of an architect and the grandson of Sigmund Freud. His family moved to Britain in 1933 to escape Nazism. Bacon, by contrast, was born in 1909 in Dublin into a wealthy Anglo-Irish family; though they cast him adrift as his homosexuality became an obvious feature of his life. (His father, a failed racehorse trainer, is said to have arranged for the young Francis to receive regular whippings from the grooms at their country estate.)

The pair first met in the mid-1940s. Freud sought out his fellow artist after Graham Sutherland told him that Bacon was the best painter in England: 'He said, " . . . He's the most extraordinary man. He spends his time gambling in Monte Carlo, and then occasionally he comes back. If he does a picture, he generally destroys it," and so on. He sounded so interesting.'[29]

Freud started visiting him in the afternoons, then in the evenings they drank in the same Soho bars and pubs as their many mutual friends, who included Frank Auerbach and Stephen Spender. His first encounter with an unfinished Bacon painting in a studio setting seems to have occurred in a South Kensington flat in 1950, part of a house that had formerly belonged to Millais. It was *Painting* – a man dressed in black sitting beneath an umbrella, surrounded by animal carcasses. It was, Freud thought, absolutely marvellous. For a period the pair were inseparable. Freud's former wife, Lady Caroline Blackwood, remembered dining with Bacon nearly every day while she was married to the artist between 1953 and 1958. Perhaps surprisingly, Bacon exerted something of a moral force on the younger artist, encouraging Freud to modify his behaviour to get what he wanted; to get into fewer fights; and to use charm rather than aggression.

The pair remained comradely in 1962, when Michael Andrews painted them in conversation in his group portrait of drinkers at the famous Soho drinking club the Colony Room. And the friendship presumably still endured in 1969 when Bacon painted *Three Studies of Lucian Freud* (though he worked from photographs rather than from life as Freud did).

However, by the time Freud's small copper portrait of Bacon disappeared in 1988 – it was stolen from an art gallery in Berlin – the pair were not on speaking terms. Exactly why is hard to pinpoint. Superficially it may have been to do with a dispute over the ownership of a painting. Bacon's *Two Figures* from 1953, showing two blurred naked men on a bed, belonged to Freud – it had been sold to him for £80 by the art critic David Sylvester. For whatever reason, Freud never allowed it to be exhibited in his erstwhile friend's lifetime, which angered Bacon, who had particularly wanted it to be included in the Tate's 1985 retrospective of his work. The falling-out may also have been because Freud did not get on with Bacon's lovers, Eric Hall and Peter Lacy.

Perhaps another source of grievance was that Freud once relied on Bacon's generosity to tide him over when funds were tight: Bacon had a habit of producing wads of banknotes – sometimes enough money to live on for three months – and asking if Freud might like some of them. Or maybe it was because Bacon disapproved of what Freud actually did with this money, which was gamble it away (although this strikes me as odd because Bacon was himself a compulsive gambler).

Or was it to do with jealousy? In terms of international standing, Freud lagged behind Bacon until after the latter's death in 1991. 'When my work started getting some notice, [Bacon] turned bitchy,' Freud revealed in 2006. 'What he really minded was that I started getting rather high prices. He'd suddenly turn and say, "Of course, you've got lots of money".'[30] The other possibility is that there was something about the paintings, something in Bacon's technique, that made Freud – whose work was, on the surface, more conventionally figurative and observational – feel insecure. Smee suspects Freud felt 'accusations of backwardness, of timidity, of naivete'[31] emanating from Bacon, certainly in the early phase of their friendship.

As someone who took a long time over paintings, Freud was amazed by how fast Bacon worked and by how much faith the other artist placed in the random or accidental. He also viewed ruthless self-editing as a key part of creation. As Freud later explained: 'Sometimes I'd go around in the afternoon and [Bacon] would say, "I've done something really extraordinary today." And he'd done it all in that day. Amazing . . . He would slash them sometimes. Or say how he was really fed up and felt they were no good, and destroy them.'[32]

Freud began to absorb Bacon's influence, using bigger, thicker brushes and stringy Cremnitz White paint. He was also astounded by something you might think had no bearing on anything much – Bacon's ability to walk up to total strangers and strike up interesting conversations with them. The admiration flowed both ways. Bacon was impressed by Freud's facility as a draftsman, which he lacked, and his compelling, intelligent way of talking about art.

But their paths diverged in the 1960s and '70s when Bacon was producing his best work – existential horror shows full of blood and boneless, sagging flesh. He became openly contemptuous of Freud's paintings, which were all about the psychological intensity of unflinching scrutiny. ('The trouble with Lucian's work,' Bacon once said, 'is that it's *realistic* without being real.'[33]) Freud liked his sitters to remain still for hours, days, weeks at a stretch, to give time for a proper relationship to unfold – in other words, for emotion to leak into the situation from both sides, painter and sitter.

What Freud learned from Bacon most of all was to suppress an innate sentimentalism that cropped up in his early work and become more daring so that he was not relying to such a degree on what came naturally to him, which was drawing. Instead, he used great thick lashings of paint to produce extraordinary textural effects, yet in 1984 insisted to the BBC's *Omnibus* programme: 'I never think about technique in anything, I think it holds you up.'

The influence of Bacon is what leads so many people to find Freud's paintings cruel and unsparing in their focus on ugliness, deterioration and decay. Like Bacon, he focuses more on corporeal mass than on individual features; on the way skin, bone, muscle and fat behaves when the light hits it in a certain way. In the process, as Smee concludes, he 'undermines the whole traditional idea of portraiture as a function of both psychology and social status'.[34]

Artistic rivalries are grimly fascinating because they are often so extreme and theatrical. They rise, like menacing, alien flowers, from the soil of what seem to be genuine friendships, making observers wonder whether it is ever possible for stable, uncomplicated camaraderie to exist between artists working in similar or complementary fields.

The painters Vincent van Gogh and Paul Gauguin were once close, despite Gauguin being very much the senior partner in the relationship – older, with an established career and, to match it, a high sense of his own worth. Van Gogh saw him as someone to follow and emulate. But the pair disagreed intellectually over such questions as the role of abstraction (Gauguin was keen; Van Gogh was sceptical, comparing it to a brick wall) and whether painting should be 'poetical' or concerned with what was observable in nature.

It was after a row with Gauguin that Van Gogh drew a razor and cut off a piece of his left ear. Van Gogh had worked hard to persuade Gauguin to stay at his 'studio of the south', the yellow house he was renting in Arles in the south of France and which he hoped to turn into a commune for like-minded painters. He had been thrilled when Gauguin arrived. But their personalities failed to gel and Gauguin spent only nine weeks there, writing in his memoirs: 'Between two human beings, he and myself, the one like a volcano and the other boiling too, but inwardly, there was a battle in store, so to speak.'[35]

However unpleasant it is to be caught up in, the *Sturm und Drang* of these kinds of artistic disputes often results in the production of startling new work and the opening up of new possibilities. Without friction, you would have stasis. But when that rivalry involves a man and a woman the narrative can take a wearyingly familiar turn, especially when that man is already a superstar in his field.

Take, for example, the very male field of sculpture. The *Dictionary of Employment Open to Women*, published by the London Women's Institute in 1898, lists the sort of commissions that women artists desiring careers as sculptors in the late nineteenth century might expect. They include jewellery, the stone decoration of light fittings, cutlery, racing cups, medals and presentation plates. The restoration of domestic facades, occasionally an option, was 'nice work, but poorly paid' and 'difficult to obtain without personal acquaintance with architects'.[36]

When Camille Claudel met Auguste Rodin in the early 1880s she was a seventeen-year-old woman with a remarkable artistic talent that needed honing. She had struggled to get herself to Paris to be trained, only to find when she arrived that most prestigious art schools such as the Ecole des Beaux-Arts did not admit women. She had brought her brother, younger sister and fiercely disapproving mother along with her. Her father, a middle-ranking government employee, stayed at home in Wassy in north-eastern France, working to earn the money to support his vanished family.

By this time Rodin, who took over her teaching after her original tutor Alfred Boucher moved to Florence, was forty-one and a successful sculptor winning lucrative commissions such as the 10,000 francs he earned designing the portal to the Museum of Decorative Arts. Claudel and her friend Jessie Lipscomb were employed as assistants at Rodin's studio on rue d'Université. Rodin recognised Claudel's talent and enlisted her to work on the feet and hands of his sculpture, *The Burghers of Calais*. His and Claudel's subsequent relationship – sexual and pedagogic – lasted ten years and was enshrined in an extraordinary contract that Rodin drew up for her:

I will have for a student only Mademoiselle Camille Claudel and I will protect her alone through all the means I have at my disposal through my friends who will be hers especially through my influential friends.

I will accept no other students so that no other rival talent could be produced by chance, although I suppose that one rarely meets artists as naturally gifted . . .

Mademoiselle Camille promises to welcome me to her atelier four times a month until May.[37]

The association displeased Claudel's mother and resulted in Claudel's banishment from the new family home in Montparnasse. She and Rodin never actually lived together. Nor did Rodin ever marry Claudel as he promised he would: he remained in the longstanding relationship he enjoyed with Rose Beuret, later his wife and the mother of his son. But before long Claudel began modelling for Rodin and creating sculptures with him. Some unsigned pieces bear evidence of having been sculpted by more than one pair of hands. She mastered the art of working with a variety of materials, including plaster, bronze, onyx and marble. She also produced her own pieces such as *The Wave* – three small female figures bending their knees as a wave of onyx marble breaks over their heads – and the sexually graphic *Sakuntala*, a life-size sculpture of a naked, slumped woman with her eyes closed while a kneeling man reaches up to envelop her in his arms.

When *Sakuntula* was exhibited in 1888, one critic, Paul Leroi, called it the most extraordinary work in the Salon; another, Mathias Morhardt, said that it ranked among the purest masterpieces of this century. But although she had Rodin's talent, Claudel lacked his connections and confidence. On the whole, her work was rarely exhibited and, once sold, records of ownership were not kept. Unlike Rodin, Claudel preferred not to use assistants, which limited her output.

As a woman, Claudel was subject to censorship in a way that Rodin was not. To get a clay maquette made in bronze, she had to obtain official funding and approval from the French state. When the inspectors visited Claudel's studio, they refused permission for her to cast her sculpture *The Waltz* because its depiction of two bodies touching was deemed too risqué. Under Claudel's influence, Rodin produced some of his most passionate, explicit work, for example *The Kiss*. But critics seemed to be more interested in identifying Rodin's influence on Claudel and implying that she was 'stealing' his style.

Although she received a good deal of acclaim, in her lifetime Claudel was often judged through the prism of her relationship with Rodin. Rodin knew this to be unfair; that Claudel deserved to stand in her own light – 'I have showed her where she could find gold, but the gold that she finds is entirely hers,' he said.[38] Still, the constant battling ground her down. And Rodin did not always support her. In 1898, wanting greater independence, Claudel opened her own studio, only for a lucrative commission for her sculpture *The Mature Age* to be cancelled, possibly because Rodin had expressed his dislike of it to the French state's Inspector of Fine Arts.

Did this stem from jealousy? Claudel had split with Rodin in around 1893, and financial worries then began to overwhelm her. Towards the end of the decade she became more and more reclusive, focusing on work that was, she wrote to her brother, no longer anything like Rodin's (not least because her subjects were clothed). She collected cats and began to show signs of confusion and paranoia, accusing Rodin of stealing her ideas in what were assumed to be delusional rants. She barricaded herself into her house, only receiving food through a window. In 1909 her poet brother Paul visited his sister, now aged forty-four, and wrote: 'Camille mad. Wallpaper ripped in long strips, the only armchair broken and torn, horrible filth. Camille huge, with a dirty face, speaking ceaselessly in a monotonous and metallic voice.'[39] Eventually Claudel was taken from her studio and confined to the first of a series of asylums.

Was she 'mad'? If so, her letters from the asylum are surprisingly lucid: 'I am so devastated at having to continue to live here that I am no longer a human being,' she wrote. 'I can't stand the cries of all these creatures, it really upsets me.'[40] It was a tragic fall from the heady days of 1897 when she was included on the jury at the prestigious Champ de Mars Salon and a journalist wrote: 'Mademoiselle Claudel is without rival when it comes to her will power, her hard work, her incredible integrity, her faith in truth, which to her is Beauty.'[41]

But is any artist ever 'without rival'? Rivalry can express itself in strange ways. Another painter Sebastian Smee considers in his book is Jackson Pollock. The paint-splattering inventor of abstract expressionism was consumed by real and imagined rivalries with other artists – a function of his insecurities about his lack of technical ability. (Pollock was notoriously bad at drawing.) The most obvious one was with his friend and fellow abstract expressionist, Willem de Kooning, who channelled the freedom and energy of Pollock's poured and dripped paintings into his own more uptight, controlled canvases.

Together, Pollock and de Kooning embodied the macho, competitive culture of postwar American art. 'I was jealous of him – his talent,' de Kooning admitted. They were forever wrestling and punching each other, vying to see who could drink the most, wondering who among their circle was the 'greatest' painter in America, as if such a thing was possible to quantify. The idea of painters being rivals was one they embraced as it positioned art as a rugged American pursuit rather than a decadent Old European one. 'Everyone's shit but de Kooning and me,' Pollock told the artist Grace Hartigan in 1950.[42] More than one critic has linked Pollock's 'action painting' technique to his drunken habit of urinating in public.

Pollock was like a damaged child in constant need of help and reassurance. The person who had to provide this was his wife Lee Krasner, also an artist. Once dismissed as his inferior – dwarfed by his talent, overcalculating where he was instinctive – she is now regarded as having the same stature. A 2019 exhibition at the Barbican, *Lee Krasner: Living Colour*, played to huge audiences and rave reviews. A sexist myth casts her as the conniving mastermind of her husband's success. The dealer, John Bernard Myers, said: 'There would never have been a Jackson Pollock without Lee Pollock and I put this on every level.'[43] People say she was manipulative, that he was her creation, her Frankenstein's monster. The rivalry between them is curious and complicated and in some ways does not look like rivalry at all. As Elaine de Kooning, wife of Willem, remarked, Krasner became 'kind of the opposite of competitive with Jackson. She wiped herself out.'[44] (De Kooning too was often assumed to be her husband's rival in a simple, straightforward way. When she was asked what it was like to work in de Kooning's shadow, she replied that she didn't work in his shadow, but in his light.)

It would be naive to think that two artists living and working together did not share the obvious goal of success and acclaim for their work. For both Krasner and Pollock, artistic rivalry was bound up with loyalty, intellectual respect and a kind of selfless love. Having watched her husband experience a fame unlike anything previously bestowed on an American painter – *Life* magazine hailed Pollock as the greatest living artist in the US – she was not sure she wanted it for herself, as it would have a bad effect on her work.

Lee Krasner was born Lena Krassner in Brooklyn in 1908, the daughter of Jewish refugees from Odessa in the Ukraine. When she and Pollock first met in the early 1940s she was a clever, connected New Yorker who had studied at the School of Fine Arts and knew all about European developments in art. He was a 'misfit hick', a hard-drinking farmer's son from Cody, Wyoming. They were exhibited together at the McMillan gallery on East 55th Street in January 1942. She was the only woman in the group.

Krasner said that when she saw Pollock's paintings, she almost died she was so impressed. She taught him about modernism, whose idioms she had mastered. They became a couple and in autumn 1945, with the help of a $2,000 loan from the gallery-owner Peggy Guggenheim, moved from New York to a village called Springs near East Hampton on Long Island. They found a nineteenth-century clapboard farmhouse without water or heating and worked hard to make it habitable. The life seemed to suit them. For three years Pollock stopped drinking. They lived simply and cheaply, enjoying the view and the nearby beach. They worked at their art – she (controversially) in a small upstairs bedroom, he in the vast barn adjacent to the house. They were respectful of each other's work and working practices, only visiting the other's studio by invitation.

But there were problems not far below the surface. Meeting Pollock caused Krasner to question her assumptions about art so severely that between 1942 and 1945 she did not make a single painting. Something about Pollock's work made her feel her own did not matter. 'I had a conviction, when I met Jackson, that he had something important to say,' she said. 'When we began going together, my own work became irrelevant. *He* was the important thing.'[45] She made it her business to control him, to structure his life and, as Smee says, to protect him despite the appalling way he treated her, knowing perhaps that this was the only way to get him to achieve anything.

During this period Pollock produced his best work. Typically, he got up late and had his breakfast while Krasner had lunch, sometimes sitting over the same cup of coffee for two hours. By the time he left to work in the barn it was afternoon and he would have only a few hours' daylight left as the studio had no electric lights. He worked intensely during this time and, as Krasner remarked, what he managed to do in those few hours was incredible: bold, urgent, lyrical paintings made by dripping and pouring industrial paint onto unprimed canvases. Krasner helped give them the names that would soon be world-famous: *Galaxy*, *Phosphorescence*, *Full Fathom Five* . . .

Krasner also created a group of her own poured and dripped 'all over' paintings between 1946 and 1949. She called them her *Little Images* and, as the art critic Anne Wagner says, they 'view and review Pollock, profiting from . . . his example in ways which are strategic and intentional'.[46] Krasner too wanted to do something new with paint, something that involved using the language her husband had created, but in a more controlled way. She had the same problem as Camille Claudel, though. Because she was Pollock's wife, her paintings were judged alongside his – and to complicate matters further, they did owe something to him. Critics of the time called her work a neatened-up version of Pollock's. 'Lee Krasner (Mrs Jackson Pollock) takes her husband's paints and enamels and changes his unrestrained, sweeping lines into neat little squares and triangles,' wrote *Art News* of a 1949 group show called

There were laughs along the way, but Microsoft co-founders (and childhood friends) Paul Allen and Bill Gates drifted apart when the more 'hardcore' Gates started to assert his dominance.

Writer Virginia Woolf (right) and her artist sister Vanessa Bell had an intense sense of themselves as a duo – and of what Virginia called 'a very close conspiracy'.

Choreographer George Balanchine and composer Igor Stravinsky rehearsing their 1957 ballet *Agon*, in which the African-American dancer Arthur Mitchell and the white ballerina Diana Adams danced the *pas de deux*.

Married couple William and Ellen Craft escaped from slavery by hiding in plain sight: fairer-skinned Ellen dressed as a man and pretended to be William's master.

Lady Eleanor Butler and Sarah Ponsonby, AKA the Ladies of Llangollen, out walking with their dog. Their close friendship was stylised and performative but emotionally sincere.

A glass jellyfish created by the father-and-son duo of Leopold and Rudolf Blaschka in the late nineteenth century. Even today, experts struggle to explain exactly how the Blaschkas made their models.

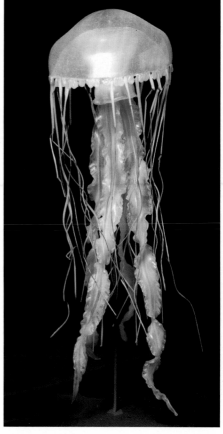

The spies who lived next door… Peter and Helen Kroger presented as an ordinary suburban married couple but were later revealed to be Soviet agents.

Darlings of French salon society, scientist couple Antoine and Marie-Anne Lavoisier commissioned this portrait of themselves by Marie-Anne's art teacher, Jacques-Louis David, showing them surrounded by laboratory equipment.

Among scientist Henry Cavendish's repertoire of quirks were intense shyness and introversion. Without the help of friend Charles Blagden, none of his achievements would have been known about.

A still from Ken Russell's 1968 film *Song of Summer*, which dramatises Eric Fenby's fraught stint as amanuensis to composer Frederick Delius. Meals *chez* Delius were conducted in silence as he could not bear the sound of conversation or the rattle of cutlery.

A breakfast meeting at society hostess Hester Thrale's house in around 1770. Seated opposite her, in full flow, is her close friend and rumoured lover Dr Samuel Johnson.

Sept 1853

The artist and muse Elizabeth Siddal, one of the 'stunners' adored by the Pre-Raphaelite Brotherhood, sketches her future husband Dante Gabriel Rossetti…

…who in turn painted her after her premature death idealised as Dante's Beatrice in the eerie *Beata Beatrix*, completed in 1870.

Folk singer Joan Baez wanted her 'little vagabond' boyfriend Bob Dylan to be a committed political activist, as she was. But he had the more trivial quarry of rock stardom in his sights.

War reporter Martha Gellhorn remained so furious about the conduct of her ex-husband Ernest Hemingway that, later in life, she refused to discuss him.

Paul Gauguin's *The Painter of Sunflowers* from December 1888 is an affectionate portrait of his fellow artist and one-time housemate Vincent van Gogh.

Van Gogh returned the compliment by painting Gauguin in *Man in a Red Beret*. But their friendship foundered. 'Between two human beings, he and myself, the one like a volcano and the other boiling too, but inwardly, there was a battle in store, so to speak,' Gauguin wrote later.

Even artists need to wash the dishes… Lee Krasner and Jackson Pollock in the kitchen of their clapboard farmhouse on Long Island.

Cyclists Laura and Jason Kenny show off their gold medals at the 2016 Olympics in Rio de Janeiro – bonded by love, for sure, but also by a shared understanding of what being a world-class athlete involves.

'Artists: Man and Wife'. What Krasner took from him was what she had put there in the first place by educating him, stabilising him, improving him. Cleaning up after him. And handling his domestic affairs, for instance going to a train station and buying him a ticket – something he was incapable of doing. Pollock was inarticulate, taciturn. 'Words were never his thing,' Krasner once said. 'They made him uncomfortable.'[47]

Krasner subordinated her ambitions to his, looking after him like a child. Her job was to stand back and let the forces that would propel her husband to fame gather strength. As a result, Krasner was unfairly neglected, though some critics suggest she was complicit in this neglect by not fighting for herself hard enough. The marriage undoubtedly had an impact on her work and identity, but was it a good one or a bad one?

Krasner did not mind that she was the one who had said yes when her husband turned to her one day, gestured to one of his new works, and asked (as he allegedly did, naively unknowing): 'Is this a painting?' And she seems not to have been too fussed when Hans Hofmann, the German émigré Krasner won a scholarship to study under in the late 1930s, commented that one of her paintings was so good you would not know it was painted by a woman.

Though not a feminist, Krasner did picket at the Museum of Modern Art in Manhattan with the Women in the Arts group in 1972 in protest at their discrimination against women artists. She would not enjoy a retrospective of her own work at MoMA, however, until 1984, the year of her death.

As for Pollock, the world knows that he was killed on the night of 11 August 1956 at the age of forty-four. He was driving drunk and at high speed when he lost control and hit a tree, his hard-won sobriety having lapsed following the tortuous making of the famous film of him painting in his studio in 1950, which contributed to his sense of himself as a fraud and a phony. The quality of his work had lapsed and his champions in the art world were beginning to lose patience with his erratic, abusive behaviour. He and Krasner were estranged by the time he died – he was seeing the much younger artist Ruth Kligman, the only survivor of the car crash; Krasner was in Paris when she heard the news – but she still became manager of his estate, a role so huge that her art had to be put on the back burner.

After Pollock's death, stories circulated that Krasner had had his signature forged on unsigned works to increase their value. She was accused of driving up prices for his paintings by releasing them to the market deliberately slowly. It is hard not to detect anti-Semitism at work here. As Wagner writes in a prescient essay, Krasner was given a cartoon identity to complement the chaotic white Protestant country boy Pollock, by being cast as his opposite – 'urban, Eastern, Jewish, the daughter of immigrants, homely, capable, good with money, a wily bargainer and strategist, intellectually competent but lacking "inner fire"'.[48]

Why wasn't Krasner's own art taken more seriously? The obvious – and I think correct – answer is: sexism. Le Corbusier once wrote of Pollock and Krasner: 'This man is like a hunter who shoots without aiming. But his wife, she has talent – women always have too much talent.'[49] Meaning: she tries too hard and is too uptight. The critic Arthur Danto went one step further, writing that 'there is no recurrent touch, or whatever may be the pictorial equivalent of voice, in Krasner's canvases', only 'the echo of other voices'.[50]

In other words, she had no signature style, no brand. But that was the whole point of her work. Krasner moved through styles and was always trying new things out. That was how she liked it.

In the early 1950s, as Pollock was disintegrating and unable to paint, Krasner produced a string of collages which redeployed sections of discarded paintings and drawings by her husband, mixing them with her own design elements. As Ellen Landau comments, this 'completely recontextualised Pollock's aggressive physicality'[51] – it is not hard to see it as Krasner's way of reasserting herself during a period of acute domestic turmoil.

Did Krasner yearn for the big barn studio her husband had? Did she efface herself deliberately as part of a long game, knowing she would 'win' in the end? Krasner's paintings provide clues, but not answers. 'Painting is not separate from life,' she once said. 'It is one. It is like asking – do I want to live? My answer is yes – and I paint.'[52]

The Pollocks' marriage was dysfunctional – blighted by addiction and mistrust. 'I want to talk about my self-destruction,' Krasner wrote in a journal fragment, 'my disgust and stupidity . . . (waiting and trapped).'[53]

In healthy relationships it would be nice to think a different standard applies. 'One can live magnificently in this world,' wrote Tolstoy in 1856, in a letter to his young lover Valerya Arsenyev, 'if one knows how to work and how to love, to work for the person one loves, and love one's work.'[54]

Couples who work in the same field have it harder in

some ways and easier in others. On the one hand, there is a greater probability of friction between a couple if they are measuring themselves by the same professional yard-stick. On the other, you might expect less friction in such a relationship because it is easier to adjust to the peaks and troughs of someone else's demands when you understand them.

There will be rivalry, for sure. But in an ideal world the competitive impulse would give way to empathy, so that when something good happens to their partner, they are happy for them, rather than jealous.

Perhaps this is why people who are really dedicated to their careers are often attracted to – or deliberately limit their choice of partners to – people within their field. This means never having to ask each other: 'Why do you have to go to that meeting?' 'Why are you painting at three o'clock in the morning?' 'Why are you going to the gym again?'

As someone who has been known to get home from work and, perhaps eccentrically, clamber straight onto the exercise bike, this last question has a special resonance for me. My husband, who doesn't exercise enough, is very understanding (except when it's late and he's cooked something special and would rather I eat it NOW). But my energy and his tolerance pale into insignificance when compared to dual-career sporting couples.

Laura and Jason Kenny are the golden couple of British sport. They are both cyclists but with different specialisms. Laura excels in team pursuit, omnium, scratch race and Madison disciplines: she won both the team pursuit and the omnium at the 2012 and 2016 Olympic games and is Britain's most successful female Olympic competitor. Jason's disciplines are individual and team sprints. At the 2012

Olympics he won gold in both the team and individual sprints, repeating his wins in 2016.

The pair are bonded by love, for sure, but also by a shared understanding of what being a world-class athlete involves – something that can't help but elude anyone not involved with a sport at their level. Only another athlete can know the hellish rigours of training – sessions so intense you vomit afterwards; the weird restricted eating – protein gels, marshmallows for energy, a steak for supper; the constant physical pain, so intense that, as Laura has said, 'you come off the track and think your head is going to explode'.[55] For women this is aggravated even further by 'saddle soreness' – the way the vulva can be bruised or even lacerated by the saddle at high speeds. The support you require – support Laura and Jason were able to give each other – is psychological as much as physical. Once you are successful, an additional burden is managing the weight of the public's expectations. As Laura puts it: 'I crashed twice in the lead-up to Rio – once in training, once in a race – I was stressed a lot of the time. It's hard on your head and you have the whole country thinking: "Why aren't you winning any more?" I started sending crisis emails to my coaches and my background team, because I'd totally lost confidence.'[56]

In this situation, rivalry is the last thing on their minds. But then sportspeople seem to be better at converting rivalries into friendships than their counterparts in the arts. The rivalry between Francis Bacon and Lucian Freud consumed both painters until the end of their lives. They were never able to recapture the friendship they had enjoyed when they were starting out. In the sporting arena, it is hard to imagine a bigger rivalry than that between British decathlete Daley Thompson and West German Jürgen Hingsen in the 1980s.

The pair vied constantly to smash world records. At the Los Angeles Olympics in 1984, Hingsen bragged that he would be winning gold. Thompson begged to differ: 'There are only two ways he is going to bring a gold medal home,' he said. 'He'll have to steal mine or win another event.' Sure enough, it was Thompson who triumphed, while Hingsen, suffering from a stomach bug, threw up twice before the pole vault event.

These days, however, the two men enjoy spending time together. 'I am always happy when I am in Daley's company,' Hingsen explained in 2012, 'because there is something that connects us. It's something I want to cherish for the rest of my life. We don't see each other very often. It is sometimes every two or three years. When I turned fifty, four years ago, I wanted to invite Daley. There is nobody in the world that would give me more joy and fun than Daley.'[57]

4

Tension

Romantically speaking, there are odd couples and there are odd couples. And then there are couples you would never in a million years believe were couples because it seems so improbable and ridiculous. Into this category we must put the reclusive Hollywood actress Greta Garbo and the flamboyantly unreclusive photographer and society man about town, Cecil Beaton. I had no idea they were an item until I started researching this book.

Greta Garbo's retreat from the world has become part of her legend, helped by the famous line she utters as Russian ballerina Grusinskaya in the 1932 film *Grand Hotel*: 'I want to be alone.' In fact, Garbo was not *that* reclusive. She was just self-sufficient, wary, a little closed-off. Also, she disliked big groups, preferring to socialise on a small scale with people she knew well and trusted.

The bizarre relationship between Garbo and Beaton began in 1932, when they first met, and ended in 1971, when Cecil betrayed her by publishing diaries revealing an account of their every meeting and almost every conversation the two ever had. He had long been fixated on her. 'How I long to get at Garbo,' he wrote in his diary in December 1929.

The following year, in his *Book of Beauty*, he called her 'the most glamorous figure in the whole world': 'There is no one with a more magnetic, romantic or exotic personality.' Despite what he called her 'slightly insane' look, she was, he wrote, like Leonardo's Gioconda, 'a clairvoyant who, possessed of a secret wisdom, knows and sees all'.

As a photographer Beaton had access to most of the celebrities of the times – writers, artists and socialites as well as actors. However, he was particularly enamoured of Garbo and, like a crazed superfan, kept a scrapbook of cuttings and publicity shots. Garbo existed for him not as a real human being so much as a quarry, a rare butterfly to be pinned and mounted. And of course he was transfixed by her beauty and glamour and aloofness. Many times he had requested to photograph her. Always she refused.

This confused Beaton. He was so good at making women look beautiful, even when they weren't. Why on earth wouldn't Garbo take advantage of his skills? The answer is that she existed in her own world. The woman widely considered to be the world's most beautiful was rumoured never to comb her hair or look in a mirror. If she did not care much about herself, she did not always care much about other people either. She failed to turn up to her own wedding to the actor John Gilbert in September 1926, telling a friend simply: 'I have been very naughty.' She was happier walking in the mountains than starring in a film, despite the fact that she was such a gifted actress. Cecil loved this about her, or thought he did: 'She is so casual and dreamy, she doesn't give a damn and the fact that she doesn't give a damn and will not come out of hiding only increases the frenzy and . . . desire to see her.'[1]

In her book about the couple, Diana Souhami points out

that 'relationship' is too concrete a word for what transpired between them. 'They contrived, or inhabited, a world of elusive gender and identity, reflected image, posed photographs, projection, fantasy and façade,' she writes.[2] Cecil was fond of dressing as a woman; Greta often spoke of herself in male terms. Souhami thinks Cecil saw himself in pictures of her. Certainly, in his photographs he liked to blur the line between viewer and viewed by using mirrors and sometimes appearing in the photos himself. He wanted to blend with his sitters, to see himself reflected in their image.

Beaton and Garbo had a mutual friend in Mercedes de Acosta, a playwright and socialite known for her lesbian affairs with famous Hollywood actresses. Garbo was rumoured to be bisexual and certainly had lesbian relationships: she wore trousers and had, it was commonly observed, a 'masculine' way of walking. Mercedes went on holiday with her in the summer of 1931. The pair stayed on their own for six weeks in a log cabin in the Sierra Nevada mountains near Silver Lake. '[Greta] is a creature of the elements,' she wrote. 'A creature of wind and storms and rocks and trees and water.'[3] (Mercedes too would betray Greta by publishing scurrilous details of their friendship.) Mercedes tried to insinuate herself into Greta's life, to exert authority over her wardrobe and choice of films. But Garbo could look after herself and Mercedes was swiftly discarded when the star tired of her. She realised that, just as Clive James once wrote of Philip Larkin, the 'need for affection was matched by an equally consuming need to be alone'.[4] She did need companionship. But she demanded the right to withdraw from the world when it suited her, however callous and whimsical her behaviour looked to others.

Cecil's eventual meeting with Greta, in 1932, was

random. She turned up unexpectedly at the house of friends with whom he happened to be staying in Hollywood. Cecil looked out of his bedroom window and saw, in the garden, an apparition in a white sweater and shorts and with her hair tucked beneath a cap. He later wrote: 'If a unicorn had suddenly appeared in the later afternoon light of this ugly, ordinary garden, I could have been neither more surprised nor more amazed by the beauty of this exotic creature.'[5]

Within minutes his long-cherished fantasy had come true and he was sipping a bellini beside her on a leather pouffe. Greta exclaimed, in her accented English: 'But you're so yorng!'[6] She admired Cecil's shoes and told him he was beautiful. He said she was beautiful too, which seemed to annoy her. At the end of the night she plucked a yellow rose from a vase and gave it to him. (Cecil had it framed in silver and took it back to Ashcombe, the country house in Wiltshire he had just bought, where he hung it above his bed.) He took her up to the turret room where he was staying and showed her photos of Ashcombe. She said she despised Hollywood and always felt excluded, an outsider looking in. They kissed and Cecil thought she smelled like freshly mown grass. She compared him to a young Grecian boy and said: 'If I were a young boy I would do such things to you.' They went downstairs and danced to the radio with the others. Greta left at dawn. Cecil asked if he might visit her at the studio where she was making her latest movie. She said no. Was this really goodbye, then? 'Yes I'm afraid so,' she replied. 'C'est la vie.'[7]

They would not meet again until 1946. In the meantime, Cecil dined out on the encounter, writing in one magazine that 'her hair is biscuit coloured and of the finest spun silk and clean and sweetly smelling as a baby's after its bath'. Greta had, he declared, 'the tragic quality of a child'.[8]

The odd thing was the sexual dimension to his obsession with Greta, given that Cecil presented as flamboyantly gay. (On the day he met her, he was sporting tiny shorts made of white sharkskin and a white kid jacket.) But Cecil had a hatred of gay sex and as a young man once wrote that gay men 'frighten and nauseate me and I see so vividly myself shadowed in so many of them'.[9] His bedroom at Ashcombe had a circus theme. The bed, designed by Rex Whistler, resembled a gaudy carousel: Cecil had originally wanted it to revolve to the sound of steam-organ music. But rather than put the bed to the carnal use he had had in mind when he commissioned it, Cecil threw himself at men who were not interested in him sexually, then obsessed over them until they grew bored and weary.

Greta had grown up poor in a cramped apartment in southern Stockholm. Her father did what jobs he could, including as a street cleaner and an abattoir assistant. As a child Greta developed the trick of escaping in her mind and grew to love solitude and private reverie. (The miserliness for which she was famed may have been a result of this childhood deprivation.) In adulthood she preferred to live only in a couple of rooms and hated being waited on. She also had fits of melancholy which manifested as an urge to detach herself from others.

Cecil, meanwhile, had grown up in leafy Hampstead in north London, the eldest of four. His father was a wealthy timber merchant and Beaton attended the same prep school as Cyril Connolly and George Orwell. An academic underachiever, he blagged his way into Cambridge using family connections, leaving without a degree. While at university he became obsessed with photography, especially once he acquired a gadget that made it possible for him to photograph himself – an early twentieth-century selfie!

At weekends while at Cambridge he would go partying in London and took pictures of the so-called Bright Young People cavorting decadently. All the time he was struggling with his own sexuality. As Souhami puts it: 'He wanted to behave affectionately toward the men he fancied and to sleep in the same bed with them, but that was all.'[10] His affairs with men ended in disappointment and misery. He had flings with women too, but these were no more successful.

Professionally, though, he was in clover. By 1934 he had a contract with US *Vogue* and sailed out twice a year to New York. He stayed at the Waldorf Astoria where he decorated his suite with original Picasso and Matisse paintings that he brought with him in a trunk. He photographed all the stars of Hollywood's Golden Age, including Marlene Dietrich and Gloria Swanson. Cecil also designed sets and costumes for theatre and opera as well as film and, to cap it all, was appointed court photographer to the royal family.

By the time he and Greta next met – on 15 March 1946, at the home of Margaret Case, society editor for *Vogue* – the war had been and gone and Greta had given up acting entirely, exhausted by Hollywood and stung by bad reviews and poor box office returns for her final film, *Two-Faced Woman* (1941), which had required her to play a ski instructor who pretends to be her own twin sister in order to win back her unfaithful husband. Meanwhile, Cecil had found renown as a surprisingly effective official war photographer.

Case had invited Cecil at the same time as Greta quite deliberately, knowing of his obsession. When he saw Greta again, he wrote, he felt 'knocked back – as if someone had opened a furnace door onto me: I had almost to gasp for the next breath.'[11] She looked older – after all, she *was* older, having turned forty. A great noticer of superficial details, Cecil observed unkindly that her hands were rough and that her legs had 'the scrawny look of a waif's or of certain poor, older people'.[12] They went outside onto the roof garden to look at the Manhattan skyline and she allowed him close enough to detect again the cut-grass scent of her hair and face.

So recommenced one of the most unusual relationships ever, one governed by rules imposed largely by Greta. Sometimes she came to tea with him at his hotel. Sometimes they met for dinner. They had little in common and their temperaments were opposed – Beaton needing people desperately, Garbo needing solitude. Did she notice his creepy idealising of her? Or did he conceal it, saving it for his diaries and letters? When, one day, she wondered aloud if she should get married, Beaton pounced and proposed. She told him to stop being frivolous. Still, they continued to meet: to walk together in Central Park; to visit museums and galleries.

One day, Cecil offered to take Greta's passport photo – she genuinely needed one. She arrived at his hotel suite where Cecil, unable to believe that she had finally agreed to be photographed, snapped off a volley of pictures. In some of them she wore costumes from the dressing-up box he always brought with him on his travels. Ever ambitious, he took these photos straight to *Vogue*, who were astounded. Greta had grudgingly given consent to the publication of one of them. Without consulting her, Beaton allowed *Vogue* to publish fourteen. When she heard what he had done,

Garbo was livid and from then on played a wary game, alternately ghosting him and leading him on – for instance, inviting him to her New York hotel room on the condition that he came 'now', when she knew that that was impossible for him because (for example) he was in London or Los Angeles.

Gradually, though, there was a thawing. Towards the end of 1947 Cecil went to New York again and managed to coax her into his hotel room. A routine developed of meeting in hotel rooms where – sometimes – they had sex, even though Garbo was in another relationship (with a married man). It was almost always in the afternoons and Greta never stayed the night. She exuded, wrote Cecil, an ambiguous sex attraction, as if she were half boy, half woman. What exactly their sex life constituted is hard to say. Certainly, he liked her trim, athletic figure and broad shoulders. Cecil wrote that 'we talked of many intimate things that it is difficult to talk about, but managed to achieve a happy understanding and mutual enjoyment'.[13]

As the years ticked past Greta grew lonely and depressed. Sometimes she drank too much. She worried about ageing and its effects on her face. When Cecil went to stay with her in Hollywood she took him for a long walk along the shoreline at Santa Monica, cooked him lamb chops with steamed vegetables, then packed him off to a hotel so she could get an early night. Time and again, writes Souhami, Cecil wilfully deceived himself about what it was that Greta was offering him: 'She seemed to want refuge in his superficiality, to have him as her lover because he need not be taken seriously as a lover.'[14]

Greta had weirdly little need of human ties. She had other suitors – her business adviser George Schlee; Mercedes de Acosta – but kept them at a distance. Cecil was probably the neediest of them all. He pestered her with phone calls and wrote her long letters which she usually ignored. Cecil wanted her to live with him and Greta did visit him at Reddish House in Wiltshire, to which he had moved in 1947. But she argued with his mother during the stay and it was not a success. She led him along and teased him; played on his insecurities, such as when she called him 'Mr Beaton' in front of mutual friends. It was a friendship with benefits – not just sex, but the glamour of association. He loved the mystery and gossip that attended her every move. And she knew this – knew he wanted her as an ornament first and foremost.

It was, perhaps, Cecil's growing realisation that the relationship was never going to solidify into something lasting and significant that led him to betray Greta. In 1960, when Mercedes de Acosta was sick with a brain tumour and in need of money to pay for her treatment, Mercedes had published a memoir, *Here Lies the Heart*, which spilled the beans about her and Greta's lesbian relationship. Greta was so upset that she never spoke to or contacted her again, even when Mercedes was on her deathbed.

Cecil was in the habit of publishing his diaries, though he edited them carefully to exclude references to his sexuality, tone down bitchy comments and downplay his ambition. In November 1971 he published what became the most notorious instalment, called *The Happy Years*, covering the period 1944–48. He had used his diaries to keep detailed track of all the meetings and conversations he had had with Greta in the course of their relationship. The reaction, upon publication, was little short of nuclear. The newspapers went wild, but once the initial thrill of the attention had passed Cecil began to appreciate the extent of what he had done and suffered a host of psychosomatic symptoms. 'The awful feelings of guilt and anxiety continue to dog me,' he wrote. 'I have headaches and feel very rotten.'[15]

All contact with Garbo lapsed, as he must have known it would.

They did see each other one last time, though. It was in October 1975. Cecil had suffered a stroke. His speech was slurred and he was partially paralysed. Having been persuaded to visit him in Wiltshire, Garbo turned to Cecil's secretary and said: 'Well, I couldn't have married him, could I – him being like this.'[16]

They never saw each other again and she did not attend his funeral.

Garbo and Beaton were in their own way an alpha couple. Although attached to some degree, they never actually had to live together, or help each other out, or look after each other. There was no discharging of the mutual responsibilities that most couples elect to shoulder. It is perhaps a relief that two such idiosyncratic people never married. Even though there were, by the mid-twentieth century, many different ways of being married, the likelihood is they would have been terribly unhappy. We have to hope, though, that they would not have been as unhappy as the Victorian author Edward Bulwer Lytton and his wife Rosina.

History has not been kind to Lytton, the opium-addicted, bisexual dandy best known now for originating the phrases: 'It was a dark and stormy night', and 'The pen is mightier than the sword'. But in his day he was one of the most successful writers around – a playwright and essayist, as well as a novelist who outsold Dickens and Walter Scott. Not only was he one of the early pioneers of science fiction, he was also a successful politician, rising to the post of colonial secretary.

Throughout his life, however, Lytton's notoriously rickety marriage threatened to eclipse his professional achievements. And until fairly recently, Rosina's reputation was for being 'unhinged'. One academic blames the 'partisan distortion' of then-influential male critics, who naturally sided with Edward, and the embarrassment generated by people such as Rosina who have reached the end of their tether, which 'quickly turns the person with a grievance into a social liability'.[17]

Edward and Rosina met in around April 1826 in the West End drawing room of a bluestocking called Elizabeth Benger. Edward was a dandy, excessively concerned with clothes and style. The late 1820s found him at his most resplendent – a vision in lace shirts with turn-back cuffs, his hair hanging in golden ringlets below his shoulders. Rosina, for her part, was a good mimic with a clever, cutting sense of humour. She was beautiful, too; even Lytton's mother agreed, though she grew to hate Rosina, telling her son that if he married her, he would in less than a year be the most miserable man in England. Within months the couple had consummated their passion. Edward would later claim that he had only married her out of a sense of honour. But the feverish letters he sent her at the time suggest this was not true.

Rosina had had a hard childhood. Born in Ireland, she was spurned by her alcoholic father and brought up – 'dragged up', Rosina would say – by her mother Anna

Wheeler, a radical feminist who was always 'deep in the perusal of some French or German philosophical work that had reached her translated via London'.[18] Anna was not much interested in children. Rosina remembered trying to draw as a child but, 'being no genius, I only succeeded in making a most atrocious squeaking of the pencil against the slate, which would so irritate my poor mother's philosophical nerves that I generally received so strong a rebuke that it sent me screaming into the garden'.[19] There were rumours of insanity in the family, which Edward came to believe. But then it suited him to think this.

During their courtship Edward and Rosina called each other 'puppy' and 'poodle' and used a baby language that substituted 'oo' for 'you'. Lytton wanted his wife to be his intellectual equal. The problem was, he also wanted her to be the sort of innocent, ethereal heroine he was fond of featuring in his novels.

Edward's mother continued to be suspicious of Rosina, worrying that she had had a 'forlorn childhood and unguided girlhood',[20] and obsessed with the idea that Rosina had lied about her age and was a year or two older than she claimed to be. (Opinion varies as to whether or not she was.) Edward's mother's opinion mattered because at this early stage, before his books made him rich, he was financially dependent on her. When, at one point, he broke off the engagement, Rosina wrote to him: 'May you find in the affection of your mother all that you have lost in me.'[21]

But they made up and did, in the end, marry at St James's, Piccadilly on 29 August 1827. They sent Edward's mother a slice of wedding cake, but she refused to eat it. Instead she stopped his allowance, leaving him with no income save Rosina's dowry (the exact amount is disputed); a small lump sum he had inherited from his father, and whatever he could make from his writing.

The Bulwer Lyttons lived at first at Woodcote House near Reading. The marriage started well enough. The couple idealised each other and the transforming role they would play in each other's lives. 'We are alone in the world,' Edward wrote to her, 'let us cling to one another for support.'[22] In another letter he called her 'my Rose of Roses' and the 'Quintessence of Darlingry'. They were obsessed with dogs and encouraged visiting guests to bring theirs too.

Soon, however, cracks started to show – as they were always going to, considering Edward's narcissistic view that falling in love was 'less an appreciation of another person than the meeting of an inner need': 'Responding to the need, spouses are moulded to a preconceived pattern. Inevitably, expectations are never realised, and the result is misery.'[23]

'Till very lately I always hoped that I *could* make you happy,' Edward wrote to Rosina around this time. 'If now, dearest, I doubt it, it is both from a knowledge of my own faults and a discovery, I will not say of a *fault* in you, but of a proud and resentful principle in your mind, which does in my opinion detract from its perfection.'[24]

That much of this was standard Victorian sexism is plain from the sort of statements relating to gender politics that Edward was fond of making, for example: 'No attachment can be permanent where the woman does not make greater concessions than the man, and does not even feel that those concessions are the most real sources of pride.'[25] Rosina came to hate this attitude and realised that, whatever her faults as a parent, her feminist mother had been right. The patriarchy, which controlled every institution, was an 'infernal machine of occult power'.[26] Men covered up each other's mistakes and indiscretions, even if they disliked each other. The preservation of the system demanded as much – and it had to be kept going at all costs.

Without his mother's allowance, it fell to Edward to fund his and Rosina's lavish lifestyle by his writing. Their annual expenditure in 1830 was £3,000 – a massive sum. To make anything near the necessary money, he had to write like a demon. Between 1827 and 1837 he wrote eleven novels, two long poems, a play and a history of Athens in three volumes. He was also a regular essayist and book reviewer – and an MP. Even Rosina was forced to admit that Edward 'undertakes a degree of labour that . . . no three persons could have the health and time to achieve'. This involved neglecting his family and wearing himself out. However, neither he nor Rosina could curb their spending. 'I never suffer myself to be troubled, if I can help it, with the vile details of household affairs,' Rosina wrote, while her husband celebrated the success of his 1828 novel *Pelham* by buying 36 Hertford Street in Mayfair and filling it with antiques, including two Louis XIV clocks. (He bought other houses too which he used as meeting places for his lovers.)[27]

Two children were born – Emily in 1828, Robert in 1831. But the couple were starting to get bored in the country, especially Edward. His workload, his sadness at being rejected by his mother and his frustration at having to count the pennies combined with his gross egotism to create the father of all bad moods. He invited Rosina to criticise his novels, then got cross when she said bad things. She found literary society tedious, writing: 'It is astonishing what bores I find all authors except my own husband, and he has nothing author-like about him, for this reason, that his literary talents are his very least.'[28]

As the marriage deteriorated, Edward buried himself in work and started to worry excessively about his health. He spent more and more time in London. On the rare occasions when he was at home at his Knebworth estate, he would remove himself from family life, breakfasting on his own in the library while Rosina had hers in her dressing room. They had violent arguments, exacerbated by alcohol. Rosina once threw one of his favourite shirts on the fire.

In 1833, Rosina wrote an essay called 'Nemesis', which took the form of a letter from Byron. In it she claimed that while she was pregnant with Emily and working with Edward in the library on one of his books, Edward had kicked and beaten her when she excused herself to lie down because she was tired. (Whether or not this is true – and it most probably is – Edward certainly attacked Rosina later on, biting her on the cheek. Their cook had to intervene and pull Edward off her. Edward was ashamed and later sent her an apologetic letter admitting 'I have eternally disgraced myself', though he later denied it all.) Rosina also hinted at depraved sexual appetites – 'other little incidents which women cannot tell even to their lawyers'.[29]

Certainly, Edward continued to have affairs, most controversially with a Mrs Stanhope. He suggested they divorce, but only if Rosina admitted to infidelity and stayed silent about his own affairs and his domestic violence. She refused, fearful of destitution and loss of reputation if she fought him in court. In 1836 they separated, though they continued to use their weird baby language in letters: 'No, my sagacious Poodle, no, me does not wish oo to be a bit more stupid than oo is . . .'[30]

Rosina moved with the children to Ireland. She stayed with an old friend, Mary Greene, and requested maintenance from Edward, on whom she was financially dependent as she no longer had the independent income she had enjoyed before they married. Cad that he was, Edward took full advantage of this. He put Rosina under surveillance, hoping to catch her with another man. (She was indeed having a relationship with a Mr Hume.) He also managed to win Mary to his cause: what exactly transpired isn't clear, but by 1838 the children were in the custody not of their parents, but her.

Reeling from her friend's betrayal, Rosina went first to Bath, then spent the next eight to ten years living abroad in relative poverty. Her decision to start writing was partly to make some much-needed money and partly to tell the world what Edward Bulwer Lytton, Great Man of Letters, was really like. In 1839 she published *Cheveley: Or, The Man of Honour*, a vicious roman à clef featuring a matriarch based on Edward's mother, who 'resembled a withered crab-apple'. Edward was transformed into Lord de Clifford, a violent, abusive husband. What upset Edward most was that some critics quite liked it. 'They praise the talent of the wretched trash. They who have denied ME talents!'[31]

Encouraged by the success of *Cheveley*, Rosina followed it with *The Budget of the Bubble Family* and a further eight novels, many of which Edward tried to stifle at birth by taking out injunctions or putting pressure on publishers not to accept them. The question of whose side to take, his or hers, dominated conversation in literary London. Charles Dickens told his friend Edward that Rosina was 'the misfortune of your life'. (Dickens himself had his own 'misfortune' in the form of his wife Catherine, whom he attempted to get certified as mad so that he could continue his affair with a young actress called Ellen Ternan.) Thomas Carlyle and his writer wife Jane, novelist William Makepeace Thackeray and the poet Walter Savage Landor, on the other hand, were on Team Rosina.

The situation worsened after the death in 1847 of the Lyttons' daughter Emily from typhoid. Edward had put her to work at Knebworth translating books from German into English (he was a poor linguist). For reasons that are not clear, when she became ill he packed her off to a run-down boarding house in west London. Learning of this at the last moment, Rosina travelled to London, took the room upstairs and went to see Emily, ignoring the nurse who had been given instructions to stop Rosina from entering.

Rosina's rage intensified as Edward's fortunes rose. Not only were his novels and plays great commercial successes, but in 1844 he had inherited a large sum of money from his mother. Rosina sabotaged productions of Edward's plays by orchestrating booing campaigns. She wrote letters to his friends and associates and to him (addressed to 'the Reptile Sir Liar Coward Bulwer Lytton' and such like), repeating her allegations of violence and abuse. A particular target of her rage was Charles Dickens – Edward's co-star in one of the plays whose performance she disrupted, *Not So Bad As We Seem: Or, Many Sides to a Character*. As she wrote: 'One has only to look at his [Edward's] hideous face and that of that other brute Dickens to see that every bad passion has left the impress of its cloven hoof upon their fiendish line-aments.'[32] She hated the way Charles's reputation as a compassionate moralist continued to flourish despite the facts of his private life.

When, in 1858, Edward was offered the post of colonial

secretary in Lord Derby's administration, Rosina was livid. But she also knew that, according to the rules of the time, it meant he had to seek re-election. This gave her a unique opportunity to embarrass him.

Rosina's confidence had been boosted by the passing the previous year of the Matrimonial Causes Act which made divorce legal under British law, moving it from the ecclesiastical to the civil courts. So Rosina dared to hope it would facilitate a fair severance from Edward. A plan formed in her head, as she later explained: 'The month of June 1858 had arrived, and the Hertford election was to take place on the 8th, a Wednesday, I think. The Sunday before, I was in bed with one of my splitting headaches, from ceaseless worry of mind and want of rest. I got up, and in a perfect agony prayed to God to direct me, to send me some help in my cruel, cruel position. I went back to bed exhausted, and the sudden thought struck me, I would go to the Hertford election, and publicly expose the ruffian.'[33]

Rosina had posters printed announcing her arrival in Hertford which she paid a local tradesman to paste up over the town. These invited people to meet her at the Corn Exchange before walking up to the site of Lytton's hustings at the edge of the town. She also took with her copies of a pamphlet she had published, 'Lady Bulwer Lytton's Appeal to the Justice and Charity of the English Public'.

Edward won his Hertford seat, but as he was delivering his long acceptance speech Rosina strode towards the stage in a yellow dress and started shouting: 'Make way for the member's wife!' Edward staggered backwards before turning white and vacating the stage, accompanied by their son Robert. Whereupon Rosina clambered onto the podium and gave a speech in which she asked how the people of

England could bear to have as colonial secretary a 'fiend' and 'monster' who 'ought to have been in the Colonies as a transport [convicted criminal]'.[34]

The evident sympathy shown Rosina by the crowd tipped Edward over the edge. First, he spread rumours (possibly true) that Rosina had a drink problem. Second, he resolved to deal with her once and for all using Britain's famously lax lunacy laws, which provided ample facilities for the disposal of inconvenient wives.

So it came to pass that at 11 a.m. on 11 June 1858 a team of lawyers, a nurse and a Dr Hale Thomson insinuated themselves into the hotel in Taunton where Rosina was living and subjected her to a barrage of tests to determine whether she was mad. They also interviewed the hotel staff, none of whom had a bad word to say about her. The team slunk off after Rosina told them that all she wanted from Edward was an increase in her allowance.

It was ostensibly to discuss this that Rosina was tricked into making a trip to London on 22 June. Accompanied by two friends, she arrived at Dr Thomson's house in Clarges Street at noon. He greeted her cordially but dodged her questions about the allowance. Rosina grew frustrated and said that if a decision was not made by 6 p.m. she would hand over incriminating letters from Edward to a magistrate. When she returned at 6 p.m., Rosina was pounced on by heavies employed by the alienist (as psychiatrists were then called), Dr Robert Gardiner Hill. When it became clear that the police could not intervene to help her – Hill had all the necessary paperwork – she agreed to go without a struggle. She was taken by carriage to Wyke House, an eighteenth-century mansion in Brentford used as an asylum.

Rosina's stay there was, by all accounts, rather comfortable.

The regime was relaxed. Patients were allowed to gather strawberries and take restorative walks; though their windows were nailed shut, apart from a three-inch gap at the top. Dr Gardiner Hill, says historian Sarah Wise, 'based his regime on the illusion that this was a family home and that the patients were there as house guests'.[35] Rosina struck up a friendship with Mary, his fourteen-year-old daughter, as well as the asylum's resident cow and tortoiseshell cat.

Rosina stayed there from 23 June to 17 July. While there she threatened to kill herself and repeated claims she had made earlier that Edward had murdered their daughter Emily. She told them that Edward was Benjamin Disraeli's gay lover. She also told the story of Edward biting her cheek. Dr Hill expressed surprise that she spoke of this openly and was not ashamed by what had happened. While men could do as they pleased and were protected by male codes of honour and secrecy, women were not supposed to speak of such things. Rosina insisted she was not mad and that the Commissioners in Lunacy – who oversaw asylums – were 'patent humbugs'.[36]

It seems likely Rosina was believed as she received what appears to be special treatment – moved to a lodge down the road; given the use of a maid; allowed trips out in a brougham with Mary, access to whom would hardly have been granted if her father thought Rosina represented any sort of serious danger.

When Edward and his solicitor forced their way into the Giles Court Hotel to try to find Rosina's papers, they were stopped by a guest who, finding that they had no official permit, called the police. Local opinion rallied around Rosina. The *Somerset County Gazette* wrote that the whole plot was like a cheap romance novel. The *Daily Telegraph* joined in, though not *The Times*, which was edited by one of Edward's friends.

The plan backfired on Edward when Rosina became a celebrity and public opinion turned against him. Terrified that Rosina might expose him in the new divorce court, he agreed to her release; also to pay off her debts and increase her allowance to £500 a year. Rosina demanded £1,000. Edward acquiesced (though reduced it stealthily to £500 again later). At 3 p.m. on Saturday, 17 July 1858, Rosina was set free. Edward tried to spin the story that Rosina had simply been staying with a doctor and his family in the countryside. Rosina's part of the bargain was that she had to leave the country immediately, which she did, accompanied by their son Robert.

Rosina evidently found it more difficult to comply with Edward's order that she was to cease her whispering (or rather shouting) campaign against him. She fell out with Robert, whom she suspected of being on his father's side, and returned to England. There, she continued to write letters to everyone in her husband's circle, accusing him of every possible vice. Edward resigned his post and fled to the Continent to recuperate. Incriminating letters found their way into the press, and even steadfast friends abandoned him, including Dickens.

In the end, says Edward's biographer Leslie Mitchell, 'both found a kind of therapy in sustained hatred'.[37] Sarah Wise is right too, though, when she says the real tragedy is the way Rosina's hatred of Edward became so all-consuming that it stopped her from being the feminist campaigner she might have been, despite realising that men's 'one trick, worth our thousand, is *power*'.[38]

For some couples, pairing up is a performance. But what happens offstage, afterwards, once that performance has stopped – if indeed it ever stops? If the public relationship between a couple is toxic or combative, as in the case of the Bulwer Lyttons, then these questions become even more urgent. It suited Rosina for her marriage to be as public as possible: it was a way of turning up the heat on Edward and amassing sympathy for herself. The risk – and it is a real one – is that the spectacle becomes unseemly and degrading; a feast of oversharing so frenzied that the human relationship at the core gets lost.

We are all familiar with the concept of the double act, which has its roots in the music hall tradition of two comedians performing together. In a double act the humour often depends on an uneven relationship between the two comics. They may, for example, have radically contrasting personalities. The 'straight man', or stooge, generally assumes the role of the reasonable, rational foil to the excesses of the 'funny man'. In American vaudeville, the pioneers of the double act were Abbott and Costello. The birth of motion pictures gave rise to Laurel and Hardy, one of the few silent-film brands to carry over successfully to 'talkies'.

The recent biopic *Stan & Ollie*, with Steve Coogan and John C. Reilly, showed the duo touring dingy venues in Britain in the early 1950s, their golden days having long since passed. Writer and comedian Charlie Higson, himself part of a writing double act with Paul Whitehouse, rightly praised the film as being 'particularly good on the dynamics of a double act: the rivalry, the jealousy, the sense of "he'd be nothing without me" and, ultimately, the mutual understanding that, in fact, they would both be lost on their own . . . In a classic double act the pull is not between straight and funny, it's between order and chaos. One of the pair is always trying to make sense of the world and the other is forever pulling it apart.' In Laurel and Hardy routines, says Higson, Stan Laurel is 'the eternal child, forever getting things wrong, tangling his words and thoughts and falling foul of everyday objects, but Oliver Hardy was equally funny. His pomposity, his physical precision and delicacy, his affronted dignity, and his belief that he was superior to Stan in every way, despite being only marginally less stupid, made his performances sublimely entertaining.'[39]

This sounds distractingly like TV chefs Fanny Cradock and her fourth husband Major Johnnie Cradock, a pantomime double act who brought a touch of aspirational glamour and (from some quarters) incredulous laughter to a country that had emerged battered and bruised from the war.

Fanny famously worked in ball gowns without the customary cook's apron – a slightly bizarre way of making the point that women should feel cooking was easy and enjoyable, rather than messy and intimidating. Shows such as *Fanny's Kitchen* were the 1950s and '60s equivalent of *Bake Off*. She was Cruella de Vil in caked-on make-up (including thin, drawn-on eyebrows), while her on-screen husband Johnnie was, writes the chef Antony Worrall Thompson, whose mother worked on Fanny's early TV shows as floor manager, 'like a sponge absorbing the vitriol'. He was 'Maggie to her Dame Edna or perhaps Denis to Maggie Thatcher'.[40]

With his monocle and moustache, Johnnie was the very model of a former services man, at sea in the modern world but keen to learn the ropes – even if doing so required constant self-dosing with alcohol.

A former Royal Artillery major, Johnnie had met Fanny in November 1939 at a stage show she had devised to entertain troops in Hackney Marshes, east London. He was thirty-five, five years her senior. She had dismissed him at first as 'the sort of man who'll invite me to the Savoy, buy me champagne and give me a horrid mauve orchid with a pin in it'.[41] Johnnie pursued her, proved that this was not an accurate portrait, and left his first wife Ethel and four children for her. They disagreed on a fair bit. He, for example, was passionate about rugby. She hated it and once said: 'The only things which keep us apart are rugby and the lavatory.'[42]

Johnnie had been discharged from the Royal Artillery after temporarily losing the sight in one eye – hence the monocle. In his first marriage he had not even been allowed to set foot in the kitchen, let alone to actually set about cooking. Fanny's route to his heart was to allow him to lick out saucepans, which he did the first time he came to dinner. She reported being 'fairly disconcerted at the sight of a large, fair, balding man licking with such excessive rapture'.[43] Ahem.

Fanny's terrible temper alienated most of those who worked for her and blinded people to her better qualities. She was snobbish and egocentric, sure, but also energetic and innovative. Johnnie's talent, meanwhile, was for knowing when to stand back and let her get on with it. The pair started cooking together on stage in 1953, four years after Fanny's first taste of success with a book called *The Practical Cook* written under the nom de plume Frances Dale. These performances, which often ran for over two hours and encompassed matinees as well as evening shows, were hugely successful. By the mid-1950s the pair were packing thousands into venues across Britain, teaching them the rudiments of Fanny's beloved French cookery.

Their high point, arguably, was a 1956 televised show at the Royal Albert Hall which featured Fanny's attempt to recreate culinary king Auguste Escoffier's Peche Melba recipe inside an 80lb swan sculpted from ice in the kitchens of the Savoy Hotel. Unfortunately, Fanny and Johnnie's success did not last. They overstretched themselves, buying a Grade II-listed pile in Essex called Dover House, fitting it out with nine gas cookers and a gold ceiling frieze in the dining room, just as their TV careers were beginning to wane.

The gimmick of Fanny and Johnnie shows such as *Kitchen Magic* and *Fanny's Kitchen* was that they featured Fanny teaching know-nothing Johnnie how to cook. (Johnnie's permitted area of expertise was wine.) Her mission was to demonstrate, as she put it, that 'men are responsible for the low cooking esteem and lower ambition of their wives'.[44] *Kitchen Magic*, their TV debut, was filmed at the Shepherd's Bush Empire in front of 500 people. Fanny later wrote: 'Johnnie was so appallingly egg-bound with stage fright that, when he was cued on, he couldn't move. A shocked technician gave him a kick and said, "Go on, Johnnie, you're on you silly sod, you're on."'[45]

Sometimes Fanny called him 'darling' or 'my love'; sometimes just 'Cradock' or 'silly old fool'. In interviews she interrupted or talked over him or asked questions to which there was only one possible answer. 'It's all great fun, darling, isn't it?' she asked him in front of Maeve Binchy, then a journalist for the *Irish Times*. 'Great fun,' he replied, warily, before settling back into muteness.[46]

Fanny's background was complicated. Her first husband had died; a second she ditched; her third she also rejected, this time for Johnnie. Twice she married bigamously after her second husband, who was Catholic, refused to grant her a divorce. She changed her name to Cradock by deed poll in 1942. Fanny and Johnnie didn't actually marry until 1977 after her third husband Arthur Chapman's death – or, should we say, 'alleged death': he was actually still alive and Johnnie had got confused while reading an obituary of a different Arthur Chapman.

Fanny professed love for Johnnie and spoke of their 'insane enjoyment of life together',[47] but could be as harsh and abusive to him in private as she was on television. His response was to go quiet and wait for the fusillade to cease. As Fanny's fame grew, she became regal and haughty. When Johnnie once answered her back, their assistant Wendy Colvin remembers Fanny responding: 'Don't you ever speak to me like that again or you will be back where you came from so fast you won't know what's hit you. You're not indispensable to me. I am Fanny Cradock and don't you forget that.'[48] Fanny once said that the test of a good rolling pin was 'to slosh father or husband over the head with it. If he falls unconscious it's all right for cooking.'[49] (Johnnie once repeated a version of this 'joke' himself on *The Generation Game* in 1973, adding: 'When I go to the barber's now, if I haven't got a mark on my head, he says, "What's wrong with the old woman, is she ill?"')

Fanny had started off not as a cookery writer – her first cookbook was not published until 1949 when she was forty – but as a children's novelist. Before she became a TV star she worked tirelessly in journalism, as women's editor for the *Daily Graphic* and as a food and travel columnist for the *Daily Express*, the *Daily Mail* and the *Sunday Express*. For over thirty years she and Johnnie wrote a joint column for the *Daily Telegraph* under the pen name 'Bon Viveur'.

Fanny's real name was Phyllis Pechey. She had been 'given' to her grandmother as a birthday present by her mother, and grew up in a grand house in Leytonstone, east London called Apthorp, long since demolished. Her grandparents introduced her to smoking and drinking at an early age. Academically ambitious for her, they made her translate the *Times*'s leader into French or German every day at breakfast. As an adolescent, Fanny became obsessed with spiritualism and the supernatural and was expelled from her boarding school for holding a seance.

Fanny and Johnnie enjoyed professional success for nearly twenty years. As their TV career spluttered and died, however, Johnnie dropped out of the picture. He was nowhere to be seen when, in 1976, Fanny was recruited as culinary adviser on a BBC show called *The Big Time*, a sort of proto-*Masterchef* produced by Esther Rantzen. On this show, unable to restrain herself, Fanny played up to her own myth, cruelly patronising and belittling a Devon housewife called Gwen Troake for wanting to cook duck with black-berries followed by a coffee pudding. To make her point, Fanny gurned and fake-retched as the menu was described to her. (You can find the clip on YouTube.) The *Radio Times* was inundated with letters of complaint. Fanny's lack of a common touch, previously the source of her appeal, was suddenly a professional liability.

After Johnnie's death, Fanny insisted that the bickering and violent outbursts were 'all an act': 'We used to practise before-hand,' she said. 'We were devoted to each other. And now that he's gone, I don't want to live . . . Everyone thinks I ran Johnnie. But it's just not true. I did every single thing I wanted to do, but when it came to the really major things Johnnie put his foot down. Otherwise I wouldn't have loved him.'[50]

She didn't mention the fact that, as Johnnie lay dying in hospital, she was so frightened of illness that she visited him only long enough to remove his signet ring, then refused to go to his funeral.

———————————

To examine a marriage is to examine what Phyllis Rose, in her dazzling study of Victorian pairings *Parallel Lives*, calls the 'shifting tides of power'. Marriage is, she points out, a way of declaring how we plan to live, how we intend to 'find a design within the primal stew of data which is our daily experience'.[51] Marriage or any other long-term relationship that involves cohabiting is about the management of that power. In this sense it is always a political experience.

Unhappy marriages are often, Rose says, the sites of a struggle for imaginative dominance, whereas happily married couples tend to agree on a story about how and in what direction the marriage is proceeding: 'Marriages go bad not when love fades – love can modulate into affection without driving two people apart – but when this understanding about the balance of power breaks down, when the weaker member feels exploited or the stronger feels unrewarded for his or her strength.'[52]

One difference between marriage and more casual, ad hoc relationships has traditionally been that, by virtue of being a legal contract, marriage enforces limits. And people often live more intensely, more *interestingly*, when they have limits imposed upon them. Still, marriage can be a mystery. We cannot get to the bottom of some, except to say that they seem to work on the level of social or professional performance. Remember how important it seemed to self-confessed 'terrible homosexualist' Cecil Beaton to marry Greta Garbo? It would have been his greatest social triumph, never mind the gossip about it being a 'lavender' marriage. Diana Souhami puts it well: 'For Cecil, Greta was the Queen of Queens. Were he to marry her, he would be her Duke, the commoner who conquered. Such a marriage would tantalise society and set him above it. Something of her allure might brush off on him and her androgyny free him from any need to be a conventional man.'[53]

Fanny Cradock insisted people call her 'Mrs Cradock' for decades – when for most of her career, of course, she was nothing of the sort. The idea that she and Johnnie were married, with all that that implied, added not just pathos but a dark, perverse energy to their stage and TV shows. You couldn't quite believe it. Part of you didn't want to believe it.

Beaton's marriage to Garbo would probably have been a disaster. At least nowadays it is relatively easy for couples to extricate themselves from bad marriages. Before the Matrimonial Causes Act of 1857 full divorce with permission to remarry afterwards was only achievable by bringing a private bill to Parliament – something only very wealthy men were able to do. Among the poor, the most common exit strategy was simply to walk out of the door and not return. In practice, though, this option was easier for men, who often took advantage of wars to enlist and escape their domestic responsibilities, leaving their abandoned wives and children at the mercy of the parish. Others stuck together for reasons not directly to do with gender – though gender inequality was always there – but because it was socially expedient and, on some level, mutually gratifying, even if it looks like a bizarre sort of gratification to us.

The marriage of Thomas Carlyle and his equally intellectual but less feted wife, Jane, has long been notorious. It was discussed as a phenomenon when both were alive and at greater length after Jane's death, when Thomas courted comment by publishing a self-pitying book called *Reminiscences*, in which he chastised himself for his poor behaviour towards her. Like many Victorian marriages, the Carlyles' is believed not to have been consummated for, as Thomas's biographer Fred Kaplan explains, they were both naive and prudish: 'Puritanical inhibitions and romantic idealisations were in the seven-foot-wide bed with two sexual innocents.'[54]

The marriage achieved notoriety because Thomas was extraordinarily grumpy and difficult and Jane made sure everyone knew it. A one-time maths teacher from Ecclefechan in Scotland, Thomas had been raised as a strict Calvinist. Many of his books – for example the six-volume history of Frederick the Great over which he laboured for many years – promoted the 'great man' theory of history I discuss in the Introduction. His works informed Nietzsche's theory of the *Übermensch* (superman) and were enjoyed by Goebbels and Hitler. We cannot blame him for this any more than we can blame Marx for Stalin; though we can certainly take him to task for his racist 1849 essay defending slavery, *Occasional Discourse on the Negro Question*.

Thomas admired Jane hugely and thought her a fascinating person with whom 'everybody fell in love'. 'She could do anything well to which she chose to give herself,' he wrote after her death. 'She had a keen clear incisive faculty of seeing through things, and hating all that was make-believe or pretentious. She had good sense that amounted to genius.'[55] Casual observers of the marriage might have been surprised that this was his view.

The couple's lengthy, mostly epistolary courtship had been what Phyllis Rose calls 'a comfortable relationship based on the exchange of books and responses to books'.[56] But while Jane had held her own in their early correspondence, the sense that she was a pupil in thrall to her tutor – a situation crystallised in one of her favourite books as a young woman, Rousseau's *La Nouvelle Héloïse* – came to dominate. Jane's early scepticism about marriage faded, helped along by her need to get away from her mother, and the pair moved to her family's farm in Craigenputtock, Scotland. In 1834, however, they made their home on Cheyne Walk in London's Chelsea, then a modest area beloved of artists.

As Thomas's reputation grew, the pair became unlikely salonnières. But what did London literary society think of their union? Samuel Butler famously said that it was 'very good of God to let Carlyle and Mrs Carlyle marry one another, and so make only two people miserable instead of four'. 'Being married to [Thomas],' said Jane's friend Anna Jameson – having just braved the consequences of interrupting Thomas during one of his monologues – must be 'something next worse to being married to Satan himself'.[57]

The full extent of Thomas's mistreatment of Jane is hard to discern. One of her letters refers obliquely to 'blue marks on my wrists', so it is possible he was physically aggressive towards her. What is certainly true is that, having trained Jane up, Thomas found he had no use for her as an intellectual companion. He needed a domestic help, a 'true-hearted dainty lady-wife' to take care of him, despite his self-confessed tendency to be sulky and bad-tempered. Thomas's cleverness transfixed Jane. She felt it had an unstoppable force, whereas her own could be turned off and on: it was more versatile and could even be directed into running the household. She wrote to her uncle's wife that Thomas was 'among the cleverest men of his day'; therefore she was bound to live in the 'Valley of the shadow' of his reputation.[58] There was never any question of his writing career not being her number-one priority, even though she was so smart that she was believed for a while to be the secret author of Charlotte Brontë's novels.

Over time this ground Jane down and she became bitter and depressive at the thought of the books she would never write. Instead, her genius found its fullest expression in her lively, witty, funny letters and journals, which often mock Carlyle by adopting his own lofty style. These resonate across the centuries, unlike Carlyle's attempts at humour in his breakthrough book, *Sartor Resartus* (1836).

But of course there can be something patronising and belittling about praising a woman for this sort of writing. It is even worse when the person doing the 'praising' is a woman herself. The social reformer and salonnière, Elizabeth Montagu, once told Jane: 'Everybody is born with a vocation, and yours is to write little notes.' The early nineteenth-century view of letter- and journal-writing was that it was quintessentially female – humdrum, domestic, concerned with trivialities rather than the sort of big, bold subjects (Frederick the Great, for instance) that men liked.[59] In one letter, for instance, Jane writes to her mother-in-law that she is always as busy as possible 'and yet, suppose you were to look thro' a microscope – you might be puzzled to discover a trace of what I do – nevertheless depend on [it] my doings are not lost – but invisible to human eyes they "sail down the stream of time onto the ocean of eternity" and who knows but I may find them after many days?'[60]

This is self-deprecating, for sure, but also ironic at Thomas's expense. In fact, many modern scholars argue that Jane's letters work as a deflation of Thomas's 'self-assertive egocentricity' and are 'subversive rather than conformist'.[61] This is certainly how I see them. Jane's letters are a glorious performance, as she well knew – for she admitted that when she felt 'sick and dispirited' she found them hard to write: 'A letter behooves to tell about oneself, and when oneself is disagreeable to oneself, one would rather tell about anything else.'[62]

'How one is vexed with little things in this life!' Jane observed. 'The great evils one triumphs over bravely, but the little eat away one's heart.'[63] Both she and Thomas worried about their health – he called them 'a pair of poor sickly creatures' – and Jane's was worse than Thomas's. He was more obsessive. Of the 'little things' that vexed him, none was greater than noise. He became obsessed with dogs barking, cocks crowing and (later on) steam trains whistling past his window. As Jane wrote in a letter, he was disturbed by 'men, women, children, omnibuses, carriages, glass coaches, street coaches, wagons, carts, dog-carts, steeple bells, doorbells, gentleman raps, twopenny-post-raps and footmen-showers-of raps'.[64] He and Jane built a soundproof room on the top floor of the Cheyne Walk house for him to work in (you can see it today when you visit the house, which is now owned by the National Trust). But it was stuffy and uncomfortable to work in and still noisy, so Thomas rarely used it.

In one brilliant letter Jane paints a domestic picture of

the breakfast table one morning: 'Figure this: (Scene – a room where everything is enveloped in dark-yellow London fog! For air to breathe, a sort of liquid soot! Breakfast on the table – "adulterated coffee", "adulterated bread", "adulterated cream", and "adulterated water"!) Mr C at one end of the table, looking remarkably bilious; Mrs C at the other, looking half dead! Mr C: "My dear, I have to inform you that my bed is full of bugs, or fleas, or some sort of animals that crawl over me at night."'[65]

The marriage was stable insofar as it conformed to its own rules, even if those rules favoured Thomas. Jane's mind, though of a different order to Thomas's, was admired, not least by Charles Dickens and George Eliot. She turned being Thomas's put-upon wife into an art form. She also became incredibly accomplished at running the house and, especially, handling finances so that visitors always left thinking the Carlyles were better off than they really were. When Thomas was summoned to see a tax assessor he decided that 'the voice of honour' was calling on him to pay the required visit; Jane archly noted that that voice 'did not call loud enough' and went herself.

Things really started to go wrong in the 1850s as Jane's health declined. As Rose writes: 'She feels herself taken for granted. She feels herself slighted and somebody else favoured.'[66] The complicating factor was Lady Harriet Ashburton, with whom Thomas had struck up a close friendship. Jane often tagged along to her house parties but disliked them (and Lady Ashburton) and the way she was treated: 'I was thinking the other night, at "the most magnificent ball of the season", how much better I should like to see people making hay, than all these ladies in laces and diamonds, waltzing!'[67] She lacked the energy to dress up and go out and was quietly devastated by Thomas's non-sexual but intense interest in Lady Ashburton and visiting 'that eternal Bath House' where she lived. When Lady Ashburton died suddenly in May 1857, Jane was relieved and resolved to cheer up and cease 'egotistical babblement'.[68] (It is worth pointing out that Jane did herself have an intimate semi-romantic friendship with someone who wasn't her other half. The object of her desire was a woman, the writer Geraldine Jewsbury, who once wrote to Jane, 'I feel towards you much more like a lover than a female friend.'[69])

Jane talked about 'the demoralisation, the desecration, of the Institution of Marriage'.[70] It took her sudden death in April 1866 of suspected heart failure – she was found dead in her carriage while driving in Hyde Park – and Thomas's subsequent reading of her diaries and letters to understand how awful he had made her feel. As Rose notes, instead of train whistles he became obsessed with his own regret – 'the high-pitched wail of past disharmony'.[71] He enshrined his guilt in writing about her: 'I doubt, candidly, if I ever saw a nobler human soul than this which (alas, alas, never rightly valued till now!) accompanied all my steps for forty years.' Obsession with his own 'heavy-laden miserable life' had blinded him. Preparing her letters for publication, he found, was a 'mournful, but pious, and ever interesting task'.[72]

Indeed, everything about Jane became suddenly interesting to Thomas, even sentimental stories from her childhood, such as one she had once told him about how she illicitly sampled a row of custard puddings. After being caught, she was made as a punishment to eat them all and tell the guests what had happened to their desserts. 'The poor child hated custards for a long time afterwards,'[73] notes Thomas sadly. He appraises her former suitors and says she was a terrible flirt. He admits that people thought Jane was making a 'dreadfully bad match' when she married him. 'Long afterwards, when the world began to admire her husband, at the time he delivered the "Lectures on Hero Worship", she gave a little half-scornful laugh, and said, "They tell me things as if they were new that I found out years ago."' Her literary insight, meanwhile, 'was like witchcraft'.[74]

Rose sees the Carlyles as uniquely compatible. 'She gave him the stability and affection he needed to work; he gave her the frustration and annoyance she required to thrive.'[75] This might seem a harsh conclusion – and understanding of coercive behaviour is more sophisticated now than it was when Rose was writing in 1982: nowadays we would be much less inclined to make excuses for Thomas. But they undoubtedly had a system that yielded more or less satisfactory results until the equilibrium was disturbed.

That this system worked, after a fashion, for the Carlyles does not of course mean it worked for everyone. In the eighteenth century, marriage was governed by religious, or canon law, administered in the ecclesiastical courts. Their archives yield some of the saddest examples of aristocratic marriages gone bad – with accounts of the slow-motion disarray, often drawing in a cast of hundreds, that ensued when, for example, a wife was accused of adultery. As the historian Lawrence Stone explained, it was the practice in these courts to deal with written accusations and to write down everything litigants and witnesses said. Stone went through the raw data – sometimes as much as 250,000 words for each case – and presented the results in his fascinating *Broken Lives: Separation and Divorce in England 1660–1857*.

The kinds of marriages I am thinking of predated the

ideal of the companionate marriage, where an emotional bond was considered important. Really they were little more than business deals between propertied families. While in the mid-eighteenth century both halves of a couple had some individual power when it came to the choice of partner and courtship rituals, the dominant ideology of patriarchy still reigned supreme.

Since women are diminished, sad figures in so many accounts of marital separation, it's cheering to read accounts where the wife fights back, or seems to be having a good time, as happened in the case of Beaufort v Beaufort.

Henry Beaufort, 3rd Duke of Beaufort inherited a vast estate from his father at the age of seven. In 1729, aged twenty-one, he married the heiress to an almost equally impressive portfolio – Frances Scudamore, seventeen-year-old daughter of the late 2nd Viscount Scudamore. It was an arranged marriage, as was normal at the time in this world, but an exceptionally potent one in terms of the wealth any male heir would inherit.

The couple got along reasonably well until the late 1730s, when their childlessness, which had long been noted by gossips, became the most obvious thing about them. With a vast array of houses to choose from, and the duke increasingly sickly, they started to spend large amounts of time apart from each other.

In February 1740, the duchess met William, Lord Talbot of Hensol, a gentleman of leisure whose good fortune had been made better still by marrying an heiress worth some £70,000. Lord Talbot and his wife had one child, whose delivery had been so traumatic that Lord Talbot had taken to using his wife's 'weakly' constitution (and, presumably, fear of sex and pregnancy) as an excuse to sleep around. The duchess became his quarry and by May that year they were lovers.

Wary of using the marital bed at the Grosvenor Street house, where the affair had kicked off, the couple had to use other rooms and items of furniture, sometimes pushing dining chairs together to form a sort of sofa. Because the rooms they chose were ones to which servants needed frequent access to carry out daily chores, their secret was discovered almost immediately, when one day a servant walked into the dressing room and found the duchess sitting on Lord Talbot's lap, her hair and clothing in disarray. He observed that Lord Talbot crossed his legs and thighs and turned away in order to stop the servant seeing his exposed penis. The next day, the servant and the butler listened by the locked dining-room door and heard the sound of kissing followed by the duchess saying: 'You make me very hot. I am not able to bear it. What would you have me do? My precious Lord, I am afraid the servants suspect us.'[76]

She was right about that, but as long as Frances and Lord Talbot continued their affair knowledge of it was only going to spread. They paid off her groom, John Pember, doubled his salary and gave him some horses. But it was no use. Rumours reached the duke. He agreed to a private separation, but his real goal was to obtain proof of their continuing adultery so that he could sue Lord Talbot for damages for 'Crim Con' – 'criminal conversation' – conversation being an old euphemism for sexual intercourse. The lovers knew this and determined to be more discreet. The problem was, they weren't very good at it.

By this time the duchess was living in a rented house in New Bond Street. Lord Talbot would visit her three times a week, staying for up to five hours each time. When the duchess became pregnant, it became clear even to the lovers that cursorily paying off staff would not be enough. Lord Talbot rented safe houses, including one in Golden Square in London – hardly a discreet locale – and hired a sixty-one-year-old midwife. When he visited the duchess at Chipping Warden near Banbury, where she was staying, he arranged to meet her in fields adjacent to the house rather than at the property itself. But he was an obvious, loud presence in his bright red hunting jacket and when they went for walks in the grounds the pair were trailed by curious servants to a lodge on the river bank. One servant, John Pargiter, saw the duchess on her back with her petticoats pushed up to her waist. He went home and made notes in case he needed to blackmail her later.

When the duchess unexpectedly went into labour, she was in Chipping Warden rather than the Golden Square house that Lord Talbot had designated for the birth. This meant involving and paying off scores of new 'emergency' servants, midwives and doctors, which in turn meant the duchess's hope of keeping the baby a secret until her husband's death ('which should not be long, since he is an infirm man') looked more and more forlorn; ditto her belief that the baby – a girl – could be passed off as the duke's and so claim a portion of his inheritance.[77]

In fact, this was the beginning of the end of the affair. Lord Talbot was angry that the duchess had not made use of the house he had spent so much money readying for her. He had no time for her secret scheme and made a tellingly ungallant remark to the gardener's wife they had used as an emergency midwife: that he had only started sleeping with the duchess to avoid the danger of making his sickly wife pregnant. 'I heard that the Duchess of Beaufort had a passion for me, and I thought it was better to make use of her in that way than common women.'[78] Nice!

Over the next few weeks Lord Talbot was smuggled into the house to see the duchess and his daughter by a little-used entrance and continued the cover-up, paying off staff and dressing a servant in the duchess's clothes, 'with an intent that the neighbourhood might imagine it was her Grace herself taking the air'.[79] The baby, who was being suckled by a maidservant, was packed off to Golden Square where she was christened Fanny Matthews. Lord Talbot drained the duchess's engorged breasts himself by sucking on her nipples and spitting out the milk into a bowl. (Lawrence Stone notes that Fanny's fate is not mentioned in the court records and concludes that like so many other babies at this time, particularly illegitimate ones, she fell victim either to irregular feeding from her wet-nurse or some infantile malady.)

Whatever became of Fanny, it did not stop the duchess and Lord Talbot from resuming their affair in rented London houses. By the time the duke got his act together and sued his wife for adultery in May 1742, the affair was all but over. Servants were summoned and swiftly spilled the beans, seduced by the prospect of even more money and a possible position in the duke's household, never mind the efforts the duchess and Lord Talbot had put into bribing them. Stone thinks it likely that some of the staff were spies, placed deliberately in the duchess's household by the duke, as it is suspicious that so many witnesses made written memoranda. The duke's goal was not financial, but personal. He wanted his honour restored; to get revenge on the duchess; and to humiliate Lord Talbot (and bring his behaviour to the attention of Lord Talbot's wife) by launching an action for

Crim Con. Ultimately, he intended to divorce the duchess the expensive way by an Act of Parliament so that he could remarry and beget an heir. 'His case was watertight,' remarks Stone. 'But he had reckoned without the Duchess, who, as we have seen, was a bold, impetuous and obstinate woman.'[80]

The duchess launched a countersuit for nullity on the grounds of impotence, claiming that their eleven-year marriage had never been consummated: 'The privy members [sic] of the Duke were never to my knowledge turgid, dilated or erect in such a way as (in my opinion) may be usual and necessary to perform the act of carnal copulation.' His penis 'never did penetrate or enter my body'.[81] The duchess had had a baby, so her fertility was not in doubt. Which placed the burden of proof on the duke.

Some unseemly business followed as the duke insisted he was perfectly capable of intercourse and summoned an array of chambermaids to insist that they had found stains on the sheets and the duchess's shift consistent with sex having occurred. His defence was clearly good enough for the duchess's suit to be rejected by the London Consistory Court. But it was upheld on appeal by the Court of Arches in December 1742. The only course of action now available to the duke was to undergo the humiliating 'virility test' which medieval canon law insisted upon. This involved masturbating behind a screen – in the presence of two physicians, three surgeons and a court official.

'I should never have been potent again!' quipped Horace Walpole in a hilarious letter: 'Well, but he was [potent]. They offered to wait upon his Grace to any place of public resort [i.e. a brothel, where they would have watched him have sex with a prostitute] – "No, no he would only go behind the screen, and when he knocked, they were to come to him, but come that moment." He was some time behind the scenes: at last he knocked, and the good old folks saw what amazed them – what they had not seen many a day! Cibber [the poet and actor-manager Colley Cibber] says "His Grace's [penis] is in everybody's mouth." He is now upon his mettle, and will sue Lord Talbot for fourscore thousand pounds damages.'[82]

The result of this extraordinary occurrence was that in May 1743 the Court of Arches reversed its judgement and threw out the duchess's suit. The duke sued Lord Talbot for Crim Con for the then-enormous £80,000, and formally divorced the duchess by Act of Parliament in March 1744.

Sadly, the years that followed were not happy for either party. The duchess and Lord Talbot rekindled their romance in the immediate aftermath of the trial. But he had moved on to other mistresses and it soon spluttered out. The duke intended to marry again and had found a likely partner in a Miss Windham. However, the poor health that had blighted his life finally claimed it in February 1749 at the age of just thirty-nine. His ex-wife also married again, to a Colonel Charles Fitzroy, but died in 1750 while giving birth to their daughter.

5

Serendipity

For some reason the music of chance is always pleasing to the ear. We think of chance as random, but as any gambler knows, it isn't really – there's a science to it, a side that manifests itself in quantum mechanics and probability theory. When we experience chance, we are experiencing the tension between chaos and a kind of order, albeit one most of us aren't clever enough to grasp.

We love chance meetings and serendipitous friendships. They are a staple of novels and films, especially romantic comedies, where the initial 'meet cute' between the two main characters is often accidental. The structure of one of my favourite films, *When Harry Met Sally*, is organised around a series of chance meetings. Harry Burns and Sally Albright have never met until they agree to share the drive from the University of Chicago to New York. Their next chance meeting, five years later, is on a flight. The next is in a bookshop. This apparent randomness is the soil that allows first their friendship and then their romance to bloom.

The scientist Louis Pasteur famously said: 'In the field of observation, chance favours the prepared mind.' But some chance couplings are so strange and incredible that they are impossible to prepare for. Mindful of this, the satirist Craig Brown, in his brilliantly funny book about remarkable random meetings between famous people, *Hello Goodbye Hello*, introduces 'a note of order into the otherwise haphazard',[1] by describing each of the 101 meetings he recounts in exactly 1,001 words.

Two people do not need to have known each other for long for their meeting to have unfortunate consequences. I am always cheered by meetings that are happy, unexpected accidents; but in some cases what we are dealing with is the opposite of serendipity – what the novelist William Boyd has called 'zemblanity': 'the faculty of making unhappy, unlucky and expected discoveries by design'.[2]

Consider, as Brown does, the case of 1960s DJ and TV star Simon Dee and actor George Lazenby. The unhappy discovery both men made after Lazenby's catastrophic appearance on Dee's ITV chat show on 8 February 1970 was that both their careers were en route to the toilet.

Lazenby was a good-looking, self-assured Australian who had moved to London in 1963 and worked as a used-car salesman before drifting, with some success, into male modelling, notably in a TV advert for Fry's chocolate. After Sean Connery decided he had had enough of playing James Bond, Lazenby won the part by engineering a meeting with the spy series' producer Cubby Broccoli – he arranged to have his hair cut at a salon Broccoli frequented at a time when he knew that the producer would also be there – and impressing the women working in Broccoli's office with his rangy masculinity. His performance in the subsequent film, *On Her Majesty's Secret Service*, received mixed reviews – he had fibbed about the extent of his acting experience – and his arrogant behaviour on set alienated both cast and crew. Despite this, Lazenby had been offered $1 million to reprise the role. But he had decided that playing Bond again was beneath his dignity and spent the publicity tour for *On Her Majesty's Secret Service* telling journalists as much.

Dandy radio and TV star Simon Dee had actually auditioned for the role of Bond himself but been rejected. ('Another dream shattered!' he later harrumphed. 'I still happen to think I'd have been pretty good at it, though. Well, let's face it, I couldn't have been much worse than Lazenby.'[3]) Dee had recently moved to ITV from the BBC, lured by a then-massive salary of £100,000. Like Lazenby, Dee was given to arrogant, entitled behaviour enhanced by a top note of marijuana-fuelled paranoia. Starting off at the pirate station Radio Caroline, Day had by 1970 become what his biographer Richard Wiseman calls 'British television's single most fashionable face'[4] – louchely emblematic of the Swinging Sixties, with a top-rating show, *Dee Time*, which ended every week with its presenter zooming off in an E-type Jaguar accompanied by a beautiful model; (not for nothing was Dee reputedly the model for spoof spy Austin Powers).

When Dee's three-year contract came up for renewal, however, the BBC's Head of Light Entertainment, Bill Cotton, refused his outlandish pay demands – hence the star's decision to jump ship. But Dee was not comfortable in his new home. The platform ITV created for him, *The Simon Dee Show*, was awkwardly scheduled at 11 p.m. on Sunday nights and so struggled to build the audience Dee felt it deserved. Never mind, though, because Dee could still at this point command high-grade talent. For the 8 February 1969 show, George Lazenby and his Bond co-star

Diana Rigg were booked as the first guests. They were to be followed, in the second half, by Dee's old chum John Lennon and his wife of a year or so, Yoko Ono.

The first shock for Dee was that Lazenby, when he wandered in from the green room, seemed to have gone to extraordinary lengths to distance himself from the character of James Bond. His hair was long and unkempt and he had grown a beard. Unbeknownst to Dee, this change of look was a salvo in Lazenby's ongoing battle with Cubby Broccoli, who Lazenby claimed was attempting to control how he dressed and behaved when he was not on set. However, what really threw Dee was when, a few minutes into the interview, a distracted, slightly stoned-seeming Lazenby produced a piece of paper from his pocket, turned to the camera and announced: 'I would like to draw everybody's attention to the fact that the following senators were involved in a plot to kill President Kennedy!'

As Lazenby began to recite his list of names, Dee turned panicking to Diana Rigg and tried to enlist her help in changing the subject: 'That's very interesting, George. What does Diana make of all that then?' But Lazenby was in full flow and would not be stopped, despite Dee's best efforts to close the conversation down and move on.

Dee's confident expectation was that Lazenby's bizarre rant would be edited out of the final show, which was recorded shortly before transmission rather than broadcast live. That this didn't happen aggravated both men's already tricky relationships with their bosses. Lazenby jumped before he was pushed, announcing that 'Bond is a brute . . . I've already put him behind me. I will never play him again. Peace – that's the message now.' Dee was hauled before

Stella Richman, managing director of London Weekend Television, the ITV franchise that made his show, and asked: 'Who said you could talk about Kennedy?' Dee made the fair point that it was Lazenby who had raised the subject, not him, but then vacated the moral high ground by insisting it was his guests' right to talk about anything they liked. 'It really was an amazing moment,' he said later. 'Here was this female terrier telling me that she had the right to tell me who I could or couldn't book on my show and what I was supposed to say to them! And if I disagreed with her then I was out of a job!'[5]

Unfortunately for Dee, this is exactly the fate that befell him: *The Simon Dee Show* was cancelled after one series. Dee never worked in TV again. True to character, he blamed dark forces rather than himself for his Icarus-like fall: 'It was pretty obvious that the CIA, who controlled our media and still do, would be on my case.'[6]

The tragedy of Simon Dee and George Lazenby is that they never, to my knowledge, met again. Their encounter was a chance moment in time, never to be repeated; magical not because of any fairy dust it left on either Dee or Lazenby, but because it's a funny story about egotism.

In the Introduction I discussed TV presenter couples who had been brought together to do a specific job, that is: host a programme. The nation has, however, a special place in its heart for television couples who have been brought together serendipitously. This might be on a show such as *Celebrity Hunted*, on which Boris Johnson's father Stanley found himself paired surprisingly effectively (albeit temporarily and platonically) with *Made in Chelsea* star Georgia 'Toff' Toffolo. Or – and I touched on this earlier – it might be a magazine programme like *Good Morning Britain*, where the goal is to combine two well-defined but contrasting personalities (in this case Susanna Reid and Piers Morgan) and hope the tension that results is productive.

In the case of *Good Morning Britain* it clearly is. Susanna and Piers first met in 2006 when Susanna interviewed him for a BBC show she was presenting. 'I seem to remember being glad it was only a brief encounter,' she recalls.[7] The decision to pair them on-screen in 2015 could have gone horribly wrong. But they work fantastically as a 'TV husband and wife' and the whole point is that watching them resembles watching 'mum and dad argue in front of the kids', as Susanna puts it. 'It's a dynamite dynamic,' she says. 'However strongly Piers argues his point, I'm there to represent the other side, even when it's unpopular. He needs me to be the yin to his yang.'[8]

Obviously, Susanna and Piers's relationship is not a romantic one. Programmes more likely to act as petri dishes for *that* sort of enduring union are competitive shows like *Dancing On Ice* and *Strictly Come Dancing*, where prolonged physical proximity means one thing can lead to another. *Coronation Street* star Samia Ghadie found love on the ice in 2013 when she was partnered with pro skater Sylvain Longchambon. When they met, he was already dating *Hollyoaks* actress Jennifer Metcalfe, whom he had also met on the show, two years earlier.

After winning *Strictly* together in 2018, TV presenter and journalist Stacey Dooley and dancer Kevin Clifton also became an item. 'Kev's amazing, I'm happy, life happens, I've got an amazing career and I'm very lucky,' she told the

Guardian, correctly identifying serendipity as the agent of their life-changing coupledom.[9]

The birth of twins feels like the ultimate serendipitous happening. Twins are central to the idea of the power of two – of coupleness, in the broadest sense, being an enhanced state. Never mind the existence of triplets, quadruplets, etc.; the idea persists that it is twins who have the most to tell us about who we are. After all, world mythology teems with twins: in Greek and Roman mythology alone we have Apollo and Artemis, Castor and Pollux, Hypnos and Thanatos, et al. Sometimes twins embody the opposing forces of good and evil, sometimes the harmonious conjunction of complementary powers.

Twins are special in almost all cultures, but particularly in the Yoruba tribe of south-west Nigeria. This might be because twins are so common among the Yoruba (around fifty sets of twins in every thousand births) – so common that they often share a given name with other twins from the same tribe: either Taiwo (meaning 'the first twin to taste the world') or Kehinde (meaning 'the second-born'), depending on their birth order.

Until the day he discovered otherwise, James Springer always believed his identical twin had died at birth. Born in August 1939, he and his brother were adopted by different families in western Ohio when they were only a few weeks old. Both families were told that the other baby twin was dead. It was Lucille Lewis, the adoptive mother of James Springer's brother, who discovered this was not true, quite by chance, when she went to probate court to complete the adoption procedures. When she revealed that her son was called James, the court clerk said: 'You can't do that. They named the other little boy James.'[10]

Who, she wondered, were 'they'? And who was 'the other little boy'?

Unlike James Springer, then, James Lewis did know he had a twin brother called James. For most of his life, he resisted the urge to find him. Trying to do so would, he worried, stir up problems. But then he reached thirty-seven and realised he felt differently. He decided to try and make contact with the other James and succeeded in finding his contact details through an Ohio courthouse. The pair spoke on the phone and eventually agreed to meet.

When this momentous event finally took place, on 9 February 1979, the similarities the twins discovered between them were astonishing, not to say uncanny. Both were six foot tall and weighed 180 pounds. Both had married women called Linda, been divorced and their second wives were both called Betty. Both had owned a dog called Toy. Both liked carpentry and mechanical drawing and holidaying in the same part of Florida. Both liked Miller Lite beer and chain-smoked Salem cigarettes. Both ground their teeth in their sleep and suffered from migraines. The names of their eldest children were James Alan Lewis and James Allen Springer.

The case of the 'Jim twins', as they became known, was widely reported in the US media, which is how they came to the attention of the psychologist and geneticist Dr Thomas Bouchard of the University of Minnesota. Bouchard was conducting research into twins who had been separated at birth and reared in different families. The Jim twins had grown up only forty miles apart from each other, so some cultural similarities were to be expected. Even so, that did not account for coincidences such as the fact that each Jim lived in the only house on his block and had placed a white bench around a tree in his backyard.

How to explain the mystery-magic of doubleness? 'Reunited twins' stories are tabloid staples. But why do we care so much? Why is it so much more astonishing when twins, rather than mere siblings, are reunited? Maybe because it feeds the common myth that any one of us could have a doppelganger: what the Pulitzer Prize-winning American journalist Lawrence Wright, in his book *Twins: Genes, Environment and the Mystery of Identity*, calls 'someone who is not only a human mirror but an ideal companion'.[11] The fantasy rests on the idea that someone who looks like you is psychologically the same as you and therefore in a unique position to understand you. They are genetically identical to you, but at the same time living another life: 'An identical twin could experience the world and come back to report about choices we might have made.'[12]

Separated-twin research is a tricky moral area within the field of behavioural genetics because of the conclusions it has led some to reach: principally, that a person's genes play a much greater role in shaping their destiny than the environment in which they were raised. According to the starkest reading of this 'hereditist' viewpoint, traits such as criminality are genetically determined, so why bother trying to rehabilitate offenders?

This kind of thinking gave rise, in the 1930s, to the eugenics movement, informing not just the Nazis' theories about Aryan perfectibility but SS doctor Josef Mengele's horrific attempts to prove them by performing experiments on twins in Auschwitz. (One twin who survived the camp, Jona Laks,

says Mengele removed organs from people without anaes-
thetic, and if one twin died the other would be murdered.
Another, Vera Kriegel, remembers being led into his laboratory and seeing 'a whole wall of human eyes'.[13] Mengele was
especially interested in the colour of twins' eyes.)

In his book, Wright excavated the story of the Jim twins
and other comparable cases which had comparable outcomes.
Among the twins he discusses are 'Amy' and 'Beth' (not
their real names), identical Jewish girls who were deliberately
separated and placed with different families by an orphanage
complicit in an ethically dubious 'nature versus nurture'
experiment conducted in the 1960s by the late Dr Peter
Neubauer, Clinical Professor of Psychiatry at New York
University. The adoptive families were told that their children
would be studied, but not why.

When the twins found out later that they had identical
siblings they had never known about, the emotional consequences for some of them were devastating. Tim Wardle's
much-praised 2018 documentary, *Three Identical Strangers*,
focuses on the sole group of triplets studied by Neubauer:
three identical boys raised by their adoptive families as David
Kellman, Eddy Galland and Bobby Shafran. All three struggled with mental health issues. Galland committed suicide
in 1995. Perhaps realising the implications of what he had
done, and fearing that his seemingly hereditist conclusions
would be a gift to the far right, Neubauer instructed that
the study records, stored at Harvard, be sealed until 2065.

Inevitably, the biological picture is much more complicated than clickbaity stories about identical twins'
similarities suggest – though we have those same twins to
thank for our understanding of this. It is twins' identical
genomes that have made them ideal subjects for studying

the effects of so-called epigenetic modifications – changes to DNA which control the expression of genes but not the DNA sequence itself. In other words, just because your genes are encoded with a predisposition, that does not mean environment is irrelevant. To give one obvious example, there is a significant genetic component in alcoholism, but if you, say, live in a country like Saudi Arabia, where alcohol is banned, then you will never develop it.

Epigenetic modifications are why identical twins sometimes look different: their genes are subject to different mutations. Twins develop differently in utero, the point at which they separate from each other being especially important. As Wright explains, studies show that an identical twin who is gay has a 50 per cent chance of having a gay twin. 'But if homosexuality is genetically determined, why wouldn't the chances be closer to 100 per cent? . . . What is it in the environment that affects us and makes us different from each other, and different, in some respects, from ourselves, the selves we might have been if genes alone control who we are? The differences in identical twins may turn out to be more informative than their similarities.'[14]

———

As potent a mythic staple as identical twins are wild children – untamed and feral, living in jungles, raised by animals. The two traditions combine in the case of Romulus and Remus, founders of the city of Rome. These twins were abandoned on the bank of the river Tiber to die by King Amulius, only to be rescued by the god Tiberinus and a she-wolf who took them to her cave lair, the Lupercal, and suckled them.

This story would have been deeply familiar to Reverend Joseph Amrito Lal Singh, a missionary in the district of Midnapore, near Calcutta, in the 1920s. Singh ran an orphanage with his wife, taking in abandoned or parentless children with the ultimate aim of converting them to Christianity. To this end, he was in the habit of making regular trips into the jungle and to nearby villages in search of 'lost' children. On one occasion in September 1920, he and his team of fellow hunters happened to stop for the night in a villager's cowshed. Its owner told them there was a man-ghost in the jungle, about seven miles from the village, and asked the reverend to perform an exorcism so that locals would no longer be scared when they were walking past it.

Reverend Singh agreed to accompany the villager to the place where he had seen the man-ghost and do what he could to exorcise it. But the journey was light on evidence of ghostly activity and by the end of it the reverend decided the sighting was merely evidence of peasant superstition. The villager persisted in his entreaties, however, which is how, in early October, Singh and five other prepared observers found themselves standing in front of what looked like a giant anthill, as high as a two-storey building, with tunnels leading into a hollow at the base. This, the villagers told him, was where the man-ghost lived.

Reverend Singh and his team watched and waited. As darkness fell, several wolves slunk out of the tunnels followed by their cubs. The cubs were followed, however, by a stunted, human-like shape – 'a hideous-looking being', Singh called it in his diary – its face hardly visible behind a tangled mass of hair. As if one of them wasn't enough, 'close at its heels there came another awful creature exactly like the first, but smaller in size. Their eyes were bright and piercing, unlike human eyes.'[15]

Like the wolves, these creatures ran on all fours. Singh realised soon enough that they were actually children. His companions weren't so sure: 'My friends at once levelled their guns to shoot at the ghosts. They would have killed them if they had not been dissuaded by me.'[16] Several days later, having persuaded (with considerable difficulty) some local men to help him, Singh returned to the site again. This time, he and his team physically dug the children out of the anthill with spades and shovels, a hard job made additionally difficult by the fact that the she-wolf was protective of the children and would snap and snarl at the diggers. Singh thought this was evidence of God's wonder. The children were not her cubs – indeed, they had originally been brought as food for the cubs – but the wolves had not only allowed them to live but nurtured them alongside their own offspring: 'I was simply amazed to think that an animal had such a noble feeling surpassing even that of mankind.'[17]

The team took the rescued children to the nearby village of Godamuri so that they could be washed and tended. Singh entrusted them to the villagers while he toured the district, honouring some lecturing commitments he was unable to cancel. But when he returned five days later, he learned that they had been left to themselves, without food or drink. The villagers had been so scared of the 'ghosts' – actually two girls, one about eight, the other eighteen months' old – that they had 'left the place in hot haste . . . and gone away to a place no one knew. The panic was so great that it depopulated the entire village.'[18]

Singh named the older girl Kamala and the younger one Amala. He nursed them until they were fit to travel, then risked the bumpy journey back to Midnapore in a straw-filled bullock cart. At the orphanage, his team looked after the sorry pair – 'so weak and emaciated that they could hardly move'[19] – as best they could. If they were expecting gratitude from the girls, they did not get it. Michael Newton describes in his book, *Savage Girls and Wild Boys: A History of Feral Children*, the way they 'remained detached, indifferent, taking nourishment but forging no connection, true to their wild selves'.[20] They refused to be dressed or to eat cooked food. Their behaviour was unpredictable and sometimes savage: they befriended a baby, only to turn on it and maul it when they had tired of it. In general they preferred each other's company and barely communicated with the orphanage staff. They had, Singh observed, been physically changed by their time in the jungle. Their canine teeth had grown long and pointy, while their eyes had acquired the blue glare of cats' or dogs' eyes. Their night vision and sense of smell were both preternaturally acute. While sleeping, they would lie across each other like animals. And in the middle of the night, they would howl like wolves.

The only time either girl expressed a human emotion was when Amala died of dysentery on 21 September 1921. Kamala cried, then sat for six days in silence in a corner of the room. In the years that followed, Singh and his wife managed to teach Kamala a primitive form of speech and trained her both to urinate in a toilet and to walk partially upright. (She always preferred to walk on all fours.) But in 1928, just as she was about to go on a tour of the US, she became ill with tuberculosis and died in November 1929.

What should we make of this curious couple, Kamala and Amala? Our only real knowledge of them comes from a single source, Singh's loose-leaf diary. Their story spread to a Western world drunk on the imperial fables of Kipling and Rider Haggard, but reluctant to accept the testimony of an Indian native. Besides, was it really possible for children's teeth to grow and their eyes to change colour? Only in fairy tales, surely?

If some contemporary scientists were sceptical, others loved the idea of a 'wild child' actually existing because it fed their pet theories – for example that children are born wild and civilised during childhood. More recent research into the case has suggested that the Reverend Singh perpetrated a grand hoax. In his book *Enigma of the Wolf Children*, the French surgeon Serge Aroles concluded, among much else, that Singh's diary was not contemporaneous, as claimed, but written in 1935, six years after Kamala's death; that the photos he allegedly took of his feral charges were posed and featured models other than the girls; that Singh beat Kamala to make her act the way he wanted her to in front of visitors; and that Kamala suffered from a rare neurodevelopmental disorder, Rett syndrome, which accounted for the shape of her head and her hunched appearance.

In the annals of chance meetings between mismatched couples, none rates more highly than the encounter in the early 1950s between the existentialist Irish playwright, Samuel Beckett, and seven-feet-tall French professional wrestler and actor, André 'the Giant' Roussimoff – or as I like to think of him, Fezzik, the giant in Rob Reiner's classic film *The Princess Bride* – a role he inhabited with gusto.

There are two different versions of the story of their friendship. The most popular, first told by André's *Princess*

Bride co-star Cary Elwes in 2000, starts with the Nobel Prize-winning author of *Waiting for Godot* moving to Molien, a small village in rural France, in 1953 and enlisting a man called Boris Roussimoff to help him build a house.

One day, Elwes said, Boris told Samuel about his twelve-year-old son André who was already so tall and heavy that he could not fit in the school bus. The family were too poor to afford a car. But since Samuel owned not merely a car but a Citroën 2CV convertible that fitted André comfortably with its roof off, he kindly offered to drive the boy to and from school every day. The pair enjoyed the journeys hugely and bonded over a shared love of cricket.

Did any of this really happen? It would be lovely if so. However, the forces of reason have chipped away at the myth in the last decade. Jason Hehir, the director of an HBO documentary about the wrestler, discovered that the story did not withstand scrutiny. Although Beckett and the Roussimoffs did live close to each other in Molien, Boris did not help Samuel build his house; nor was there any bus from André's house to the schoolhouse in the centre of town. Most children walked to school. As Hehir explained to *Business Insider* in 2018: 'Beckett had a truck, and if he passed the kids, he would stop and let them hop into the flatbed of his truck and he would drive them to or from school. But it wasn't singular to André, and he had no special relationship with André any more than he did with any other child in the area. André's brother laughed at us when we told him what the legend is.'[21]

And yet, and yet . . . people strike up improbable friendships all the time. Just ask the poet T. S. Eliot and the cinema legend Groucho Marx. To understand just how odd their friendship was, you need to understand Eliot's personality and politics.

The dynamics of friendship are mysterious and unquantifiable. Tom (as it feels inappropriate to call him, but let's do it) was not a man given to easy sociability. Born in St Louis, Missouri, he had moved to England in 1914 when he was twenty-five. His first marriage, to the depressive, ultimately institutionalised Vivienne Haigh-Wood, had been a disaster, though it gifted him misery enough to write his greatest poem, *The Waste Land*. Clenched and fastidious, Tom did not put those he met at their ease. But then he was not at ease himself and struggled to connect with others. 'He doesn't understand all I say nor do we him,' wrote the literary critic I. A. Richards's wife Dorothea. 'His questions are surprising – disconcerting because so simple, sometimes also inane.'[22] Society hostess Ottoline Morrell found him 'dull, dull, dull', adding: 'He is obviously very ignorant of England and imagines that it is essential to be highly polite and conventional and decorous and meticulous.'[23]

Eliot was self-aware enough to appreciate his shortcomings. He even wrote a Lear-like poem mocking himself, in which he acknowledges how unpleasant and intimidating it must be to meet him, with 'his brow so grim', his conversation so dominated by 'What Precisely / And If and Perhaps and But'.

But while Tom was undoubtedly a victim of genteel Bloomsbury snobbery – most people were – he was a snob himself. And, as he aged, his political views shifted rightwards, revealing a simmering anti-Semitism that found its fullest expression in a series of lectures he gave in the early 1930s. In one he declared that 'reasons of race and religion combine to make any large number of free-thinking Jews undesirable'.[24] And yet he loved the Marx Brothers, free-thinking Jews to a man. Go figure.

Eliot and his wife Valerie saw Groucho Marx and his wife Eden while they were on holiday in Jamaica in early 1961: the Eliots were disembarking from a glass-bottomed boat; the Marxes were waiting to get on. They did not speak, but when he got home Tom felt moved to write Groucho a fan letter in which he requested a signed photo.

Groucho obliged with a 'straight' photo showing himself without his trademark cigar and moustache. Tom wrote back expressing his pleasure and assuring Groucho that he intended to frame the photo and hang it on his office wall alongside pictures of his other celebrity mates, W. B. Yeats and Paul Valéry. He also enclosed a photo of himself. Exactly which photo this was we do not know – a publicity still, presumably. But it roused Groucho to high sarcasm: 'I had no idea you were so handsome,' he wrote back. 'Why you haven't been offered the lead in some sexy movies I can only attribute to the stupidity of the casting directors.'[25]

The correspondence continued, characterised by what Craig Brown rightly calls a 'slightly effortful jocularity'.[26] Numerous plans to meet came to nothing – no longer youthful, both men were struggling with poor health. Eventually a date was settled on – May 1964, or thereabouts. Groucho was due in London to participate in a TV panel show. In his restrained way, Tom expressed his excitement at the prospect. But he had also found something to worry about: 'If you do not turn up I am afraid that all of the people to whom I have boasted of knowing you (and of being on first name terms at that) will take me for a four flusher.'[27]

However in June 1964, Groucho and Eden finally arrived

in London. Tom personally arranged for a taxi to bring them from the Savoy to his Kensington apartment. What we know about the evening derives from a letter that Groucho wrote to his brother Gummo. It was not a disastrous meeting, far from it. But it seems Groucho had been determined to talk about literature, specifically *King Lear* and his host's own *The Waste Land* – subjects he had researched beforehand 'just in case of a conversational bottleneck'.[28] (Groucho had dropped out of high school and was always embarrassed by his lack of formal education.) Tom, on the other hand, wanted to talk in some detail about old Marx Brothers films.

'He asked if I remembered the courtroom scene in *Duck Soup*,' Groucho wrote to Gummo. 'Fortunately, I'd forgotten every word. It was obviously the end of the Literary Evening, but very pleasant none the less.' Even so, Groucho explains, he and Eden left early as they felt the esteemed poet 'wasn't up to a long evening of conversation'.[29]

You could argue, of course, that this was not a friendship at all. It was too hesitant and superficial to be worthy of the term; too constrained by politeness. 'The transition from acquaintanceship to friendship is typically characterised by an increase in both the breadth and depth of self-disclosure,' says University of Winnipeg sociologist Beverley Fehr, author of *Friendship Processes*. 'In the early stages of friendship, this tends to be a gradual, reciprocal process. One person takes the risk of disclosing personal information and then "tests" whether the other reciprocates.'[30] By this measure, T. S. Eliot and Groucho Marx were never going to get very far. They should have quit while they were ahead, at the fan-letters stage, and not spoiled everything by attempting to meet.

For a glorious example of Fehr's friendship process working as it should, seek out the much-loved early 1970s bestseller, *84 Charing Cross Road*. This book, adapted for stage and film, chronicles the twenty-year correspondence between cash-strapped, New York-dwelling book-lover Helene Hanff and Frank Doel, chief buyer of Marks & Co antiquarian booksellers, based at the titular London address. One of its many pleasures is the ease with which the initial clipped formality falls away, to be replaced by the softness and warmth of genuine friendship.

The correspondence started in October 1949 when Hanff sent Marks & Co a wish list of titles she had been unable to find in New York. 'I am a poor writer with an antiquarian taste in books,' she explained. 'If you have clean second-hand copies of any of the books on the list, for no more than $5 each, will you consider this a purchase order and send them to me?'[31]

In his reply, manager Frank Doel addressed Hanff as 'Dear Madam' and signed it, with Eliotic fastidiousness: 'Yours faithfully, FPD'. Hanff's next letter enclosed payment but chanced a risqué PS: 'I hope "madam" doesn't mean over there what it means over here.'[32] This was her version of Fehr's 'test'. Would Doel reciprocate? Absolutely, but the relaxing of formality was a slow business: not until several years later – in 1952 – did he address her as 'Dear Helene'.

Even the most complete – the most incendiary and life-changing – relationships often start hesitantly, with something held back; or even with anger and tension. Alice B. Toklas first met her future life partner, the avant-garde writer Gertrude Stein, in 1907 at the Paris apartment of Stein's eldest brother, Michael. Alice was overwhelmed by this 'golden presence, burned by the Tuscan sun and with a golden glint in her warm brown hair',[33] and felt sure that she was in the presence of genius.

It was arranged that Alice would return to the apartment on the rue de Fleurus the next day and collect Gertrude. The pair would then take a walk together through the Luxembourg Gardens. But Alice was late – not very late (half an hour) and she had sent a note in advance to let Gertrude know. When she finally arrived, Gertrude was furious. 'She was now a vengeful goddess and I was afraid. I did not know what had happened or what was going to happen. Nor is it possible for me to tell about it now.'[34]

After telling her in no uncertain terms that she was unaccustomed to waiting for people, Gertrude left Alice to look at her paintings while she went to change her clothes: she had decided she still wanted to go for the delayed walk. By the time they reached the gardens, Gertrude's mood had improved. 'Alice,' she instructed her new acquaintance, 'look at the autumn herbaceous border.' Alice was shocked and slightly offended that Gertrude had used her first name; for her part, she did 'not propose to reciprocate the familiarity'.[35]

Virginia Woolf was not at all sure about her future lover, the poet, novelist and landscape gardener Vita Sackville-West, after their first meeting – a dinner at fellow Bloomsbury Group member Clive Bell's house: 'Not much to my severer taste – florid, moustached, parakeet coloured, with all the supple ease of the aristocracy, but not the wit of the artist,' she wrote in a letter on 15 December 1922.[36] Jealousy and contempt commingle in her observation that Vita writes fifteen pages a day (so her books must be rubbish) and 'knows everyone'. Still, she asks, almost desperately: 'But could I ever know her? I am to dine there on Thursday.'[37]

It is easy today to get yesteryear's class system wrong and

imagine that Vita and Virginia were social equals. But they were not. Measuring the distance between them seems to have excited Virginia and encouraged her to view the aristocratic Vita in a more sympathetic light. Vita's breeding meant, Virginia felt, that the gardening-obsessed author of *All Passion Spent* had no false shyness or modesty. The force of her personality made Virginia feel virginal and schoolgirlish.

Vita is kinder in her letter to her husband Harold Nicolson describing the meeting. She says that she adores how unadorned and unaffected Virginia is; when she adds that Virginia dresses 'quite atrociously' she manages somehow not to make it sound like an insult.

Gradually, over the course of several dinners, the attraction sparked fully into life. Vita became Virginia's muse as well as her lover, inspiring that revolutionary paean to gender fluidity *Orlando*.

Another slow-to-ignite friendship that ultimately consumed both parties was the one that formed between two esteemed American writers, Gail Caldwell and Caroline Knapp. They first met at what Caldwell calls an 'insufferable' literary party back in the early 1990s when they were both writing for newspapers in Boston. Nine years older than the smart, manicured Knapp, who had just published a collection of her columns, Caldwell noted the way the other writer 'seemed to wear her reserve like silken armor . . . We passed a few polite words of mutual regard, then moved apart to make the necessary rounds.'[38]

Neither came away with any sense that a friendship was in the offing. But then they met again a few years later – both childless, both with young dogs, both having 'downscaled' their appearance and settled into a comfortable early middle age in which self-respect, control, water-based exercise, solitude and dogs – especially dogs – were as important as dating. They were so close that people mistook them for siblings or lovers. For years they played 'the daily, easy game of catch that intimate connection implies. One ball, two gloves, equal joy in the throw and the return.' But there was a competitive edge: 'Each of us wanted whatever prowess the other possessed.'[39]

Knapp's writerly prowess would show itself in the form of a bestselling, much-admired chronicle of her battle with alcoholism, *Drinking: A Love Story*. Among much else, it addresses the business of solitary drinking – a particularly soothing form of self-annihilation: 'Drinking alone is enormously self-protective, at least in theory. The solitude relieves you of human contact, which can feel burdensome to even the most gregarious alcoholic, and the alcohol relieves you of your own thoughts, of the dark pressure of your own company. Drinking alone is what you do when you can't stand the feeling of living in your own skin.'[40]

Caldwell too had an alcoholic past and therefore insight into the 'empty room in the heart that is the essence of addiction'.[41] She understood in Knapp what others might have found prickly and unapproachable, that she wanted the warmth of spontaneous connection and the freedom to be left alone.

But their friendship did not stretch into old age as they hoped. Knapp fell gravely ill with Stage IV lung cancer at forty-two and died just seven weeks later. Caldwell tells us this right at the beginning: 'It's an old, old story: I had a friend and we shared everything, and then she died and so we shared that, too.'[42]

One of my favourite types of serendipitous coupling involves cross-cultural collaboration, where the intervention of an outsider from a different culture, say, catalyses innovation and gives proper shape to something that might have remained inchoate. A point Robert Winder makes in his history of immigration to Britain, *Bloody Foreigners*, is that immigrants are often entrepreneurial risk-takers with a strong sense of individual liberty.

Some of the most compelling immigrant stories involve partnerships forged with figures from outside those immigrants' communities. Sometimes these are romantic, sometimes professional. Both types have important implications for our understanding of integration and belonging. Focusing on specific partnerships helps us to understand not just the process by which newcomers become friends, neighbours and associates, but the intricacies of our globalised world – one in which it makes less sense than ever to talk about 'native' populations.

No one knows exactly when Michael Marks left the city of Slonim in Belarus, but most accounts estimate it was in 1882, when he was nineteen years old. Slonim had a significant Jewish population and its Great Synagogue, built in 1642, would go on to survive the liquidation of the Slonim Ghetto by the Nazis in 1942. By the late nineteenth century, Slonim's Jewish population had risen to more than 10,000. But it was around this time that many Jews started to look west: Michael was far from alone in his desire to move to Britain in search of safety and prosperity.

Historian Andrew Godley talks about the 'exceptionality of the East European Jews' upward mobility relative to the host populations'.[43] This exceptionality is all the more, well, exceptional when you consider the toughness of the lives many of these Jews had led. Michael's mother had died in childbirth, leaving him to be brought up by his elder sister. When he arrived in Hartlepool, Michael had little money and could speak only a few words of English. He is thought to have slept on the floor of the local synagogue for a few nights while he decided where to move next. This turned out to be Leeds, where he settled in 1884 on the sensible basis that he could count for support on the then-strong Jewish community concentrated in the Leylands area of the city.

Like many other immigrants at the time, Michael Marks became a pedlar, or travelling salesman. With his merchandise in his 'pedlar pack', he walked the Dales trying to interest the impoverished inhabitants of small mining and farming villages in buttons, socks, needles, wool and the like. Much of his stock he bought from Isaac Dewhirst, a wholesale clothing merchant. Dewhirst was so impressed by the physically frail Marks's dedication that he advanced him a loan of £5 to get him started in business. Marks used it to hire a stall in the new covered market in Leeds, just around the corner from the Dewhirst warehouse. It consisted of a trestle table, six feet by four feet, laden with baskets containing the sort of small items he was used to hawking around in his pedlar pack. The gimmick was that, in some baskets, everything cost a penny. Above these a sign hung which proclaimed: 'Don't ask the price, it's a penny.'

Michael soon applied the 'penny' price point to everything on sale and the stalls became known as 'penny bazaars'. They did so well that he opened others in the markets of a host of other northern towns such as Wigan and Manchester. The sheer variety of products that Michael was able to sell for a penny was amazing: crockery, ironmongery, soap, candles, stationery, toys . . . It was the modern 'department' store in microcosm.

And yet Michael's profit margins were low: he needed a massive turnover to make decent money. The burden of running his network of stalls weighed heavily on him, especially after he got married and had children. Michael's talent had always been for running the bazaars and working out where might be good places to open new ones. The pressures of opening a new warehouse in Wigan and his first proper shop in Cheetham Hill in Manchester in 1894 convinced him that he needed help if the business was to survive and thrive.

Michael had always been good with people – honest and direct. He inspired, as his son-in-law put it, 'confidence and affection in even casual acquaintances'.[44] He never argued with people. Also, because he had come from a humble background, he understood the needs of his mostly working-class customers. An example of this is the clever design of the early shops, where customers were able to inspect the goods for sale on open display on a horseshoe-shaped counter but felt under no pressure to make a purchase.

Michael possessed entrepreneurial flair in spades, but he had an idiosyncratic approach to accounting. Which is to say, he never actually kept accounts, preferring to work out (and retain) everything in his head. It is unlikely this would have put anyone off becoming his business partner. Still, his quest for one turned out not to be straightforward. First of all he asked a fellow stallholder in Leeds called Bernard Sloman, who specialised in candles. He said no, so Michael asked his original contact Isaac Dewhirst. He also declined the offer, but spoke highly of his cashier, who had a talent for numbers and well-honed skills as a bookkeeper. His name was Thomas Spencer. Perhaps Michael should ask him? He might be interested.

Thomas Spencer was born in Skipton on 7 November 1851. He moved to Leeds before he was twenty-one and worked as a bookkeeper for a wholesale company started by Isaac Dewhirst. After his first wife died, he married again – to a clever, spirited woman called Agnes who would later help Michael with his broken, hesitant English. It was, as historian Asa Briggs says, a partnership which rested on contrasting, if complementary, qualities.[45] Spencer was the polar opposite of Marks – a burly, no-nonsense Yorkshireman eleven years Michael's senior, who liked his food and a drop of the hard stuff. As Goronwy Rees puts it in his history of the firm: 'He was sharp and authoritative in manner . . . He had little imagination or enterprise, but was something of an organiser, with an eye to small economies.'[46]

This undersells him significantly. Thomas was not scared of driving a hard bargain and understood the value of big as well as small economies. He was good at disciplining workers and commanded the respect of his workforce. He was also fiercely loyal to Michael. Organisation, particularly financial organisation, was what Michael's shops and stalls badly needed, and Thomas provided it. He had built up useful contacts with manufacturers in the years he had spent at Dewhirst's. As one associate remarked at the time, Thomas possessed 'precisely those qualities in business of which Michael Marks stood in need, and he took off his shoulders a distasteful and heavy burden' – never mind that, until he met Marks, he had held only 'minor positions' and 'knew nothing of the world of industry and commerce'.[47] In addition to the accounting, Thomas managed the supply chain, ensuring products found their way from manufacturers into the bazaars.

One of the Victorian high-street heroes whose brands endured into the twenty-first century, Thomas Lipton, once said there was no great secret to his success, 'just advertise, advertise all you can'. But the success of M&S stemmed from one person recognising that he did not have what it took to achieve his goals on his own and – quite by chance – finding the right person at the right historical moment to perform a complementary role. Nowadays we call this 'co-founding' and there is almost always a degree of luck involved. Michael Marks, it turns out, was lucky in the extreme.

Thomas Spencer left Dewhirst's on 22 September 1894. His partnership with Michael Marks was formed six days later when he put £300 – his life savings – into the business. The pair's working partnership lasted nine years and encompassed further expansion (by 1903 there were forty fixed Marks & Spencer stores) and a massive infrastructure project which Spencer oversaw – the building of a specially designed warehouse at Derby Street in Manchester, then the hub of England's cotton industry, with an electric lift running from the basement to the top two floors.

The relationship, which laid the foundations for the world-conquering store Marks & Spencer was to become, ended earlier than we might have expected, with Spencer's retirement in 1903 to farm chickens in Lichfield. (It is possible the state of his health wasn't great.) If this sounds odd, remember that Thomas was free to pursue whatever hobby he chose as he no longer had to worry about money. The value of his original £300 investment had grown to £15,000 (nearly £2 million in today's money). Shortly before his retirement, Marks & Spencer had become a limited company, each partner receiving 14,995 out of a total of 30,000 £1 shares. By 1905, Thomas was earning £3,000 a year – equivalent to £400,000 today. Sadly, he did not have long to enjoy his chickens. He died on 25 July 1905, at the age of fifty-three. Michael died less than two years later, after collapsing on his way to visit a store.

Asa Briggs calls Michael Marks 'one of the key figures in the first real transformation in retailing in the late nineteenth century and the prelude to the still greater transformation in the last decades of the twentieth century'.[48] But he too diminishes Thomas's influence, keen to keep it a Marks family story. He emphasises instead the work of Michael's son, Simon Marks, and his friend, Israel Sieff, for bringing the M&S concept to fruition and developing a company philosophy, which admittedly they did successfully: by the time Simon (Lord) Marks died in 1964, the company's turnover was £201 million. But it was Marks and Spencer who did all the crucial work at an initial stage.

Michael Marks's partnership with Thomas Spencer was close and mutually respectful, but it would have had boundaries. They would not, I'm sure, have eaten at each other's houses or spent time with each other's families.

An equivalent partnership, but in the creative sphere – and characterised by an extraordinary intellectual affinity as well as close personal friendship – was forged by the film-maker Michael Powell and screenwriter Emeric Pressburger. In the 1940s they created some of the best-loved, most successful films ever made in Britain, from the steamy Himalayan psychodrama *Black Narcissus*, to the ingenious riff on Britain and America's wartime relationship, *A Matter of Life and Death*, and *The Red Shoes*, a dazzling Technicolor extravaganza set in the world of ballet.

Their relationship is another tale of immigrant ambition, its catalyst the film producer, director and screenwriter Alexander Korda. A Hungarian, born Sándor László Kellner, Korda had already worked for a spell as a journalist in America and France before arriving in England where, in 1933, he set up a film production company – London Films, based at Denham in Buckinghamshire – surrounded by as many Hungarians as he could find, including his brothers, Zoltan and Vincent. He soon had great success with films such as *The Private Life of Henry VIII* – the first British film to win an Oscar (for Charles Laughton as Best Actor).

As a young, rookie director, Michael Powell ended up at London Films where one of the first movies he was given to direct was a thriller called *The Spy in Black*. Powell found its script unworkable, so Korda got him together with one of his newly arrived Hungarians to sort it out. This turned out to be Emeric Pressburger.

Born Imre József Pressburger on 5 December 1902 in Miskolc in northern Hungary, and educated in Prague and Stuttgart, he had abandoned a career in civil engineering after his father's death, reinventing himself as a journalist called 'Emmerich Pressburger', then as a contract writer at the German film studio UFA. As the Nazis rose to power, he fled Germany for France, arriving in Britain in 1935 where he became one of the many Hungarian émigrés employed at London Films.

At the story conference for *The Spy in Black*, where the pair met for the first time, Emeric introduced himself to Michael formally, even making a small bow: 'Excuse me,' he said, 'I am Pressburger.' Emeric shook hands with everyone present. Then he went through the particulars of the rewrite he had done on the script. Michael would remember later the way that Emeric produced a very small piece of rolled-up paper and addressed the meeting while he listened, spell-bound. 'Since talkies took over the movies, I had worked with some good writers,' Michael wrote in his autobiography, 'but I had never met anything like this . . . The day Emeric walked out of his flat, leaving the key in the door to save the storm-troopers the trouble of breaking it down, was the worst day's work that [Dr Goebbels] ever did for his coun-try's reputation, as he was very soon to find out.'[49]

As Emeric spoke, Alexander Korda and the screenwriter whose script was being pulled to pieces sat in silence with their mouths open. Michael wrote: 'Nobody had ever told them that when you buy the rights to a famous book which turns out to be useless for a screenwriter's purpose, you keep the title and throw away the book.'[50]

They went for coffee afterwards. Michael noted that Emeric was a 'short, compact man, with beautiful and observant eyes, and a broad intellectual forehead, formally and neatly dressed'.[51] He was witty and ingenious – not just a musician who had played the violin professionally, but a sportsman too. His most attractive quality was that he feared nobody. Michael realised with delight that he had found 'a screenwriter with the heart and mind of a novelist, who would be interested in the medium of film, and who would have wonderful ideas, which I would turn into even more wonderful images, and who only used dialogue to clarify the plot'.[52] He had seen a marvel: a screenwriter who could really write: 'I was not going to let him get away in a hurry.'[53]

After *The Spy in Black*, the pair worked on a war film, set in Canada, called *49th Parallel*. A huge success, it won Emeric an Oscar for Best Original Story and received nominations for Best Screenplay and Best Film. It was the top-grossing film in Britain in 1941. For their next film, *One of Our Aircraft is Missing*, they formed their own production company, the Archers, pooling their talents so that the credits of their future films announced them to be 'Written, Produced and Directed by Michael Powell and Emeric Pressburger' – an extraordinary statement, but an accurate reflection of the way the films came to be made. 'They were incredibly loyal to each other,' remembers their long-time cameraman Christopher Challis. 'I couldn't think of two more unlikely people on surface values to form a partnership, but they were perfect foils for each other, and are the only two who I've never heard one say a bad thing about the other.'[54]

These strange, idiosyncratic films about Englishness, written by a Hungarian Jew, conjure up a magical realm suffused with what the cultural historian Michael Bracewell calls 'portentous mysticism'.[55] The hero of *A Matter of Life and Death*, Peter, is an RAF pilot obsessed with the poetry of Sir Walter Raleigh and Andrew Marvell, who jumps out of his damaged Lancaster bomber without a parachute and presents himself to a startled shepherd boy at the entrance to a heaven that resembles a prep school ('I'm new. Where do I report?').

Regrettably, the Archers bowed out with a damp squib, the routine 1957 war film, *Ill Met By Moonlight*. Michael called it a sad drifting apart; Christopher Challis says they had reached a point where they wanted to do different things. In a 1971 interview, Emeric mused on the serendipity of their union: 'When we parted, Michael said to me, "Well I want to tell you that I often did things when I didn't

Greta Garbo shields her face as she leaves a reception in October 1951, accompanied by her improbable lover, the photographer Cecil Beaton. He had pursued her for decades, writing in his diary over twenty years earlier: 'How I long to get at Garbo.'

A comic double-act like no other, Laurel & Hardy – shown here in their 1933 film *Sons of the Desert* – were one of the few silent-film brands to carry over successfully to 'talkies'.

George Lazenby (left) replaced Sean Connery as James Bond. TV star Simon Dee (right) had auditioned for the role but been rejected. 'I couldn't have been much worse than Lazenby,' he harrumphed.

The so-called 'Jim twins', James Lewis and James Springer, were adopted by different families shortly after birth. Once reunited, they showed remarkable behavioural similarities.

One of the early Marks & Spencer stalls, in Cardiff's covered market in 1901. These 'penny bazaars' were the modern department store in microcosm.

Gertrude Stein (right) and her companion Alice B. Toklas walking their dog in southeastern France in 1944. Alice was late for their first meeting, infuriating punctilious Gertrude.

Moira Shearer dances for her life in a scene from Michael Powell and Emeric Pressburger's 1948 masterpiece *The Red Shoes*.

Richard Burton and Elizabeth Taylor's stormy affair nearly derailed production on *Cleopatra* (1963).

Opposite top: In his battles against racism the Edwardian composer Samuel Coleridge-Taylor had a ferocious ally in his wife, Jessie.

Opposite bottom: Ain't no mountain high enough... Ruth Williams (left) was working as a clerk when she met future husband Seretse Khama, paramount chief of Botswana's Bamangwato people.

Opposite top: The grass is always greener…? During JFK's presidency, Jackie professionalised the role of First Lady. But her peerless elegance didn't stop her husband's eye from wandering.

Opposite bottom: After the Beatles split, Paul McCartney found sanctuary in domesticity with wife Linda and their children – including James, pictured here as a baby.

Beyoncé and Jay-Z have often made their marriage the subject of their art – a means of reflecting on the pressures of being one of America's foremost black power couples.

Victorian cross-dressers
Thomas Ernest Boulton
(right) and Frederick William
Park are better known by
their respective drag names
'Stella' and 'Fanny'.

Forgotten for decades,
surrealist artists and
political activists Claude
Cahun (left) and Marcel
Moore are now seen for the
pioneers they were.

understand what you meant by them but I just did them blindly and they were all right most of the time." Now this comes about because one trusts one's partner very much but also because . . . there was an inner response like a violin that would respond to an outside sound if it is tuned in a similar way; that must have been the case.'[56]

Once the partnership collapsed, Emeric more or less retired from screenwriting. Michael Powell went on to make several more films, mostly commercial duds. Some of them, for instance *Peeping Tom* – so reviled at the time that it never received a proper British release – have been reclaimed as classics by the likes of Martin Scorsese, but in truth none came close to touching his work with Emeric. On a couple of occasions it looked as if they might reunite and a Children's Film Foundation film Michael directed in 1972, *The Boy Who Turned Yellow*, was based on a story by Emeric. But it never happened. When Emeric died in 1988, Michael wrote in a moving obituary: 'They tell me he died in his sleep, but I am sure it was in the middle of a joke.'

———————

The moment of finding the missing piece of the jigsaw, the fresh perspective, often arrives when two different temperaments and talents collide, then combine. The randomness and spontaneity of these encounters is what makes them special and keeps us all on our toes.

I began this chapter talking about the 'music of chance'. Funnily enough, a good example of this phenomenon comes from the world of classical music. Earlier I talked about the piano accompanist Gerald Moore, who wrote extensively and funnily about how he became good by acquiring sensitivity to the solo musicians he worked with. He became their partner in performance by striking a balance between his playing temperament and theirs. 'Joy, sadness, passion, exultation, serenity, rage, must be experienced by each of them,' he wrote in *Am I Too Loud?*, one of his many memoirs. 'How can the singer project an emotion to the listener if the accompanist holds back self-effacingly from the scene?'[57]

One critic wrote of Moore's 'chameleonic empathy with every musical partner – whether Casals, Chaliapin or a young debutant recitalist'.[58] It is true that Moore elevated accompaniment to an art form in its own right by making a rapid set of calculations while he was playing about how far he needed to lean in to or out of a soloist's performance.

He was taught this technique by the tenor John Coates, with whom he began working in 1925. 'He would listen carefully and critically to every note in my part,' Moore wrote in *Am I Too Loud?* 'It was a tough school; after two hours of slogging study he would say it was now time to start work. "You play that as if you had never been in love." "Have you no zest for living?" "This is angry, all venom, and you sound like a blancmange." All this was hurled at me with scorn and acidity. Many a time I felt like revolting under the lash of his tongue but, thank God, I stuck it.'[59]

Perhaps the moral of the story is that what looks like serendipity is often just hard work – and that chance really does favour the prepared.

6

Love

I could have filled this book with love stories. And it will not have passed you by that love is a common factor in many of the tales included here. This chapter, however, explores the different kinds of love between different kinds of couples – and the ways it encourages us to behave as a species.

When I first began thinking about this book and the couples who might inhabit it, the ones that sprang most readily to mind were lovers in the classic, dramatic mould. For some reason, many of them were fictional: Cathy and Heathcliff bounding across the Yorkshire moors; Cyrano de Bergerac overcoming the hurdle of his massive nose to win fair Roxane; Lizzie Bennet and Darcy's love blossoming in the soil of apparent mutual disdain.

The difficulty was working out, a) whether fictional couples counted, and b) if they did, whether they were necessarily exemplary. A lot of fictional romantic couples are slightly odd, after all. Consider the tale of Troilus and Criseyde, relayed by Boccaccio and Chaucer as well as Shakespeare. It is a bizarre affair, full of abusive emotional coercion (of Criseyde by her uncle, Pandarus, the idiotic character who brings the lovers together) and unhelpful agonising over questions of fortune and free will.

As for Cathy and Heathcliff, well – that isn't really a love story, is it? Their relationship is much darker and stranger than that: more like toxic codependence. 'I am Heathcliff,' admits Cathy. 'He's always, always in my mind: not as a pleasure, any more than I am always a pleasure to myself, but as my own being.'[1] Key phrase: not as a pleasure. Cathy and Heathcliff are soulmates, not lovers as such.

Where love is concerned, 'keep faith and be patient' is an important lesson. It is the one Orpheus does not heed when, his wife Eurydice having died after she was bitten by a snake on their wedding day, he blows the chance to get her back. While leading Eurydice out of the underworld, Orpheus ignores Hades's instruction not to turn around and look at her until they reach the light of the upper world. 'Instantly she slipped away,' Ovid tells us in *Metamorphoses* Book 10. '[Orpheus] stretched out to her his despairing arms, eager to rescue her, or feel her form, but could hold nothing save the yielding air. Dying the second time, she could not say a word of censure of her husband's fault; what had she to complain of – his great love?'

The last word in tragic grandeur is the story of Mark Antony and Cleopatra – a much-told tale, not least by Shakespeare (again), though he based his plot on Plutarch's *Lives*. It's worth retelling once more, I think.

Antony was a hard-partying young nobleman who soldiered under Caesar in the Gallic Wars and became his right-hand man. After Caesar's death, a struggle for power ensued between Antony, a general called Lepidus, and Caesar's sickly great-nephew and adopted son Octavian. Eventually this 'Second Triumvirate' divided the Roman provinces between them. Antony's territory included Egypt, known as Rome's 'bread basket', then ruled by Cleopatra.

Cleopatra was no beauty, but she was clever and canny, having (as Enobarbus puts it in Shakespeare's play) 'infinite variety' and the ability to '[make] hungry/Where most she satisfies'. She had already had a child with Caesar, her co-ruler Caesarion, when Antony requested a meeting with her in Tarsus in 42 BC to seek her financial support for Rome's planned military expansion. Determined to make an impression, she arrived in a barge with a golden prow, a purple sail and silver oars, half-undressed in the manner of Venus, her waiting women dressed as mermaids.

Gloriously, she refused to come ashore: Antony had to go to her. He followed her back to Alexandria afterwards. Entranced by each other's power, they became lovers – never mind that Antony already had a wife, Fulvia, and would go on to marry plain Octavia, Octavian's widowed sister, after Fulvia died – and have three children together: twins Alexander Helios and Cleopatra Selene II in 40 BC, then another, Ptolemy Philadelphus, four years later.

It did not end well. Rome declared war on Egypt. Antony sided with Cleopatra, but his men went hungry when Octavian, a superior strategist, cut off food supplies to Antony's troops. After defeat at Actium, he and Cleopatra fled back to Alexandria – Shakespeare has Antony berate Cleopatra for making him behave in a cowardly way. When Octavian's army reached the city, Antony offered to kill himself if it would save Cleopatra's life – and duly stabbed himself with a sword when he believed she had already done the same.

But she hadn't. Instead, Cleopatra had barricaded herself into her own mausoleum with her most precious possessions.

The dying Antony was brought to Cleopatra and hauled up through a window so that she could catch his dying breath. He died in her arms. She lived for ten more days and would have been Octavian's prisoner for longer had she not devised for herself an ingenious suicide: smuggling into her rooms a cobra camouflaged in a basket of figs. *Nunc est bibendum*, wrote Horace ('Now is the time to drink'), celebrating her downfall and Egypt's full absorption into the Roman empire.

Which brings us neatly to the couple who played Antony and Cleopatra in the 1963 movie *Cleopatra* – and who embodied for a generation film stars at their highest wattage: Elizabeth Taylor and Richard Burton. Their love withered and perished as often as it blossomed and flourished, so that observing the cycle of withering/blossoming became a compulsive media sport.

Love enacted in the public eye has a curious power to console, enrage, perhaps even educate. 'Couples all over Hollywood may be crashing and burning, but you don't have to,' insisted *Glamour* magazine in 2008,[2] going on to list lessons we might learn from Anne Hathaway's relationship with Raffaello Follieri, and George 'I'm not made for marriage' Clooney's with his then-girlfriend Sarah Larson, among others. (Of course, George turned out to be made for marriage after all. Just not to Sarah Larson.)

The drunken revels of Antony and Cleopatra were matched on the set of *Cleopatra* by those of the stars playing them. The full story of the film's disastrous production, beyond the point where it was the fault of its errant leads, is beyond the scope of this book. Suffice to say *Cleopatra* cost £31 million, making it the most expensive film to have been made up to that point, and nearly bankrupted 20th Century Fox, the Hollywood studio that made it. Joseph

Mankiewicz – hired as a replacement director after the original one left the project having spent $7 million producing ten minutes of usable footage – said *Cleopatra* was 'conceived in a state of emergency, shot in confusion, and wound up in a blind panic'.[3]

The bad publicity that attended Elizabeth and Richard's scandalous on-set affair was far from Mankiewicz's only problem. It did not help, however. You know things have reached a surreal peak when the Vatican publishes an open letter attacking your leading lady for her 'erotic vagrancy'. Elizabeth, paid an unprecedented £1 million for the role, later called it 'probably the most chaotic time of my life . . . It was fun and it was dark – oceans of tears, but some good times too.'[4]

Elizabeth Taylor was born in London in 1932, the daughter of an art dealer and an actress-turned-stage mother who moved to Hollywood to further their daughter's career as an MGM starlet in movies such as *Lassie Come Home* and *National Velvet*. In 1950, having cast off her child-star shackles, Elizabeth married first Nicky Hilton, scion of the hotel dynasty (MGM paid for the wedding); then, when that collapsed, her much older co-star in *Ivanhoe*, Michael Wilding; then, in 1956, film producer Mike Todd, who invented the widescreen process Todd-AO in which *Cleopatra* was shot. Tragically, Todd was killed in March 1957 when his private plane crashed in a storm.

Initially significant, public sympathy for Elizabeth's loss ran dry after she was discovered to have found comfort in the arms of the singer Eddie Fisher, then married to the actress Debbie Reynolds, adored as 'America's sweetheart'. Taylor's reputation as a marriage-wrecker was now set in stone.

The president of 20th Century Fox, Spyros Skouras, had

not wanted Elizabeth in the movie in the first place because he feared she would be too much trouble. On top of the Eddie Fisher business, she was known for sudden, dramatic, long-lasting illness, at least some of it self-inflicted by drug and alcohol abuse. Sure enough, on the third day of shooting in London, she called in sick with a cold and self-isolated in her suite at the Dorchester Hotel. The supervision of the Queen's personal physician failed to stop her excessive drinking and prescription drug use over the next few weeks.

But Elizabeth's absenteeism wasn't always fraudulent. On one occasion during filming she developed double pneumonia. Transferred to an oxygen tent, she nearly died on the night of 4 March 1961 – and in fact some newspapers did report that Elizabeth Taylor was dead, provoking her wonderful comment: 'I had the chance to read my own obituaries. They were the best reviews I'd ever gotten.'[5]

Richard Burton was a different kettle of fish – the twelfth of thirteen children, born into poverty in the Welsh mining village of Pontrhydyfen; raised by his sister, known as Cis, after their mother died of puerperal fever. A kindly teacher, Philip Burton, had recognised Richard's cleverness and talent for acting, and worked with him on developing his rich baritone voice and appreciation of literature. Richard duly became Philip's legal ward and assumed his surname. At Oxford, where Richard went to study for six months in 1943 on an RAF scholarship, he was talent-spotted again, this time by John Gielgud and theatre manager Hugh 'Binkie' Beaumont.

Acclaim and celebrity followed swiftly, for Richard was a magnificent stage actor; though also a bruiser, a drinker and a compulsive philanderer. His first wife Sybil, a one-time actress who had a successful second career as a nightclub owner, would later divorce him on the grounds of 'abandonment and cruel and inhuman treatment'.[6] 'He flirted like mad with me, with everyone, with any girl who was even remotely pretty,' remembered Elizabeth years later. 'I just thought, "Ohhh, boy – I'm not gonna become a notch on his belt."'[7]

It was when production of *Cleopatra* moved to Rome – an event designed to encourage Elizabeth to be more present and punctual – that the affair began. Ironically, Richard and Elizabeth did not initially hit it off. Richard was contemptuous of 'MGM's Little Miss Mammary', who was, he said, 'good at getting sick and getting married'. Her acting ability he described as 'quite pathetic, really'. But he changed his opinion after seeing the first rushes, realising that even though she went through rehearsals 'like a kind of sleep-walker', Elizabeth knew what she was doing. When the camera started whirring, 'she turns it on, the magic, and you can't believe your eyes'.[8] For her part, Elizabeth intuited the dark side beneath Richard's bar-room banter and charm, saying: 'If a prefrontal lobotomy was performed on his skull, out would fly snakes, frogs, worms, tadpoles, and bats.'[9] More carnally, she told a friend on the *Cleopatra* set that just listening to his voice gave her an orgasm.

Clearly, it was only a matter of time before she succumbed. Notch on his belt duly acquired, Richard walked into the men's make-up trailer and announced: 'Gentlemen, I've just fucked Elizabeth Taylor in the back of my Cadillac!'[10] (If you think this sounds callous and dismissive, remember that at the same time Burton was also sleeping with a dancer he had met while performing on Broadway in the musical *Camelot*.) As news of the affair seeped out, Burton was surprised by the media reaction and the hundredfold increase in his celebrity. 'I've had affairs before,' he mused, 'but how did I know the woman was so fucking famous?'[11] '*Le Scandale*', he called it. And it really was.

Taylor had been tabloid catnip ever since Mike Todd's death. Well before her affair with Burton began, Roman newspapers had been planting spies in Cinecittà studios, where *Cleopatra* was being filmed. Richard drank heavily on the set. Elizabeth, who also liked a glass or two, became even more erratic than usual in her habits. Sometimes she would show up unprecedentedly early to work on scenes with Burton; sometimes she would fail to show up at all. Sometimes, when she did show up, she was in no fit state to do any acting. A production diary kept for MGM indicates that on one day Elizabeth was sent home for 'having great difficulty delivering dialogue'.[12]

The affair ended, after much drama including suicide attempts, when filming was completed and Richard returned to Sybil. In early 1963, however, he and Elizabeth reunited to make another movie, *The V.I.P.s*, and picked up where they had left off. Unable to tolerate Richard's behaviour any longer, Sybil filed for divorce that December. Richard was playing Hamlet in Toronto when Elizabeth's own divorce from Eddie Fisher was finalised. The pair married in Montreal on 16 March 1964. The following night, after taking his curtain call in Toronto, he showed off Elizabeth to the audience and announced: 'I would just like to quote from the play – Act III, Scene I: "We will have no more marriages."' The audience roared.

In fact, Elizabeth and Richard went on to marry each other twice and make a series of (mostly terrible) films together. The one good one is *Who's Afraid of Virginia Woolf?*, in which Richard played a failed academic and Elizabeth his raging wife. Against the odds it was Elizabeth who won an Oscar for it; though she stayed away from the ceremony in protest that her also-nominated husband was not going to win.

Richard Burton and Elizabeth Taylor are significant because they ushered in the era of the world-straddling but dysfunctional super-celebrity couple. I have included them in a chapter celebrating 'love', and they clearly did love each other in their own way; but their relationship is not many people's idea of love. It was messy, abusive and booze-sodden, and it took as long to end as it was quick to begin. The couple separated in 1973; divorced a year later; then remarried a few weeks after that. 'We are stuck like chicken feathers to tar – for lovely always,' Elizabeth wrote shortly after their final wedding. 'Do you realise that we shall grow old together and I know the best is yet to be.'[13]

Three weeks later they separated again, for the final time.

———————

It would be nice to think Hollywood's days of dysfunction and abuse are behind us, especially now that Harvey Weinstein is safely behind bars. Ironically, one of the relics of Weinstein's regime at Miramax (he distributed it) is a film I have always loved: *The English Patient*.

In one scene the couple whose romance forms the core of its plot – Ralph Fiennes's Hungarian cartographer Count Almásy and Katharine Clifton, the British explorer, played by Kristin Scott Thomas – are talking about adjectives, specifically Almásy's habit of not using many of them. 'A thing is still a thing no matter what you place in front of it,' he insists. But Katharine disagrees: 'Love? Romantic love, platonic love, filial love – ? Quite different things, surely?'

One of the strongest, most intense loves is often sibling love. Even when siblings do not get on, they (mostly) still love each other. Which is just as well, because for most of us a sibling relationship lasts a long time, much longer than our relationships with our parents or partners.

For those of us who have siblings, this bond shapes us in more ways than we realise. Jeffrey Kluger puts it well in his book *The Sibling Effect*: 'From the time they are born, our brothers and sisters are our collaborators and co-conspirators, our role models and cautionary tales. They are our scolds, protectors, goads, tormentors, playmates, counsellors, sources of envy, objects of pride. They teach us how to resolve conflicts and how not to; how to conduct friendships and when to walk away from them. Sisters teach brothers about the mysteries of girls; brothers teach sisters about the puzzle of boys.'[14]

On 26 September 1796, the following report appeared in the *Morning Chronicle*:

On Friday afternoon the Coroner and a respectable Jury sat on the body of a Lady in the neighbourhood of Holborn, who died in consequence of a wound from her daughter the preceding day. It appeared by the evidence adduced, that while the family were preparing for dinner, the young lady seized a case knife laying on the table, and in a menacing manner pursued a little girl, her apprentice, round the room; on the eager calls of her helpless infirm mother to forbear, she renounced her first object, and with loud shrieks approached her parent.

The child by her cries quickly brought up the landlord of the house, but too late – the dreadful scene presented to him the mother lifeless, pierced to the heart, on a chair, her daughter yet wildly standing over her with the fatal knife . . .

For a few days prior to this the family had observed some symptoms of insanity in her, which had so much increased on the Wednesday evening, that her brother early the next morning went in quest of Dr Pitcairn – had that gentleman been met with, the fatal catastrophe had, in all probability, been prevented . . .

The above unfortunate young person is a Miss Lamb, mantua-maker, in Little Queen-Street, Lincoln's-inn-fields. She has been, since, removed to Islington mad-house.

The Jury of course brought in their Verdict, Lunacy.

The daughter in question was Mary Lamb, sister of the poet and essayist Charles. The 'mantuas' she made were loose-fitting dresses, common in the late eighteenth century. Mary, Charles and their older brother, John, were raised in London's Temple district, close to where their father worked as a clerk. Their mother neglected the two younger children. John, the favoured son, was mostly absent and had little to do with his siblings who, perhaps as a consequence, formed a close bond that would last all their lives. Charles started work in his late teens as a clerk in the accounts department of the East India Company: the organisation that controlled much of Britain's empire. He remained there until he was fifty – a tiny cog in an unfathomably intricate machine.

Mary was not the only Lamb to suffer from mental illness. Charles had had a breakdown of his own not long before the grim September day when, as the newspaper story relates, Mary chased her apprentice dressmaker around the room with a knife. She only stabbed the old woman because she happened to get in the way. Still, her mother was high on the list of triggers that had caused Mary to snap. Mary's mother and father were both senile and incapacitated. Mary had to look after them and an elderly aunt on top of managing her own workload, which included training up an apprentice and managing the household. Sleep was a rare luxury.

Thanks to the liberal laws that existed then – even a few years later her situation might have been very different – Mary did not have to stand trial for the murder. Instead, the coroner's court declared her insane and she spent a period in a private madhouse in Islington before being placed under Charles's guardianship, her brother having stated that he would accept responsibility for her care. For the rest of her life, Mary lived with Charles, occasionally checking herself in to a madhouse when she felt a bout of psychosis returning. She and Charles were always alert to premonitory symptoms. Whenever they travelled, they took a straitjacket with them, just in case.

Committing Mary was always an unhappy business – friends reported seeing the pair weeping in the street as Charles led Mary to the asylum door – but the siblings were unembarrassed by the ailment which Charles was proud to share, despite his not being on the same scale. He once wrote to his old school friend Samuel Taylor Coleridge: 'Dream not, Coleridge, of having tasted all the grandeur & wildness of FANCY, till you have gone MAD.'[15] (Charles's real problem was alcoholism.)

The phrase Charles used to describe their lives – 'double singleness' – suggests contented independence within a framework of supportive companionship. The pair lived together for almost the whole of Charles's life. (He died at fifty-nine. Mary, who was eleven years' his senior, outlived him by thirteen years.) 'She is older, & wiser, & better than me, and all my wretched imperfections I cover to myself by resolutely thinking on her goodness,' Charles wrote to

Dorothy Wordsworth, who understood what it was to have an intense relationship with a sibling – in her case her brother William. 'She would share life & death, heaven & hell with me. She lives but for me.'[16]

The closeness of their affinity astonished observers. Thomas De Quincey wrote: 'As, amongst certain classes of birds, if you have one you are sure of the other so, with respect to the Lambs . . . seeing or hearing the brother, you knew that the sister could not be far off.'[17] Similarly, the poet Bryan Procter remembered the way Mary often had 'an upward look of peculiar meaning, when directed towards [Charles]; as though to give him assurance that all was then well with her'.[18]

But the relationship was also co-dependent (as we would now think of it) in ways that were not so healthy. 'When Mary calls, it is understood that I call too, we being univocal,' Charles once said. For her part, Mary admitted that depression experienced by one of them frequently spread to the other: 'You would laugh, or you would cry, perhaps both, to see us sit together looking at each other with long and rueful faces, & saying how do you do? & how do you do? & then we fall a crying & say we will be better on the morrow.'[19] They were gregarious, however – especially Charles, who had a child's hard-to-control boisterousness – and were keen, generous hosts: the variety of houses they rented were frequently full of friends, many of them eminent Romantics like Coleridge, De Quincey, William and Dorothy Wordsworth and Robert Southey.

Late in his life, after he had tried his hand at playwriting, poetry and radical journalism, Charles acquired fame writing pseudonymously as 'Elia' in the *London Magazine*. His wry, conversational, whimsically satirical essays on everyday subjects – such as saying grace before meals and the perils of lending people books – were much loved. Mary appears in them as 'Cousin Bridget'. Their apparent lightness belies the difficulty Charles had writing them. He found it hard to concentrate and organise himself so that he could meet deadlines. Mary described them writing together: 'I taking snuff & he groaning all the while & saying he can make nothing of it, which he always says till he has finished and then he finds out he has made something of it.'[20] Charles always told himself that he could write best when drunk – a dangerous conviction for someone with alcoholic tendencies.

Mary was known to be gentle and wise when she wasn't having a manic episode. Her writing has a more explicitly political edge than her brother's. Much admired by feminist critics is her radical essay 'On Needlework', which argues that middle-class amateur sewers are taking money from the working-class professional needlewomen who need it more. Additionally, Mary contends, by sewing in their spare time, these middle-class women were reducing the opportunities to improve their minds through reading and conversation.

The book for which the Lambs are best known, however, was a joint effort. *Tales from Shakespeare* was first published in 1807 in the Juvenile Library series of William Godwin (father of the future *Frankenstein* author Mary Shelley) and his second wife Mary Jane Clairmont. Since then it has never been out of print. Adapted from Shakespeare's best-known plays – such as *Hamlet*, *King Lear*, *Macbeth* – the tales are clever summaries designed to introduce children to the Bard so that, when they finally see or read the actual plays, they will be familiar enough with them to understand what is going on.

Although Mary wrote approximately two-thirds of the

tales – tackling the comedies and problem plays, while Charles worked exclusively on the tragedies – she did not get her name on the title page until the seventh edition in 1838. This was because of her reputation as a matricide rather than because she was a woman – though it is true that female authors were, as a rule, sidelined in those days.

The Lambs shared a clear sense of the sort of books they thought children should be reading. It was wrong, they believed, for children's books to be about conduct and science and morality. Rather, they should contain what they called 'wild tales' that fostered the childish part of the imagination to which you would, Romantic ideology decreed, hark back as an adult if you wanted to stay mentally balanced.

Shakespeare's world was a place where, as the Lambs' biographer Sarah Burton points out, 'good did not inevitably triumph over evil, where there was often no "right" course of action, where virtues could bring their own attendant problems. In addition to affording children a more sophisticated range of moral possibilities, Shakespeare's stories of course also offered them adventure, romance and magical transformations.'[21]

As the Lambs put it themselves in their preface: 'What these tales shall have been to the young readers, that and much more it is the writers' wish that the true plays of Shakespeare may prove to them in older years – enrichers of the fancy, strengtheners of virtue, a withdrawing from all selfish and mercenary thoughts, a lesson of all sweet and honourable thoughts and actions, to teach courtesy, benignity, generosity, humanity: for of examples, teaching these virtues, his pages are full.'[22] Charles expresses the odd view, to us, that 'the plays of Shakespeare are less calculated for performance on a stage, than those of almost any other dramatist whatever'.[23] He genuinely believed they were better enjoyed in private tranquillity than in a public theatre.

For Charles and Mary, the success of their book depended on the stories feeling as authentic as possible, even though they had been edited and sometimes bowdlerised to be appealing to minors. To achieve this, they used a good deal of Shakespeare's original language, putting his images and rhythms through a sort of sausage machine. It is all there if you look – just minced for easy spoon-feeding. As the writer Marina Warner says: 'Long passages of *Lambs' Tales* consist not of paraphrase, but of edited quotations; they read sometimes like bits of the plays someone has learned by heart but has not quite got word perfect, with gaps and stumbles.'[24] They also unscramble the chronology of the plays so that, for example, Hamlet starts not with the ghost appearing on the ramparts, but with Gertrude suddenly widowed.

Charles's commitment to taking care of Mary meant he was never able to marry. He did fall in love, though, at the age of forty-four, with an actress called Fanny Kelly who refused his proposal of marriage. It is possible he was also in love with a young orphan, Emma Isola, whom the Lambs adopted in the decade before Charles's death in 1834, though this is hard to verify.

The idea of siblings living together in a kind of sexless marriage is alien to us now, but in the nineteenth century it was not uncommon. 'Close brother-and-sister bonds provided a supportive alternative to marriage in a way that we tend to have difficulty comprehending,' writes literary historian Valerie Sanders.[25] The Lambs constructed a version of this support structure to underpin their very particular emotional and psychological needs. Nobody at the time thought their situation particularly odd.

However, as Sanders observes, there was a certain amount of prurient speculation surrounding another pair of literary siblings – William and Dorothy Wordsworth. Both had had complicated childhoods. Aged seven, Dorothy had been separated from her older brother, William, after their mother's death, upon which she was sent to live first with an aunt in Halifax, then with grandparents in Penrith until her early twenties. When she and William were reunited in 1794, they formed a deep emotional connection. Into this charged situation came Mary Hutchinson, an orphan whom Dorothy had befriended in Penrith. Mary went on to marry William, who lived with her and Dorothy until his death in 1850.

William's friend Thomas De Quincey had heard a story – an 'abominable accusation' put about by 'coarse-minded neighbours' – that William and Dorothy's relationship was sexual. It is impossible to know if this was true, though Dorothy's behaviour was definitely . . . odd. She collected William's half-eaten apple cores and stored them in her pinny pocket. When he was away, she slept in his bed because she missed him so much.

Kathleen Jones, author of *A Passionate Sisterhood: Women of the Wordsworth Circle,* thinks Dorothy showed 'all the symptoms' of lovesickness. 'William was the centre of her world and she was deeply attached to him in a way that we might not consider healthy,' she says.[26] However, she thinks the relationship stopped short of being sexual.

An oft-quoted story relates how, on the night before her brother's marriage to Mary in 1802, Dorothy wore the couple's wedding ring. When she took it off and gave it to him, he briefly replaced it on her finger with a blessing before leaving for the ceremony, which Dorothy was too upset to attend. When she heard that the marriage had taken place, Dorothy wrote that she 'could stand it no longer and threw myself on the bed neither hearing nor seeing anything till Sara came upstairs to say, "they are coming"'.[27] Make of that what you will.

———————

The halo of claustrophobia and co-dependency around the legend of the Lambs suggests a story can be remarkable, inspiring and say something truthful about both couples and the power of love, even if on closer inspection it is not quite the story you thought it was or wanted it to be.

When it comes to grand gestures, it is almost impossible to match the Mughal emperor Shah Jahan, who immortalised his third wife, Mumtaz Mahal, by building the Taj Mahal in her memory after she died giving birth to their fourteenth child in 1631. I have always felt this must have been a reward for endurance as much as love. (*Fourteen* children!)

Love between couples – any kind of love, any kind of couple – can last a lifetime. But it can also be transient, and no less significant for that. When the great African American writer James Baldwin was on his deathbed, one of the people who looked after him was the American artist Fred Nall Hollis (known to all as Nall), his neighbour in the French town of St-Paul-de-Vence. While Nall massaged James's feet, the pair had deep, confessional conversations about the bigotry that had been instilled in Nall as a white man growing up in Alabama and the difficulties this caused when Nall realised that he, like James, was gay.

Nall was present on the night of 30 November 1987, when James died and was the recipient of James's final piece of writing, scrawled on an old envelope a few hours before he passed away: 'Safety and Honor both adore each other but are doomed to discover that they cannot find a way to live, or sleep, together. Honor's demands are brutal, and so are those of Safety. One, or the other, must give way. One, or the other, must surrender.'[28] It was a charged, intimate moment between two friends – a loving moment that yielded something remarkable. Yet the pair had not previously been especially close; they were not lovers, and the bulk of the caring for James was done by his brother, David. It was David who gave Nall the envelope, saying: 'Here's a piece of paper I think Jimmy wanted you to have. It's the last thing he wrote.'[29]

Painter Joseph Severn nursed the poet John Keats on his deathbed in 26 Piazza di Spagna by the Spanish Steps in Rome. Keats was in the final stages of tuberculosis and had been advised by his doctors to spend the winter of 1820 in Italy if he wished to prolong his life. Mere acquaintances at the point when they left England for Rome on 17 September, the pair were bonded by the journey's difficulties. Keats was pining for Fanny Brawne, the fiancée he had left behind and intended to marry on his return, while Severn was pondering excommunication by his family: his father had been so angered by his decision to accompany Keats to Italy that he had punched him upon learning of it. When they arrived in Naples they were required to spend ten days in quarantine before travelling to Rome.

Keats's death from tuberculosis was grim and protracted. And Joseph's proximity to Keats as he continually coughed up blood put him in grave danger of picking up the infection. On the evening of 23 February 1821, Keats called out to Severn: 'Lift me up – I am dying. I shall die easy. Don't be frightened. Thank God it has come.' At this, Joseph took

Keats in his arms, lifted him a little then slowly released him, keeping hold of his left hand. The pair remained in this pose as the sun faded, the mucus 'boiling' in Keats's throat. 'This increased until eleven at night,' wrote Joseph, 'when he gradually sank into death, so quiet that I still thought he slept – but I cannot say more now. I am broken down beyond my strength.'[30]

It is a reliable cliché that love is heightened by proximity to death. Keats and Fanny got engaged in October 1819, just over a year after they had first met. Fanny was beguiling and flirtatious, always tricked out in the latest elegant French-style fashions. She was also bright and well read, and passionate about politics. Her hair was dark brown, her eyes blue, her skin so pale that it made her look unhealthy. She was, it has been said, striking rather than beautiful and Keats was uncertain about her character at first, attacking her for being 'monstrous in her behaviour' and 'calling people such names – that I was forced lately to make use of the term Minx'.[31] But the very fact that she was called Fanny – also the name of his mother and sister – was alluring to the poet.

The love letters of John Keats and Fanny Brawne were first published in 1878. They have lost none of their vividness and potency. Reading them now, as Andrew Motion writes, we 'live in Keats' own rapturous and bitter present, fascinated by his convulsive contradictions, infected by his fever, "tossed to and fro" by his passionate longings and tormented doubts'. As Keats's health deteriorated, love and death became inextricably linked in his imagination so that, as Motion notes, the 'proven fact of Fanny's love could not be separated from the certainty of its destruction'.[32] Keats himself makes this clear to Fanny in a famous letter: 'I have two luxuries to brood over in my walks, your Loveliness and the hour of my death. O that I could have possession of them both in the same minute.'[33]

In October 1819, Keats wrote to Fanny: 'My Creed is Love and you are its only tenet,' – an idea he developed in perhaps the best-known poem he dedicated to her:

> The day is gone, and all its sweets are gone!
> Sweet voice, sweet lips, soft hand, and softer breast,
> Warm breath, light whisper, tender semitone,
> Bright eyes, accomplished shape, and lang'rous waist!
> Faded the flower and all its budded charms,
> Faded the sight of beauty from my eyes,
> Faded the shape of beauty from my arms,
> Faded the voice, warmth, whiteness, paradise!
> Vanished unseasonably at shut of eve,
> When the dusk holiday – or holinight –
> Of fragrant-curtained love begins to weave
> The woof of darkness thick, for hid delight;
> But, as I've read love's missal through today,
> He'll let me sleep, seeing I fast and pray.[34]

As the moment of his death approached, however, Keats chose to erect a protective shield around himself. He did not wish to transmit or receive additional pain. For this reason he did not write to Fanny from Rome, nor did he open her letters to him.

———————

Thinking about James Baldwin, as I was a little earlier, brings me to another couple bonded by love, and returns me to a subject I addressed fleetingly in *Bloody Brilliant Women*: the invidious myth put about by the far right (mostly) that Britain's black population only arrived with the *Empire Windrush* in 1948. Even those who concede that this is not true might draw the line at the suggestion that there was a black middle class in Victorian and Edwardian England. And yet as historians such as Jeffrey Green have shown, there very much was.

One of the best-known black public figures at the end of the nineteenth century was the composer Samuel Coleridge-Taylor (not to be confused with the Romantic poet Samuel Taylor Coleridge, after whom this Samuel was probably named). Known as the 'black Mahler', Coleridge, as people generally called him, was both critically celebrated and commercially successful. His cantata, 'Hiawatha's Wedding Feast', was performed throughout Britain by amateur and professional music groups alike. America loved him too: he visited the country several times and in 1904 was received at the White House by President Roosevelt.

After his death at just thirty-seven (Coleridge collapsed from pneumonia, brought on by overwork, at West Croydon station while waiting for a train), the three-mile funeral procession through his home town of Croydon drew enormous crowds. A wreath in the shape of Africa was sent by the 'sons and daughters of West Africa resident in London', a nod to Coleridge's interest in black politics.

Coleridge's zenith as a composer was also, paradoxically, the zenith of British imperialism. But while racism does not seem to have directly impeded his career – Coleridge's ascent to the highest echelons of the late-Victorian classical music world was swift and frictionless, helped by endorsements from fellow composers such as Edward Elgar – it certainly impeded other aspects of his life. The daily micro-aggressions (as we would now think of them) that he was obliged to endure were noted and deflected by Jessie Walmisley, the ballsy-sounding white woman who defied her family's prejudice to become his wife. More of her later.

Coleridge's spiritual home was Sierra Leone, though he never visited the country. It was, however, where his black father was from and was known for its European-style educational and political infrastructure, a legacy of its status as one of Britain's oldest imperial territories and the long, brutal, exploitative tradition of mostly forced sexual contact between Africans and Europeans, which gave rise to the Creole identity. Middle-class Sierra Leoneans (to frame them in Eurocentric terms) often sent their children to Britain to be educated. 'For those aspiring to become doctors and lawyers it was essential to have British qualifications,' writes Jeffrey Green. 'There had been Sierra Leonean medical students in Britain from the mid nineteenth century.'[35] Coleridge's father, Daniel Peter Hughes Taylor, qualified in London in 1874 but returned to Sierra Leone before his son's birth in August 1875, probably unaware that he was about to become a parent. Coleridge and his white English mother, Alice Hare Martin, moved to Croydon, where Coleridge was raised alongside three white half-siblings, the products of his mother's subsequent relationship with his railway-worker stepfather, George Evans.

Despite being illegitimate, Coleridge enjoyed a fairly stable middle-class upbringing. He received violin lessons from a local orchestral musician and sang in the choir at his local church. In 1890 he won a scholarship to the Royal College of Music, initially as a violinist before changing to study composition with the composer Sir Charles Villiers Stanford. Under Stanford's tutelage, he won the Lesley Alexander composition prize two years running.

Between 1898 and 1900, Coleridge was probably Britain's most successful composer. A commission from the Three Choirs Festival – the result of a recommendation from Edward Elgar, who described him as 'the cleverest fellow going amongst the young men' – led to another commission to write a cantata for a choral society. For this Coleridge produced 'Hiawatha's Wedding Feast', the first part of his trilogy *The Song of Haiwatha*, which was based on the American writer Henry Wadsworth Longfellow's Native American-themed epic poem *Hiawatha*. The piece met with acclaim while it was still a work in progress. Novello & Co published the score before it had even been performed and an early performance at the Royal College of Music was attended by the composer Sir Arthur Sullivan, among other luminaries. Sullivan was in poor health on the day, but told Coleridge: 'I'm always an ill man now, my boy, but I'm coming to hear your music tonight even if I have to be carried.'[36]

If Coleridge's status within the elite world of classical music was assured, however, it did not impress the family of his girlfriend, Jessie, who at thirty was six years older than her beau. One of six daughters, Jessie was a social class above Coleridge – her father a banker, her school the smart-sounding Eden House Young Ladies School in Kent. Jessie first noticed Samuel sitting by himself at West Croydon station. They did not speak – 'We never spoke in those days, nor even nodded to each other, both being truly English with the traditional stoic reserve'[37] – but she saw that he, like her, was reading *Musical News*. In the summer of 1892, when Coleridge was seventeen, Jessie was tasked with studying some Schubert duets for violin and piano. Knowing that Samuel was a decent violinist, she asked him to accompany her. The relationship blossomed slowly as the pair worked together. 'The practices which followed this incident were, I suppose, the "beginning of the end",' she wrote later, 'as finding that we worked together successfully, Coleridge-Taylor would ask me to accompany him here or there, and frequently the morning's post would bring me a microscopically written manuscript song, with a request that I would sing it through with him at a certain hour that same afternoon.' Coleridge's evident superiority as a musician gave him an advantage. As Jessie admitted: 'He was a Scholar and I a Student (a distinction with a difference).'[38]

Over time, Jessie's father would grow fond of Coleridge. Initially, however, both her parents were dead set against the relationship and, Jessie wrote, 'my feelings were outraged when measures were adopted to separate us (outside influence was tried), vile suggestions were made to me, and horrid threats hurled right and left'.[39] When Coleridge visited Jessie's father to ask his permission to marry her he was, he told Jessie later, 'kicked out of the house' by Jessie's ill-tempered brother-in-law, a man called Robert Murton. 'Figuratively speaking, I suppose you mean?' asked Jessie. 'No, literally . . .' Coleridge replied. Jessie was indignant at the way Murton had been 'the spokesman throughout the interview' and considered it 'most unfair that Coleridge should have to face two men that evening, especially when one had such prejudiced feelings on the subject of mixed marriages, having passed so much of his life in the East'.[40]

Jessie's parents refused to meet Coleridge again until the day before the wedding ceremony, when finally Jessie's mother invited Coleridge to the family home just outside Croydon. She and her husband shook his hand to show their grudging acceptance of their daughter's fate.

Coleridge and Jessie were married at 11 a.m. on 30 December 1899. They honeymooned for two weeks, during which time Samuel worked on the third part of his *Hiawatha* trilogy. This was typical behaviour, Jessie noting that Coleridge's 'love-making was taken with a big dose of work'.[41] Often, however, they were able to work together. Jessie's musical education meant she could help him revise and correct scores. She admits that the two of them were 'matter-of-fact' rather than intensely romantic lovers: 'I always appreciated the fact that in talking of our future he confided in me that "music was his first love".'[42]

In her memoir, Jessie remembers Coleridge as modest, and shy and uncomfortable in some social situations. It is clear to what she is referring when she writes that he was often 'made sensitive by the careless, thoughtless irreverent people amongst whom he was obliged to live; often those same people received endless joy and satisfaction from listening to or performing his beautiful music'.[43] Jessie made it her mission to stand up to this racism. 'Well do I remember passing,' she said, 'two silk-hatted "toffs" going to the theatre as we were returning home from an afternoon concert, deliberately insulting us, and how I with a palpitating heart and sick with rage, darted from my husband's side in front of them, stopped them and said, "Take back what you said and apologise." When I rejoined Coleridge his remark was, "Where did you go so suddenly?" to which I replied, "I knocked some sense into two silly heads."'[44]

Sadly, this is far from the only recorded instance of racism experienced by the composer. His daughter remembered his response when confronted by a gang of local youths as he was walking down the street: 'When he saw them approaching . . . he held my hand more tightly, gripping it until it almost hurt.'[45]

One day, a distinguished canon of the Church of England came for tea at their house. Gazing at Coleridge, the canon leaned across and said: 'It really is surprising; you eat like we do, dress like we do and talk as we do.' Coleridge was, Jessie recalls, 'too flabbergasted to make any reply'.[46] On another occasion, when someone expressed to Jessie his view that black people 'make excellent servants and are most trustworthy', she exploded and said: 'What about all the talented men and women of colour; would you train them as servants, and try to suppress their ideals?'[47] When the man realised who Jessie's husband was, he tried to backtrack, saying: 'Coleridge-Taylor, oh! But he's a household word.' 'Perhaps so,' Jessie replied, 'but one of your black men, who make such excellent servants.'[48]

In the light of such treatment, Coleridge's interest in racial politics shouldn't come as a big surprise. He frequently drew on African and African American culture in his work – for example his *Twenty-Four Negro Melodies*, in whose preface he wrote: 'What Brahms has done for the Hungarian folk music, Dvorak for the Bohemian, and Grieg for the Norwegian, I have tried to do for these Negro melodies.' Inspired by the work of the African American sociologist and historian W. E. B. Du Bois, Coleridge attended the first Pan-African conference in London in 1900 and became part of a loose circle of black activists. As the historian Mike Phillips puts it eloquently: 'The manner and the style of [Coleridge's] talent drew on his ambiguous and difficult origins, without shutting him off from the currents of his time and place. He became, against the odds, part of his culture's tradition, while openly declaring the mixture – foreign and domestic – of elements and ideas which moved him, and it is his ability to flourish in between cultures and to base himself within the junction of different platforms which gives his persona, and his music, the power to speak to our times.'[49]

It was not normal practice in those days to receive royalties from music sales. For the first part of *Hiawatha*, Coleridge had been paid a flat fee of £25 15s by his publisher Novello which did not reflect the work's huge sheet-music sales. (Elgar lost out similarly with the mega-selling 'Land of Hope and Glory'.) He received £250 for the two sequels, but subsequent pieces sold for less money, which meant he had to work hard to maintain the life to which he (or perhaps Jessie) had grown accustomed. Between 1898 and 1907 he was chief conductor of the Croydon Symphony Orchestra and resident conductor at the Westmoreland Festival, as well as the Rochester Choral Society. In 1904 he became chief conductor to the Handel Society concerts. He also served as guest conductor for numerous performances of *Hiawatha* and lectured at Trinity College of Music, Crystal Palace School of Art and Music, and then the Guildhall School of Music, where he was professor of composition. On top of this he acted as an adjudicator at various festivals and competitions, including the National Eisteddfod of Wales in 1900. No wonder he was exhausted so much of the time.

I wrote earlier that stories can be inspiring and truthful without necessarily being the stories you want them to be: it is always better to err on the side of nuance, even if that involves tarnishing a person's halo. For all that Coleridge and Jessie were a trailblazing couple, it does sound as if there were three people in the marriage. An old friend remembered Coleridge saying: 'I have been very happy in my surroundings all my life, first in my mother and then in my marriage.'

'First in my *mother*'? Even Jessie acknowledged his 'deep love for his mother' which she called 'a wonderful example of devotion'.[50] There are other cracks in the golden bowl, too. Coleridge's half-sister Marjorie once said: 'Jessie had a short temper, you know, and that made Coleridge more inclined to come to see mother whenever possible. I think he was sure of a cup of tea and a biscuit at our home. They had servants, but I'm afraid that Jessie was not very kind to them and they would leave.'[51] (Gwendolen – Coleridge and Jessie's daughter – later changed her name to Avril and wrote a book attacking her mother who, she claimed, 'not only set [Coleridge] on a pedestal, but climbed up, as it were, to sit close beside him as his widow'.[52])

Shortly before he died, propped up by pillows, Coleridge raised both arms and began conducting an imaginary orchestra. One of the nurses tried to lower his arms, but Jessie intervened, saying: 'Please don't, he is doing what he loves best in all the world.'[53]

After Coleridge's death, a memorial concert raised £1,440 for the family, who were perceived to have been left in need. The Guildhall School of Music arranged bursaries for his children, both of whom became professional musicians, while Jessie received a Civil List pension of £100 a year 'in recognition of the eminence as a composer of her late husband'. Widespread indignation that Jessie and her children had not been left financially secure despite Coleridge's success was a catalyst in the formation in 1914 of the Performing Right Society (PRS), which oversees composers' rights and royalties. Thanks to the PRS, the family did at least benefit from the annual stagings of *Hiawatha* at the Royal Albert Hall between the wars.

Coleridge and Jessie's marriage is up there with other interracial relationships that pushed the story forward, encouraging tolerance and destroying negative stereotypes on both sides. One thinks of Mildred and Richard Loving, a black woman and a white man who in 1958 defied their home state of Virginia's Racial Integrity Act by travelling to Washington DC to get married, only to be arrested when they returned. A lengthy court case resulted in the Supreme Court ruling in June 1967 that the laws prohibiting inter-racial marriage were unconstitutional.

The Lovings' story was made into a powerful film. Ditto that of Ruth Williams Khama and Sir Seretse Khama. Ruth, who was white, was working as a clerk at Lloyd's of London when in June 1947 she met her future husband – no ordinary Oxford-educated law student but the son of Sekgoma II, paramount chief of Botswana's Bamangwato people. Their marriage, so soon after the introduction of apartheid in South Africa, caused a scandal as it was opposed both by tribal elders and the British government, who tried to stop it. The couple were forced to live in exile in Croydon for five years, returning to Botswana only when the Bamangwato lobbied Queen Elizabeth II on their behalf. After a spell working as a cattle farmer, Sir Seretse went on to become the country's first president in 1966.

————

And so love between couples becomes a force for social change. The more unconventional the couple, the more momentous the change, until everyone forgets what the old rules were. It isn't very long since lesbian couple Celia Kitzinger and Sue Wilkinson, both academics, sued for recognition of their marriage, which had been conducted in Vancouver in 2003. They were enraged to discover, upon returning to the UK, that it had no legal status in the country and believed the civil partnership they were offered instead to be practically and symbolically inferior. 'This is fundamentally about equality,' they explained. 'We want our marriage to be recognised as a marriage – just like any other marriage made in Canada . . . Civil partnerships are an important step forward for same-sex couples, but they are not enough. We want full equality in marriage.'[54]

Sadly, they did not get it – not in 2005, at any rate. In handing down his ruling the President of the Family Division for England and Wales, Sir Mark Potter, rejected the notion that civil partnerships were inferior to marriage and claimed marriage was by 'longstanding definition and acceptance' a relationship between a man and a woman. Eight years later, the Marriage (Same Sex Couples) Act of 2013 blew this idea out of the water.

This Act, it's easy to forget, was the work of the Conservative–Liberal Democrat coalition government of 2010. But it wouldn't have happened without people like Celia and Sue helping to change the broader culture and bring the issues out into the open so that more politicians could admit to sharing the conviction of then-Equalities minister, Lynne Featherstone, the architect of the legislation, that 'what was needed was marriage – and full marriage, exactly the same as the non-gay community knew it. And it wasn't just desirable, but a right.'[55]

Nor has much time elapsed since Barrie and Tony Drewitt-Barlow became the first gay couple in Britain to become fathers. Their twins, Aspen and Saffron, born in December 1999, were the first babies from Europe to have both dads on their birth certificates. Barrie and Tony, who first met in 1987 in Manchester, used an American egg donor and surrogate. Commercial surrogacy is ethically fraught and remains illegal in the UK, but broader societal attitudes to gay men raising children have changed beyond measure as a result of people like the Drewitt-Barlows. As they explain on their website: 'In those days, gay men didn't have children. In fact, the thought of a gay man with a child made everyone involved think that there was something funny going on.'[56]

Trans couples in the UK do not have an easy time of it. But the situation is worse in India where, despite an estimated trans population of several million and recent legislation to extend minority rights, it is common for trans people to live as outcasts.

Aarav Appukuttan met his future partner in 2014 at the Mumbai hospital where he had gone for gender reassignment. Sukanyeah Krishna was there for the same reason. Aarav was transitioning from female to male, Sukanyeah from male to female. Sukanyeah remembers the moment she first met Aarav – she had just finished speaking to a relative on the phone, updating them about the surgery, when she overheard Aarav also talking on the phone in the same language. After Aarav had finished his call, he walked over and asked Sukanyeah if she too was from the south Indian state of Kerala. She told him she was and the pair chatted non-stop for the next three hours. Both had felt strongly since child-hood that they were in the wrong body but initially met with resistance from their families, Sukanyeah remembering the way she was told to wear boys' clothes and play with boys: 'I would always ask them why they treated me like a boy even though I felt like a girl on the inside.'

From that point on, they were inseparable as friends – and a huge support to each other as they went through their gruelling, expensive surgeries. But then friendship turned into something else and they became proud to call them-selves 'India's first complete transgender couple'. When Aarav proposed, he was nervous about the significant differ-ence in their ages – he was forty-six, Sukanyeah twenty-two – and so relieved when Sukanyeah accepted. I loved reading about their story but sadly, from what I gather, the wedding did not in the end take place and Aarav and Sukanyeah are no longer together. I was sorry to hear this and hope they are both happy, wherever they are.

In 2008 the writer and historian Jan Morris and her long-term partner Elizabeth Tuckniss went through a civil ceremony. The twist was that they had been formerly conjoined before – in marriage – way back in 1949 when Jan, then called James, was an undergraduate studying English at Christ Church college, Oxford University. After Jan's sex change in 1972 – she famously travelled to Morocco for surgery – the couple were obliged to divorce because British law did not allow same-sex marriages. In fact, they continued to live together. The quiet, private civil ceremony, held in Pwllheli in Wales on 14 May, was as much a matter of personal satis-faction and tying up loose ends as anything else.

James had been a master of the macho world, ceaselessly impressed by what his masculine body could do for him, as when he joined the British expedition to Everest in 1953. He was twenty-six at the time and tingling with strength and energy; except he did not want that strength and energy because it came courtesy of a body he hated.

Jan's relationship with Elizabeth was at the heart of her new identity. You could even say that her love was the crucible in which it was forged. Jan's remarkable 1974 memoir of her gender change, *Conundrum*, is compellingly honest about the degree of accommodation they had to make as a couple so that their life together could continue happily.

James had always felt that he was in the wrong body. This tormenting anxiety worsened in his thirties as his sense of isolation from the world became more pronounced. He developed depression and suffered terrible headaches; he hated the male world and the strain of inhabiting it. His experience of being a foreign correspondent for an esteemed but establishment newspaper, *The Times*, underlined the difference in roles within the old-fashioned, gendered coupledom of the 1950s and '60s. James would pass, she wrote as Jan, from the 'ludicrous goings-on of minister's office or ambassador's study' into the private house behind where 'women were to be found doing real things' and came to feel that 'the private part of any life was the only part that mattered'. (She admits this is simplistic. The world was different in 1974 and now, more than then, we feel compelled to ask: what is stopping men doing some of those 'real things' too?)

During treatment, as James's body became Jan's, her relationship with Elizabeth 'lost its last elements of physical contact'.[57] As it did so, however, the relationship became more lucid. Elizabeth viewed Jan's fluctuating moods philosophically, knowing that they would reconcile themselves one day, and encouraged her to view the process of shedding her male role while gradually adopting a female one as an experience to be valued in itself.

This was not easy, writes Jan, for it meant that the pair 'had to devise a new overt relationship. We could not easily be sisters, for she was Mrs Morris, I was Miss. We did not wish to be merely friends, for that would deny me any kinship with my children. So we settled for sisters-in-law, the nearest to the truth that we could devise.' Jan became to their children 'a kind of adoring if interfering aunt' and a relative 'linked neither by blood nor carnality' to Elizabeth.[58]

In 1972, after preparatory hormone treatment, Jan made the decision to have full surgery. Elizabeth did not accompany him (as she then was) to the clinic in Casablanca to which Jan had been lured by the surgeon's reputation. This seems surprising to me, but Jan writes that contact with the world outside was not encouraged. Perhaps it was something she needed to go through alone, after all.

In any case, when it was all over Elizabeth welcomed Jan home 'as though nothing in particular had happened': a function of her 'fathomless understanding' of Jan's need to undergo the procedure. Jan feels closer to Elizabeth in the crucial sense that she is able to experience the casual (and less casual) sexism that Elizabeth has experienced all these years: 'The very tone of voice in which I was now addressed, the very posture of the person next in the queue, the very feel in the air when I entered a room or sat at a restaurant table, constantly emphasised my change of status.'[59] The person who had skipped down Everest to break the news of Sir Edmund Hillary's ascent to the summit was suddenly assumed to be incompetent at reversing cars and opening bottles of wine. Jan discovers the dark truth that men prefer women to be 'less informed, less able, less talkative and certainly less self-centred than they are themselves'. Elizabeth 'professed it only a relief to be in my true company at last'.[60]

Elizabeth's voice is silent in *Conundrum*. She hovers on the margins, just out of focus. But it is clear her rightful position is at the centre of the story. 'Though Elizabeth and I are divorced,' Jan wrote back in 1972, 'we are locked in our friendship more absolutely than ever, and unless some blinding passion intervenes with one or the other of us, propose to share our lives happily ever after.'[61] That they found the ability to stay together meant the children never had to witness the collapse of love or desertion or rancour. Instead, they saw 'a troubled soul achieving serenity'.[62]

'I made my marriage vows 59 years ago and still have them,' said Elizabeth in a recent interview to celebrate the couple's civil union. 'We are back together again officially. After Jan had a sex change we had to divorce. So there we were. It did not make any difference to me. We still had our family. We just carried on.'[63]

Jan and Elizabeth are in their nineties now, but they are still together; still living in Wales not far from where Jan's father grew up – what her author blurb calls 'the top left-hand corner of Wales, between the mountains and the sea'. They have specified that when they die they want their headstone to say in both Welsh and English: 'Here are two friends, at the end of one life.'

The Lambs would, you feel, understand completely.

7

Power

We all have a pretty good idea of what a 'power couple' is. According to the most conventional reading, it is two people, usually rich and famous, who present themselves as a duo on the public stage and have a power to influence that is part and parcel of their duo-ness. One partner's power reinforces and amplifies that of the other, but (crucial caveat) only as long as they remain together: they are greater than the sum of their two parts.

The phrase is more often used to describe couples from the world of entertainment than from, say, business or politics. We already met Elizabeth Taylor and Richard Burton. Drawing only from the deep well of Hollywood's Golden Age, I could equally have written about Frank Sinatra and Ava Gardner; or Frank Sinatra and Mia Farrow; or Marilyn Monroe and Joe DiMaggio; or Robert Wagner and Natalie Wood – relationships that all came with a side order of drama and intrigue and, in the case of Wagner and Wood, untimely and mysterious death. So that must be factored in too. 'Power' in this context includes the power to fascinate.

For Mary Abbott, author of a whole book on the subject (*Power Couples*), the main criterion is equality of wattage.

Power behind the throne does not count: farewell, Lady Macbeth. Both halves of the couple must be 'big beasts' and their power must be sustained rather than momentary: 'Those "temporary lions" whose noisy matings and decouplings provide us with so much entertainment do not qualify,' she writes.[1]

One sure sign of a mated beast is the portmanteau appellation, usually bestowed by the media, which designates a 'blended' celebrity couple, for example Tomkat (Tom Cruise and Katie Holmes), Bennifer (Ben Affleck and Jennifer Lopez, then Jennifer Garner) and Brangelina (Brad Pitt and Angelina Jolie). Another recent book about celebrity power couples, the collection of scholarly essays *First Comes Love*, suggests this habit began earlier than we might think: the Beverly Hills mansion of Douglas Fairbanks and Mary Pickford was nicknamed 'Pickfair' by the press way back in 1919.

The ubiquity of the celebrity power couple feels like a modern phenomenon. But of course it isn't. The paradigm was set at least as early as the French revolution – Louis XVI and Marie Antoinette, anyone? And it was refined not just by Hollywood stars but also writers such as F. Scott and Zelda Fitzgerald, who married within less than a week of Fairbanks and Pickford in 1920 and occupied a similar amount of space in the gossip columns of the period. Zelda knew, Sarah Churchwell points out in her chapter in *First Comes Love*, that one of the things people envied about them was their union. They kept scrapbooks of newspaper cuttings about themselves, and in 1932 Scott wrote a story called 'What A Handsome Pair!' about a young couple who 'thought of themselves as a team, and it was often remarked how well mated they were. A chorus of pleasant envy followed in the wake of their effortless glamour.'[2] Of course, the reality was that Scott and Zelda's lives were not enviable at all, but blighted by alcoholism and mental illness. And Zelda acknowledged that it was all an act, that they were both merely brilliant 'showmen'.[3]

The concept of a married power couple sitting at the head of government actually dates back to Ptolemaic Egypt. A coin from the period shows 'jugate' (side by side) portraits of Ptolemy I and Berenice I, with those of their children on the other side to illustrate the line of succession and promote them as a duo. However, the man's head in these portraits is closer to the viewer, dominating the image; the female is behind, projecting forward so that her features can be seen in silhouette. As Egyptologist Dee Clayman explains: 'Though the images suggest joint rule, the male is dominant, and this was certainly the case in the context of governing.'[4]

Spain's fifteenth-century monarchs Ferdinand and Isabella were one of the most famous power couples in European history. Together they transformed Spain, uniting the disparate dominions to create a blueprint for the modern country we know today. After falsifying the papal dispensation they needed in order to marry (they were second cousins) when Pope Pius II refused to provide it, Ferdinand wed Isabella on 18 October 1469, uniting the kingdoms of Aragon and Castile. They resolved to rule as equals, an extraordinary undertaking at a time when female rulers were almost unheard of. Their royal motto, *Tanto monta* – 'as much one as the other' – signified this collaborative spirit.

Ferdinand and Isabella's best-remembered achievement is probably the sponsoring of Christopher Columbus on his expedition across the Atlantic. But we also remember them for their extreme dislike of both Muslims and Jews. At this time much of the Iberian peninsula had been ruled for over 700 years by Muslims. Fanatical Catholics, Ferdinand and Isabella determined to drive out the Moors once and for all and waged a war against the Moorish city of Granada, finally expelling the caliphate in 1492. Jews were cast out of Spain at around the same time. The duo's notorious Inquisition was designed to catch out *conversos*, Muslims and Jews who had hurriedly converted to Catholicism in a bid to save their skins. The letter of commission granting the Inquisition's enforcers the power 'to carry out inquiries into bad Christians' is signed 'I, the King; I, the Queen'. Double trouble.

In terms of formal governance, we obviously do not have married power couples running the show. But presidents' and prime ministers' wives have traditionally had considerable soft power and been crucial determinants of an administration's success. American historian Robert Watson cites Abigail Adams, Sarah Polk, Helen Taft, Florence Harding and Nancy Reagan as examples of First Ladies who were 'full political partners who appeared to function as their husbands' most trusted advisers on major political decisions and issues'.[5] This influence could extend to PR decisions too. It was Julia Tyler, wife of the tenth US President John Tyler, who in 1844 instructed the Marine Band to play the song 'Hail to the Chief' whenever her husband made a public appearance – a tradition that continues to this day.

Abigail Adams kept husband John up to speed on political events while he was away, in a series of trenchant letters which never shied from exerting political influence. In one dated 31 March 1776, she writes to John in Philadelphia, urging him and other members of the Continental Congress to keep the rights of women in mind in the fight for American independence from Britain: 'I long to hear that you have declared an independency. And, by the way, in the new code of laws which I suppose it will be necessary for you to make, I desire you would remember the ladies and be more generous and favorable to them than your ancestors. Do not put such unlimited power into the hands of the husbands. Remember, all men would be tyrants if they could.'[6]

In public, it has mostly been the sorry lot of political wives to smile and wave and not bang on about their own careers in a way that might be distracting. This was particularly painful for high-powered women such as Cherie Blair and Nick Clegg's wife Miriam González Durántez, lawyers both, whose professional identities were compromised by the widespread assumption that they should drop everything and rush to support their husbands' causes.

Of course, 'political husbands' exist too, but not in the same number, as you would expect. One example would be Philip May, who was seen as an important influence on his prime minister wife Theresa and took a step back from his job as a banker to support her. Asked what it was like being married to a prime minister, he replied: 'If you're the kind of man who expects his tea to be on the table at six o'clock every evening, you could be a disappointed man.'[7]

One man who definitely does not expect this is Clarke Gayford, TV presenter partner of New Zealand's prime minister Jacinda Ardern and technically the country's 'First Man'. Their relationship strikes me as more balanced and progressive. After all, he already had a public profile when he met Ardern. Still, there are compromises to be made.

'It sounds strange but I cannot pick up the phone and ring my partner, she's just that busy,' he admitted to one radio show. 'Some days her schedule is 15 minute blocks, with meetings in that, so it's very, very difficult just to have that communication going . . . Remember when you're growing up and that whole saying, "Who do you think you are, the Prime Minister or something?" It doesn't work in our house.'[8]

A candidate's partner matters to the public because he or she is held to be a reflection of that candidate's 'true' personality, if not an extension of it. As the historian Charlotte Lydia Riley has written: 'We don't vote based only on a candidate's practical skills or professional attributes, but also how we feel about them as a person and what we believe to be their values. And our roles in domestic spaces are part of our politics: as second-wave feminists always maintained, the personal is political. The reason partners and children work on us as an electorate is because the people that we choose to make our lives with show something about who we are ourselves.' She cites the example of 'men whose feminist partners earn them a free pass even when they behave poorly'.[9] We'll explore Bill and Hillary Clinton in a moment. But first, where would philandering John F. Kennedy have been without resolute, centred Jackie? (Not that Jackie was a feminist exactly – at least not at the beginning: 'I think women should never be in politics,' she once said. 'We're just not suited for it.'[10])

The couple's initial meeting in 1952, over chicken casserole at a Georgetown dinner party, was inauspicious. John – usually called Jack – was a congressman from Massachusetts, campaigning to be senator. Jacqueline Bouvier was a journalist working for the *Washington Times-Herald*. After dinner, the guests played charades; then Jack asked Jackie if she wanted to go out for a drink. 'Perhaps some other time?' she suggested.

Of course, there was another time. They married on 12 September 1953. From the start it was a marriage defined not just by adversity – a miscarriage; a stillborn daughter and a son who lived only briefly; Jack's incapacitating illnesses and compulsive infidelity – but by Jackie's unwillingness to perform a traditional, submissive, housewifely role. By turbo-charging Jack's success – lending him a 'society' sheen by virtue of her mother's second marriage to wealthy stockbroker Hugh Auchincloss; choosing his wardrobe; writing a campaign diary for a newspaper, etc. – she was able to promote herself too. On the campaign trail for Jack's re-election to the Senate in 1958, it was noticed that the size of the crowd was twice as big when Jackie accompanied him. When he was president, Jackie professionalised the role of First Lady. She reinvented herself as a trendsetter, remodelling the White House, hiring Oleg Cassini to design her wardrobe and a press secretary, Pamela Turnure, to manage her contact with the media. She used the White House to showcase the arts, inviting ballet and opera stars to perform in the East Room.

Intriguingly, observers noted a chilly formality to the Kennedys as a professional couple. Jack hated being touched (except during sex) and all public displays of affection. 'He would never hold hands in public,' Jackie admitted, 'or put his arms around me – that was naturally just distasteful to him.'[11] Both Jack and Jackie were independent and self-contained, their power partly consisting in the success with which they lived parallel lives. Their friend, Chuck Spalding, described them both as 'isolated' and 'alone' and believed these were qualities they recognised and responded to in each other.[12]

After Jack's assassination, despite her numerous other relationships and achievements, Jackie was fixed in the public imagination as the tragic widow cradling her first husband's shattered head in her arms. Her subsequent marriage to the shipping magnate Aristotle Onassis was seen as a betrayal – a wilful dilution, even negation, of what had come before.

Just as JFK makes more sense when seen through the prism of his iconic wife, Jack's presidential predecessor Franklin D. Roosevelt is best understood in the context of his marriage to his distant cousin Eleanor – and vice versa. The initial triad structure within the Roosevelt household (Franklin, Eleanor, Franklin's overbearing mother Sara) gradually gave way to a dyad structure (Franklin and Eleanor) after Franklin developed a paralytic illness in 1921 and needed Eleanor to campaign on his behalf. This, along with the discovery that Franklin had been having an affair with his secretary, Lucy Mercer, catalysed Eleanor's long-standing but suppressed interest in social activism.

One of America's most loved First Ladies, Eleanor did not properly fulfil her destiny as an activist and communicator until after her husband's death. But that destiny was shaped by what she experienced during her time as a political wife. In the early days of their marriage, duty was the motivating force in Eleanor's life. As she wrote in her autobiography: 'I looked at everything from the point of view of what I ought to do, rarely from the standpoint of what I wanted to do.'[13] She first became interested in politics because that was Franklin's interest: in those days she 'took it for granted that men were superior creatures'.[14] That didn't last long. What fascinates historians now is the loose, flexible nature of the Roosevelts' union – not quite an open marriage, but getting there. They were a couple and yet more than a couple.

Though Eleanor radiated modesty in her writing, it's clear that Franklin depended on her utterly and relied on her wise counsel. The economist Rexford Tugwell, a member of Franklin's so-called Brain Trust of advisers, noted: 'No one who ever saw Eleanor Roosevelt sit down facing her husband, holding his eyes firmly and saying to him, "Franklin, I think you should . . .", "Franklin, surely you will not . . ." will ever forget the experience. It would be impossible to say how often and to what extent American government processes have been turned in a new direction because of her determination.'[15]

After Franklin's death in 1945, Eleanor's activism shifted up several gears. She helped oversee the drafting of the Universal Declaration of Human Rights, chaired the first Presidential Commission on the Status of Women and sat on the board of the National Association for the Advancement of Colored People. She used her late husband's legacy as a springboard for future progressive achievements.

Of course, there was more to the power couple than met the public eye. Franklin's affairs and Eleanor's close friendships (for which read probable affairs) with her bodyguard Earl Miller and the journalist Lorena Hickok were not widely known about at the time. To a deferential press, the personal was not necessarily judged to be political.

The same cannot be said for Bill and Hillary Clinton, still widely considered to be the most powerful couple in the modern American political era.

Hillary's 2003 memoir *Living History* is revealing about the concessions and compromises she had to make when she sacrificed her career to become First Lady in January 1993. 'I supported [Bill's] agenda and worked hard to translate his vision into actions that improved people's lives, strengthened our sense of community and furthered our democratic values at home and around the world,' she writes. Then the pronoun changes, tellingly – 'Throughout Bill's tenure, we encountered political opposition, legal challenges and personal tragedies, and we made our fair share of mistakes' – before returning to the first person again: 'I became a lightning rod for political and ideological battles waged over America's future and a magnet for feelings, good and bad, about women's choices and roles.'[16]

Bill Clinton and Hillary Rodham met in 1971 in the Yale Law Library. A class year ahead of him, Hillary had started at Yale in the autumn of 1969 – one of only 27 women out of 235 students to matriculate. In *Living History*, Hillary describes Bill repeatedly as a force of nature who needs to be tamed. He looked, she wrote, 'more like a Viking than a Rhodes Scholar' after returning from Oxford in 1970 with a 'vitality that seemed to shoot out of his pores'.[17] On their first date, Bill used his charm and charisma to get them in to see a Mark Rothko exhibition in a closed gallery by offering to pick up litter that had accumulated in the gallery's courtyard: 'Watching him talk our way in was the first time I saw his persuasiveness in action.'[18]

The sense that Bill was predestined to be president gained ground. And Hillary's role evolved into feeding that sense of destiny, promoting the idea of Bill as a special person marked out by fate. She was aware, though, that their partnership might become unbalanced, that Bill's strength and certainty could overwhelm her. This is why, when Bill proposed marriage on the shore of Lake

Ennerdale during a trip to the UK, Hillary said no, she needed more time.

Coupledom for Hillary meant putting herself – her legal career, her own political interests and ambitions – at the service of Bill's ambition. But these were difficult times. There weren't many models for the kind of couple the Clintons wished to be.

Hillary's mixed fortune, writes William H. Chafe in his book *Bill and Hillary: The Politics of the Personal*, was to be a repository of almost all the attributes Bill most needed in a partner. These were, he says, 'strength of character, discipline of personality, moral direction, and the poise of a self-certain political actor'.[19]

Hillary's recent admission that staying in her marriage was the 'gutsiest' thing she has done in her personal life, raised eyebrows.[20] However infuriated and embarrassed she was by her husband's affairs, most famously the one with Monica Lewinsky, few close to the couple believe she would ever actually have left him. 'You have to remember that they are each other's closest adviser,' Carl Bernstein once noted. 'Each regards the other as the brightest star in his or her universe and despite all that's happened, nothing has changed that basic view over the years.'[21]

The problems that afflict power couples in politics do not bypass their counterparts in the parallel world of entertainment. Politics isn't far removed from showbiz: it's 'showbiz for ugly people' as the cruel old saying goes.

And as we've already seen, when those couples are linked creatively as well as romantically, slightly different rules apply. In this instance, far from being handicaps, problems within relationships can be converted into art, or music, or film, or at the very least spectacle. For showbiz couples, emphasising the imperfect nature of their union can be good box office. It collapses the distance between them and their audience: their problems reflect their audience's problems. If the downside is that this feeds an unhealthy voyeuristic impulse, the upside can be a genuine increase in empathy and understanding on the audience's part. Theoretically, anyway.

Take the superstar music couple Beyoncé and Jay-Z. They have been romantically linked since the late 1990s and first pooled their musical talents in 2003 on the track '03 Bonny & Clyde'. They married in 2008 and for the next five years or so succeeded for the most part in promoting themselves as a stable, loving couple. But then, in 2014, *TMZ* released footage of a fight that broke out in an elevator at that year's Met Gala between Jay-Z and Beyoncé's younger sister Solange. Whatever the fight was about – and the internet nearly broke under the weight of conspiracy theories – it focused attention on the couple, encouraging speculation that they might be about to divorce.

After the elevator incident, both Beyoncé and Jay-Z started to address their relationship in their work with increasing frequency. The release of Beyoncé's album *Lemonade* in April 2016 triggered a worldwide quest for the identity of 'Becky with the good hair' (allegedly the fashion designer Rachel Roy), while Jay-Z's 2017 album *4:44* was widely seen as a response.

In 2018 the pair released a joint album, *Everything Is Love*, under the name 'The Carters', Jay-Z's surname and so Beyoncé's married name: both a declaration of togetherness and a celebration of being at the apex of their imperial phase as pop stars. But making your art all about your relationship is not unproblematic, as Alexis Petridis pointed out in the *Guardian* at the time. In the context of both partners' preceding albums, which had addressed gossip about the marriage, *Everything Is Love* ran the risk of resembling 'a carefully premeditated plan to wring as much capital out of the couple's nuptial discord as possible. It doesn't take away from the musical contents of those preceding records, both artistic highlights in their respective makers' oeuvres. But it does make them look a little more obviously calculated, very clearly underlining that the whole business is as much an exercise in brand management as soul-baring artistry.'[22]

Is this calculation necessarily a bad thing, though? African American academics have embraced this aspect of the project, seeing *Lemonade* as what Oneka LaBennett has called an exercise in 'autoethnographic kinship formation' that uses representations of Beyoncé and her family to 'reimagine how black marriage, sexuality and kinship are popularly understood'.[23] For LaBennett, part of the point is that Beyoncé and Jay-Z are 'co-conspirators for whom love and marriage are both a generative artistic force and a vehicle for reflecting on the pressures and complexities of being a "power couple"'.[24]

As one of the world's biggest showbiz couples, Beyoncé and Jay-Z have enormous power to transform, reframe and educate. But being a pop or rap star has always involved a Faustian pact. You might acquire wealth and influence by tapping into a mass market, but the unrelenting exposure can be soul-destroying, even when you think you have a handle on it.

It was partly because of this, and the crippling expectation that followed their every move, that both John Lennon and Paul McCartney sought sanctuary in domestic and professional coupledom after the Beatles split in 1969 – John with artist Yoko Ono, Paul with photographer Linda Eastman.

For John, Yoko was an intellectual enabler. 'I decided to leave the group when I decided I could no longer artistically get anything out of The Beatles and here was someone [Yoko] that could turn me on to a million things,' he told *Rolling Stone*'s Jann Wenner in 1970.[25]

John and Yoko embraced peace activism and presented a united front against nostalgists who wanted the Beatles to re-form and racists who disliked Yoko for being Japanese. John's post-Beatles project, the Plastic Ono Band, was a joint venture with Yoko; several subsequent albums, including *Some Time In New York City* and *Double Fantasy*, are credited to 'John Lennon and Yoko Ono'. Similarly, Paul's post-Beatles album, *Ram*, is credited to 'Paul and Linda McCartney'. Paul insisted Linda be installed as keyboard player and backing vocalist in his band, Wings, despite her limited musical experience. He also aggravated his music publisher, with whom he was locked in a dispute, by insisting that seven of *Ram*'s fourteen tracks were 50–50 co-writes with Linda: 'If my wife is actually saying, "Change that" or "I like that better than that", then I'm using her as a collaborator.'

The main reason for this is that Paul wanted – in fact, needed – her around constantly. 'Linda saved me,' he said later. 'And it was all done in a sort of domestic setting.'[26] She was behind the couple's move to Paul's run-down farmhouse in Scotland where they lived as hippy millionaires, riding horses and growing their own vegetables. 'She was his security blanket, his inspiration, his wife and mother of his kids,' says Denny Seiwell, the drummer in Wings. 'She was the one who got Paul off his ass when he was having to sue the other Beatles. His heart was broken. He would've sat up there in Scotland and just become a drunk. If she hadn't got on his case, none of it would have ever happened.' Linda might not have been important musically, he admits: 'But she was more than an important element, she was a necessity.'[27]

When it comes to power couples, one size doesn't fit all. But for a power couple to function both halves must, in their own way, be necessities.

In terms of influence exerted and boundaries stretched, one of the most important duos is the surrealist artist Claude Cahun and their – I use the pronoun deliberately – partner Marcel Moore. Little discussed (because little seen) until the 1980s, their work is now regarded as way ahead of its time and an influence on subsequent artists and writers such as Cindy Sherman, Nan Goldin, Kathy Acker and Gillian Wearing, as well as pop stars like David Bowie, who featured it in an exhibition he curated in New York in 2007 and described Claude as 'really quite mad, in the nicest way'.[28]

Claude was born Lucy Schwob in Nantes, France, in 1894. She effaced this identity in the early 1920s, declaring: 'Under this mask, another mask. I will never be finished removing all these faces.'[29] Educated at the Sorbonne, Lucy changed her name so that it was gender-neutral and moved to Montparnasse in Paris in 1922. They (as she became) would spend the next sixteen years there, making art that questioned conventional notions of gender identity and performance alongside 'Marcel Moore', the pseudonym of their lover, lifelong partner and step-sibling, Suzanne Malherbe. (They had already been friends for eight years by the time Suzanne's widowed mother married Lucy's divorced father in 1917.)

Claude's achievements are manifold. For the pair's biographer, Gavin James Bower, Claude was the ultimate multihyphenate, 'a writer of poetry and prose, self-centred curator of tableaux, a skilled sketch artist, photographer and muse, a poseur, actress and performer, composer of objets d'art, propagandist and saboteur'.[30] On the face of it, Marcel seems like the junior partner in the relationship – a graphic artist who produced stylish illustrations for fashion magazines as well as avant-garde publishers and theatre companies. But Claude could not have been Claude without Marcel. The lovers collaborated on a variety of projects, including articles and novels, and held salons at their home. They used the phrase 'singular plural' to describe themselves and over the years it has become clear that the photographs attributed to Claude should be credited to Marcel as well. For example, a celebrated staged photographic 'self-portrait' from early on in their career shows Claude in a Medusa-like pose with strands of hair covering her face. Marcel was not simply the intended audience for this picture and others like it, where Claude is shown topless with pasted-on nipples, kiss curls embellishing her neatly slicked down hair. Marcel actually took the photos, as you can see from the way her shadow falls across their subject, and she does appear in some of them.

The couple's story took a curious turn after they moved to Jersey in 1937, little knowing that it would shortly be occupied by the Germans. In Paris they had been involved with the writer Georges Bataille's Contre-Attaque resistance group. In occupied Jersey, they put their artistic nous to political use once more as resistance fighters and propagandists, producing anti-German flyers and pamphlets made up of snippets of translated BBC reports on Nazi atrocities which they would scatter around German military events. For this they were arrested and sentenced to death in 1944.

Luckily, the island was liberated before the sentence could be carried out, but Claude never recovered from the effects of imprisonment and died prematurely in 1954.

In the course of researching my previous book about influential but underappreciated women, I came across several couples who I would call 'power couples' on the strength of their crusading zeal – their sense of shared political purpose or social ambitions. Take Esther Roper, for example, the daughter of a Manchester factory worker turned missionary, who formed a thirty-year partnership with the Anglo-Irish aristocrat Eva Gore Booth.

Esther and Eva became key figures in the political landscape of Victorian Lancashire, promoting the cause of female circus performers, pit girls, flower-sellers and barmaids. Little discussed today, they were close friends (for a time) of Christabel Pankhurst, though they were shaping the suffrage agenda long before they met her: laying the foundations for the work that she and others would do to secure the vote for women. They went on to become influential peace campaigners in the run-up to the First World War. Most intriguingly of all, they co-founded a radical magazine, *Urania*, whose ideas about gender and sexuality anticipate modern ones in startling ways.

Considered individually, Esther and Eva were remarkable. But something magical happened when they came together as a couple. They spurred each other on and helped to fight each other's battles. It was as if the romantic love they felt for each other – they were almost certainly lesbian – was too powerful to be contained by their private relationship.

It became the animating force behind their public achievements too, despite being something society obliged them to keep hidden.

Shared political beliefs also united Dora Russell with her husband, the philosopher Bertrand Russell, to challenge conventional ideas about education. The pair opened the progressive Beacon Hill school in September 1927 in the deliberately Edenic setting of Petersfield on the South Downs. Amid acres of woods and valleys, children would, Dora believed, learn in new and exciting ways: 'There was to be no corporal punishment; the children were free to come into the classroom and work and learn, or not to do so . . .'[31]

In many respects the experiment was not a resounding success. The kind of children it attracted turned out to be the ones who most needed set boundaries. Bertrand lost interest in the school after the collapse of his and Dora's marriage in 1930 and withdrew their children from it. Dora kept the school going in the face of considerable financial difficulties, finally closing it in 1943.

If it is Dora we remember today when considering the school's legacy, it is important to remember that this was not always the case. At the time and for some time afterwards, as the historian Deborah Gorham points out, Bertrand received the credit for a project that was mainly Dora's – 'the inevitable result of the imbalance of power between them'.[32] Gorham continues: 'Given the explicitly feminist, egalitarian public face of their marriage in the 1920s, Bertrand and Dora might appear to have shared the same status (Dora herself made the fatal mistake of believing this to be the case), but in fact Bertrand's fame, social position and gender always gave him far more weight than Dora would ever have. Gender, class and status inequalities meant that if the school was basically Dora's, it owed its importance to Bertrand.'[33]

Two social reform pioneers who made a longer-lasting impact were Beatrice and Sidney Webb, doyens of the British intellectual left between the wars who met in 1890 through the Fabian Society. Beatrice, who came from money, had developed a taste for the new science of sociology through helping her cousin Charles Booth research his monumental study, *Life and Labour of the People in London*. She stumbled across Sidney on the rebound from the politician Joseph Chamberlain. They struck observers as an odd, socially mismatched couple – she a handsome heiress, he the son of shopkeepers and physically unprepossessing to boot. Ever a snob, she believed his intelligence to be a 'physiological freak', given his humble background. But both were genuinely committed to improving the lot of the poor. They married in 1892 and spent their honeymoon researching Irish trade union records.

The Webbs became a celebrated working partnership and collaborated on several influential books together, including the bestselling *The Decay of Capitalist Civilisation*, which for many people captured the interwar mood of fear and impermanence. When in 1894 a wealthy solicitor left the Fabian Society £10,000, Beatrice and Sidney recommended that the money be used to develop a new university in London. The London School of Economics and Political Science (LSE) was founded in 1895. The pair travelled around the world twice, in 1899 and 1911, then in 1913 founded the still-going-strong *New Statesman* magazine.

A great team, then, in all sorts of ways; though for Beatrice it was a different calibre of relationship to the one she had perhaps imagined for herself. The ferocity of Sidney's political passions was what had drawn Beatrice to him initially. But on a romantic level it was less straightforward: 'That other man [Joseph Chamberlain] I loved but did not believe in,' she wrote to Sidney. 'You I believe in but do not love.'[34]

The couple did everything together and were seldom separated for more than a few days. Yet their marriage was reputedly never consummated and their personalities could not have contrasted more strongly. Sidney was quiet, content, optimistic. Beatrice was fretful and morbid, what *New Statesman* editor Kingsley Martin called 'a complex mixture of class superiority, intellectual impatience and puritanical morals'.[35] In their old age they retreated to their country house in Hampshire and held court, the better to enrich their young acolytes. 'All opinions were prefaced "we think" rather than "I",' says historian Richard Overy, 'testament to the extent to which the two minds had over the years grown to work as one.'[36]

Some of the most successful power couples have been unlikely matches. The two politicians who came together in Britain's Second World War coalition government were the oddest of odd couples. Charisma had bypassed the Labour leader Clement Attlee but Churchill had more than enough of it to share round. Churchill gets most of the credit for winning the war, but it was Attlee, brought into the War Cabinet by Churchill, who was what Giles Radice describes as the 'linchpin of the administration', neutralising disagreements and covering for Churchill more than competently during his absences abroad. 'A funny little mouse', Churchill's wife Clementine called him, though it is Churchill's witty summary of Attlee as a 'sheep in sheep's clothing' that has made it into numerous dictionaries of quotations.

Churchill was from an aristocratic political dynasty; Attlee from a south London middle-class family – the seventh child of eight, the son of a solicitor. Attlee was shy but industrious and dependable, while Churchill famously underperformed academically despite an expensive education at Harrow. Their childhoods informed their attitudes, as we might expect. Churchill lived extravagantly and was often on the edge of bankruptcy. Austerity came naturally to Attlee, who preferred to holiday in Frinton rather than in a luxurious villa in the south of France. Churchill believed himself to have been singled out by fate – that he 'walked with destiny'. His successes came as no surprise to him, whereas Attlee was probably as shocked as everyone else when he led Labour to a landslide election victory in 1945, then presided over a radically reforming government that would bequeath us the welfare state and the NHS.

But if Attlee was a mouse, he could still roar when it suited him. It was he who read the riot act to complacent Chamberlain, who saw no reason why he should stand down over his strategy of appeasement: 'Mr Prime Minister, the fact is our party won't come in under you. Our party won't have you and I think I am right in saying that the country won't have you either.' On 10 May 1940, the King asked Churchill to form a government. Attlee knew that he must be a part of that government if Britain was to rebuild itself fairly and effectively. 'I am quite certain,' he wrote, 'that the world that must emerge from this war must be a world attuned to our ideals.'[37]

For this reason Attlee stood firm in May 1940 with Churchill against Foreign Secretary Lord Halifax, who favoured a negotiated peace settlement with Germany. He understood what Churchill was good at – rousing speeches, keeping up morale. Attlee wrote later: 'If somebody asked what exactly Winston did to win the war, I would say, "Talk about it".' It is a reliable truism that the welfare state had its roots in the state planning that got Britain through the war. This came from Attlee and the other Labour ministers who Churchill brought on board – Ernest Bevin as minister of labour and Herbert Morrison as home secretary.

Not everyone liked Attlee. Aneurin Bevan thought he brought 'to the fierce struggle of politics the tepid enthusiasm of a lazy summer afternoon at a cricket match'.[38] But if Attlee was a behind-the-scenes politician, lacking presence and eloquence, he was more dominant than this suggests. He was brisk and efficient – 'we keep to the agenda, make decisions and get away in reasonable time', he said of the meetings he himself chaired – and knew that this set him apart from Churchill, who sometimes coasted on windy rhetoric. On at least one occasion Attlee wrote Churchill a 'stiff memorandum of rebuke, rather like a headmaster chastising the class idler' when Churchill showed a lack of familiarity with papers he was supposed to have read.[39] However, he understood better than others in the Labour Party that Churchill was the ideal wartime prime minister and remained loyal to him even in the darkest moments, when the war was going badly and Tory plotters attempted to depose him. 'What once earned him the reputation of being a reactionary and a warmonger,' Attlee wrote, 'was the same quality that enabled him to save civilisation from the greatest dangers it has ever faced.'[40]

Publication of the Beveridge Report in 1942 was a golden opportunity for Attlee and his left-wing colleagues, whose presence in the wartime Cabinet had helped to establish the party's fitness for power in the minds of voters. They were in favour of the massive changes the report proposed; Churchill dithered: 'He kept, so to speak, pushing the report away from him, because he wanted to get on and win the war,' wrote Attlee.[41]

The alliance fell apart to some degree in the unseemly election campaign afterwards, when Churchill made his notorious comments about the socialist ambitions outlined by Beveridge requiring 'some form of Gestapo' to implement them. A triumphant Attlee responded coolly, conveying the disappointment felt by the whole nation at Churchill's misjudgement. 'I had seen enough of him during the war to be sure that, unless there was a war on, he would not make much of a prime minister,' Attlee wrote later. 'What Britain required when the war was over was an architect, somebody who could build new parts into our society, and repair damage. If he had not been so inveterate a politician, so imbued with political pugnacity, I think he would have seen this.'[42]

Mutual respect remained, however. 'By any reckoning, Winston Churchill was one of the greatest men that history records,' Attlee continued. 'If there were to be a gallery of great Englishmen that could accommodate only a dozen, I would like to see him in. He was brave, gifted, inexhaustible and indomitable.'[43] At Churchill's state funeral in 1965, despite being not far off death himself, Attlee insisted on carrying out his role as one of the pallbearers, stumbling as he carried the lead-lined coffin up the steps of St Paul's Cathedral.

It is fair to say that more recent political power couples have not been so interesting. David Cameron and Nick Clegg, anyone? Much ink was spilled at the time over the tensions between Tony Blair and his fellow New Labour architect Gordon Brown, later chancellor under Blair before becoming prime minister himself. (A lot of it, I must admit, was spilled by me in my then job as a political reporter.) Given everything that has happened since, it is hard to recall all the fuss about their tiffs and temper tantrums – the 'TB–GBs', as they became known; hard to see beyond the opprobrium heaped upon Blair over the Iraq war.

But we must try because those years, 1997–2010, especially the early ones of what was effectively dual premiership, mattered. Thanks to the Blair–Brown partnership, the Labour Party experienced its longest ever period in power. And as with Attlee and Churchill, the duo's very different talents were complementary. Blair was youthful, charismatic, an excellent communicator; Brown was clever, trenchant, obsessive about policy.

The duo's fallings-out could be spectacular. One famous story tells of how Brown told Blair: 'You've stolen my fucking budget', after Blair committed on television to increasing funding for the NHS without telling his chancellor. However by working in tandem they brought peace to Northern Ireland, improved schools and public services and introduced the Working Families Tax Credit to help low-paid families.

Blair tendered his resignation to the Queen on 27 June 2007, paving the way for Brown to have a go at the top job. But the former chancellor's premiership turned out to be what Giles Radice rightly calls 'an epilogue to the New Labour era',[44] coinciding with the global recession and disenchantment with New Labour over Iraq and its aftermath. Brown couldn't connect to the public as Blair had and found it hard to define what he stood for in Blair's absence. Neither man understood properly the secret of their chemistry as a couple. If they had – if, as Radice says, the two men 'had been able to continue to combine as effectively as in the first term' – then their legacy would be much more impressive.[45]

———————————

As I said earlier, the real power today lies less with politicians and more with tech companies like Facebook and Amazon. A recent twist on the power couple is the 'tech philanthropist' couple such as Facebook founder Mark Zuckerberg and his wife Priscilla Chan, who launched the Chan Zuckerberg Initiative (CZI) in 2015, and Bill and Melinda Gates, who have overseen their own foundation together since 2000.

Both have goals so broad and momentous – the CZI wants to 'advance human potential and promote equality in areas such as health, education, scientific research and energy'[46] – that they eclipse the hows and whys. They also make criticism feel mean-spirited. Views like those of Stanford political science professor Rob Reich – who says 'Big Philanthropy is definitionally a plutocratic voice in our democracy, an exercise of power by the wealthy that is unaccountable, non-transparent, donor-directed, perpetual, and tax-subsidized'[47] – are in the minority. You could argue that making a foundation an extension of your identity as a married couple lends it a wholesome, domestic sheen, disarming suspicion. On his own, Mark Zuckerberg struggles to be appealing: he can seem cold and mechanical and odd. Pair him with his wife, however . . .

Whether couple-controlled foundations operate differently is an interesting question because research has shown that couples have distinct patterns of giving. In her book

Why the Wealthy Give: The Culture of Elite Philanthropy, Francie Ostrower found that couples function as a 'distinct unit of donor whose importance varies in different areas of philanthropy'.[48] Philanthropy is often seen by couples as a shared endeavour, one which shapes their self-identification. They tend to give money to areas they associate with themselves as a duo, for example cultural bodies such as museums and orchestras. For many of the donors studied by Ostrower, philanthropy was seen as a joint activity within which, nevertheless, a husband and wife might have 'different, individual philanthropic involvements and interests. This explains the otherwise puzzling fact that many donors regarded all their donations as having been done jointly with a spouse, but also clearly differentiated particular causes and gifts as "belonging" primarily to one member of the couple.'[49]

'Giving together not only allows partners the chance to work on issues they care deeply about, it also provides an opportunity for their relationship to grow,' says the blurb on the website for Rockefeller Philanthropy Advisors, seemingly proving the point. 'Some couples say their joint philanthropy is one of the most meaningful shared experiences in their lives.'

Zuckerberg and Chan announced the creation of CZI, to which they committed to donating 99 per cent of their Facebook shares over their lifetimes, in a joint open letter on Facebook which also served to announce the birth of their daughter Max. Max was framed as an unwitting prime mover. It was for the benefit of her generation, the couple wrote, that the initiative existed.

Based in Seattle, Washington, the Bill and Melinda Gates Foundation was founded in 2000 and is reputed to be the largest private foundation in the world, with around $46.8

billion in assets. Its focus has been on poverty, healthcare – and gender equality, a concern particularly close to Melinda, a committed feminist. In her book *The Moment of Lift: How Empowering Women Changes the World*, she writes that the foundation was so named because she was going to have a big role in running it, greater than Bill's to begin with; though for privacy reasons she decided not to make her role public while their children were small.

The foundation had its roots in a Microsoft project to make technology accessible to girls, motivated by Melinda's experience of gender bias in her own school. But it was also inspired by a trip she and Bill took to Africa in 1993, just before they married, on which they witnessed large-scale suffering caused by problems that would be simple to remedy – for instance, children dying from diarrhoea who could be saved by oral rehydration salts. Their first big investment was in vaccines targeted at the developing world. Their second, prompted by a conversation Melinda had with a mother waiting in line for her child's injection, was in contraception. Their third was in midwives.

The way Melinda tells it, these initiatives were driven largely by her, born of the horrified discovery that 'in societies of deep poverty, women are pushed to the margins'.[50] The way to help everybody and restore health and wealth to communities, is to bring those women into the fold and empower them.

Bill was involved too, of course, but the question of what it means to forge an equal partnership with someone so successful is one Melinda addresses in her book. Clearly, it has involved some delicate conversations about roles. 'We've had to figure out who's good at what,' she writes, 'and then make sure we each do more of that and not challenge each other too much on the things we're not good at. But we've also had to figure out what we're going to do in areas where we're both sure of ourselves and we have opposing convictions.'[51]

────────────

I referred earlier to the distinction political scientists make between hard and soft power. Hard power is aggressive, forceful and coercive. It can take the form of military threats or severe economic sanctions. Soft power, on the other hand, involves diplomacy, civic action, the effecting of subtle shifts in a narrative so that you persuade others to share your desired outcome. Soft power is not necessarily good. It can be propagandistic. As Joseph Nye, who helped pioneer the term, points out: 'Hitler, Stalin and Mao all possessed a great deal of soft power in the eyes of their acolytes, but that did not make it good. It is not necessarily better to twist minds than to twist arms.'[52]

Still, one way of winning people over is by attracting them (or at least making them acquiesce) to an idea which challenges their prejudices and preconceptions. One of my favourite couples, whose legacy I want to conclude this book by considering, have exactly this soft power. It enabled them to transform the wider culture by expanding people's sense of what could and should be. They are Thomas Ernest Boulton and Frederick William Park, better known by their respective drag names 'Stella' and 'Fanny' – two Victorian cross-dressers and suspected homosexuals who appeared as defendants in a celebrated trial in London in 1871, charged 'with conspiring and inciting persons to commit an unnatural offence'.

They did not have power at the time, obviously. They only have it now because they are martyrs to a cause, symbolic figures whose daring and élan makes them irresistibly attractive to us in the twenty-first century. Their joint arrest anticipated that of another, very singular martyr, Oscar Wilde – who was led from the Cadogan Hotel by two detectives on 5 April 1895, an incriminatory 'yellow book' under his arm.

Fanny and Stella are also important because they challenge our lazier assumptions about Victorian society, showing that it was not as trussed-up and repressed when it came to sex as is sometimes suggested. The cultural historian Matthew Sweet has written of Wilde that 'the sexual sensibility he represented – curious, adaptable, versatile – was much more typical of his time than our own'.[53] Victorian sexuality was, he says, 'much less systematised and tribal than our own' and LGBT identities as we understand them today simply did not exist: 'Attempting to apply modern jargon to what went on between nineteenth-century lovers can only yield a limited understanding of how their relationships were constituted.'[54]

Fanny and Stella help us plot a path from there to here. Along the way they give us glorious insights into the history of drag – that is, the exaggeration of female gender signifiers and roles for entertainment purposes. (Historically, most drag queens have been men dressing as women; though obviously this is no longer exclusively the case.)

Boulton ('Stella') and Park ('Fanny') were friends in their early twenties who toured theatres with a drag double act. In their spare time they frequented, in full costume, West End venues such as the Alhambra Theatre and the Burlington Arcade. Stella was the younger of the two, tall and slender with ruby lips. In her scarlet silk evening dress she looked uncannily female, tricking many a straight man who propositioned her. But her most famous lover, Lord Arthur Pelham-Clinton, son of the Duke of Newcastle, knew exactly what he was getting.

Fanny was plainer and less convincing. Her eyes were too small and close-set and her brows too heavy. Frederick William Park was the youngest of twelve children of Judge Alexander Park. Like his friend, Frederick craved the theatrical life, but had been articled by his father to a firm of solicitors in Chelmsford.

On the evening of 28 April 1870, dressed in full female regalia including jewellery, Stella and Fanny entered a private box at the Strand Theatre and started drawing attention to themselves – waving their fans, twirling their handkerchiefs and ogling nearby men. They also 'chirruped' – which is to say, made a sucking noise with their lips. This was a come-on signal used by prostitutes. About half an hour into the show, they left the box to visit the theatre bar, where they knocked back brandies and sherries and enjoyed the attention of the admirers who had gathered around them. Stella, in particular, attracted a lot of male attention, beautiful in her scarlet silk evening gown trimmed with white lace.

'Her pale face was captivating,' writes Neil McKenna in his brilliant book about the pair, *Fanny and Stella*, 'with large liquid violet-blue eyes, just a becoming blush to her cheeks, perfect full ruby lips and pearly white teeth . . . If she was indeed a whore, she was an exceptional whore.'[55]

They stayed in the bar for around half an hour, then Fanny asked one of the pair's gentleman companions, a puppyish fellow called Hugh Mundell, to call a carriage. As they attempted to leave the theatre, they and the hapless

Hugh were swooped upon by police who, unbeknown to Fanny and Stella, had been shadowing them for a while – waiting outside the house they used to get dressed up in. 'I have every reason to believe you are men in female attire,' said the arresting policeman. Fanny was indignant. 'How *dare* you address a Lady in that manner, sir,' she replied.[56]

They were arrested and taken to Bow Street police station where Stella falsely gave her name as Cecil Graham before deciding not to lie and retracting it. (The name was later used knowingly by Oscar Wilde for a character in his society comedy *Lady Windermere's Fan*.) Hugh Mundell told the police he believed Fanny and Stella genuinely were women. Hmm, right.

The police were mostly interested in convicting Fanny and Stella of 'buggery' (and conspiracy to commit buggery) rather than the lesser crime – a mere 'misdemeanour' and as such, McKenna says, a fair cop – of disguising themselves as women and frequenting public places with the intention of outraging public morals. To this end the pair were subjected to intimate examination by a police doctor, one Dr Paul, in order to establish not just that they were men, but whether they had had anal sex. This was strange because usually the police did not care too much about particulars and were happy to release prostitutes from custody in return for bribes or sexual favours.

The court case, held at Westminster Hall in May 1871, was a sensation, attracting massive crowds and plentiful newspaper coverage. Big guns were wheeled out: the judge was the Lord Chief Justice, Sir Alexander Cockburn, and the prosecution was led by the Attorney-General. But the prosecution's witnesses were unreliable, especially Dr Paul, so it was unable to prove either buggery or that the wearing of women's clothing by men was an offence.

The witnesses for the defence were more convincing. Mrs Mary Ann Boulton, Stella's mother, came over well, declaring that she knew of her son's predilection for women's clothes and had even lent him some of her own dresses. 'The *only* fault he ever had was a love of admiration which has been fed by the gross flattery of some very foolish people,' she told the court. By the time she had finished, says McKenna, there was barely a dry eye in the house.

After deliberating for fifty-three minutes the jury found them not guilty. It later emerged that the home secretary himself had encouraged the Attorney-General to prosecute Fanny and Stella. McKenna thinks this is a case of society having 'one of its periodic anxiety attacks' about syphilis, illegitimacy, disease, death, overcrowding and immigration: 'At the same time there was a new approach to sex between men, with the recent invention of the word "homosexual" to describe an identity rather than behaviour and there was a worry about effeminisation, that the masculinity of Britain would be diluted,' he says. 'Fanny and Stella ticked both of those boxes.'[57]

Their acquittal does not represent an instant sea change in attitudes to homosexuality. Other gay scandals were to follow, most notably Oscar Wilde's imprisonment in 1895, before the Wolfenden Report of 1957 led to reforms ten years later that made homosexual acts between consenting adult men legal provided they took place in private.

But Fanny and Stella started the conversation – a conversation which continues to this day, as new questions over sexual and gender identities are debated.

As the author Neil Bartlett, who wrote a play about Stella

in 2016, puts it: 'Every baby comes out of hospital with a whole lot of invisible labels tied to its ankle saying, "You're this gender, you're this colour, you're this class et cetera." And one of the great gifts that the Stellas of the world give us is saying, "Take all these labels off, look at yourself in the mirror and say, who are you?" And it's not just about living your own life, it's about realising that everyone has the right to be themselves and then getting on and doing something about that.'[58]

As with so many of the other couples we have met, *being themselves* was something Fanny and Stella were able to do much more effectively together. Remember Georg Simmel's definition of a dyad – his theory that 'precisely the fact that each of the two knows that he can depend only upon the other and on nobody else, gives the dyad a special consecration'? And his belief that a group of two is 'much more frequently confronted with All or Nothing than is the member of the larger group'?

Fanny and Stella, who spent their adult lives enacting that consecration, might have been custom designed to prove Simmel's point.

Epilogue

About twenty-five years ago, not long after I got my first Fleet Street job on the *Independent*, I developed shingles. Alongside the physical pain caused by the rash came debilitating feelings of anxiety and depression. I count myself fortunate that I was able to take some time off work and move back in with my parents.

Almost the worst thing about it was the insomnia I experienced. I'd lie in my narrow childhood bed, willing myself to doze off, my heart racing and sore eyes aching. The only thing that helped at all was switching the light back on and rereading the Agatha Christie books I'd loved when I was in my early teens. My favourite titles, for reasons I couldn't articulate then – I wasn't firing on all cylinders – were the mysteries involving Hercule Poirot and his stooge-like sidekick Captain Arthur Hastings. There are fewer of these than people think. Hastings appears in twenty-six Poirot short stories, for sure, but only in eight of the thirty-three Poirot novels Christie wrote, starting with *The Mysterious Affair at Styles* in 1920.

Very obviously descended from Sherlock Holmes's companion Dr John Watson, Hastings narrates all the tales in which he features. Yet he's a bit of a blank. In the course of his and Poirot's adventures, we discover a small amount about him: that he attended Eton and was wounded in the First World War; that he is attracted to women with auburn hair; that he marries a performer called Dulcie Duveen and moves with her to Argentina, where they have four children. But Christie gives us little in the way of physical description beyond the vague observation that Hastings has a straight back, broad shoulders and grey hair.

It is Hastings's personality that matters, not his appearance. And his is, on the face of it, easy to mock. He is gullible, earnest, a stickler for correct conduct. Possessing no imagination, Hastings frequently draws the wrong conclusions and lacks the obsessive-compulsiveness from which Poirot draws his ratiocinative power. As Christie's biographer Laura Thompson points out, Poirot's solving of the mysterious affair at Styles Court, for example, is rooted in Poirot's obsession with symmetry – his straightening of a pair of misaligned candlesticks. We know from Hastings himself that this exactitude carries over into Poirot's style of dress: 'The neatness of [Poirot's] attire was almost incredible,' he observes. 'I believe a speck of dust would have caused him more pain than a bullet wound.'[1]

Poirot represents, as he puts it, 'order and method'. His way of looking at the world is unswervingly rigid. But in my favourite Poirot stories, our view of the detective is filtered through Hastings. And Hastings stands for the reader. He represents our brains in 'idle' mode – a setting Poirot's brain doesn't possess. When Hastings half-understands something, or misses the point, that's okay. His point-missing is why he's there – and why it is he's telling the story in the first place. If Poirot told it himself, it would be unreadably dull.

Being given permission to miss the point is incredibly soothing, particularly when you're anxious and unsettled, as I was. So too is the promise of a neat solution to a knotty conundrum. Between them, Poirot and Hastings soothed my racing brain until it was able to function normally again.

Why do they do this so effectively? I think it's because Christie created the duo partly to help explain herself to herself – that Poirot and Hastings represent different aspects of her personality. Don't forget, the Queen of Crime knew exactly what it was to be anxious and unsettled, as her famous eleven-day 'disappearance' in 1926 attests.

Shortly after 9.30 p.m. on 4 December, the then thirty-six-year-old Christie kissed her sleeping seven-year-old daughter Rosalind goodnight before climbing into her Morris Cowley and driving away from the Berkshire home she shared with her first husband, Archie. The police found her car abandoned on the edge of a chalk pit near Guildford. But of Christie herself there was no sign. Rumours circulated that she'd killed herself, or been murdered by Archie – a former First World War pilot who was known to be having an affair with a younger woman.

The police followed a trail of clues that included letters, an expired driving licence and a fur coat. Not until 15 December was Christie finally located – at a spa hotel in Harrogate, where she was staying under the assumed name of Archie's mistress, Teresa Neele. Archie sought to draw a veil over what had happened by claiming amnesia on his wife's part. 'She does not know who she is,' he explained to journalists. 'She has suffered from the most complete loss of memory.'[2] While this wasn't strictly true, Laura Thompson thinks Christie experienced some form of mental breakdown at this time: 'She was in command of herself, to the extent that she could plan and think and function, and yet the self that she commanded was no longer really there.'[3]

Ironically, it was Christie who returned my own self to me in good working order after I'd been ill, by reminding me that books were like perfect friends – capable of supplying strength and succour whenever I needed it. As the literary critic Harold Bloom puts it: 'We read not only because we cannot know enough people, but because friendship is so vulnerable, so likely to diminish or disappear, overcome by space, time, imperfect sympathies, and all the sorrows of familial and passional life.'[4]

People think of reading as a solitary pleasure, but it isn't at all. I wrote in the Introduction that the power of two is a unique, contained bond that generates a particular kind of catalysing spark. For many of us, the strongest dual bond of all is surely the one between reader and author.

There's a famous line spoken by C. S. Lewis in the film *Shadowlands* (though it's not his own work: it was put into his mouth by the screenwriter William Nicholson): 'We read to know we are not alone.' This was true for me, in my sleeplessness, all those years ago. And I suspect it's true for you, wherever and whoever you are.

It takes two. How could it ever not?

Acknowledgements

For love, support and friendship during the frequently fraught period when I was working on this book, thank you to: Matt Baker, Harriet Bell, Rosie Bennett, Simon and Saoko Blendis, Sarah Boyd, Martin Brookes, Louise Casey, Chloe Dalton, Oruj Defoite, Becky Emmett, Federico Escher, Julie Etchingham, Ali Goldsworthy, Julia Goring, Mary-Anne Harrington, Stephen Heath, Arminka Helic, Mathew Horsman, Matthew Hotopf, Rhodri Jones, Nicole Kleeman, Gavin Knott, Emma Clark Lam, William Lam, Liliane Landor, Toby Litt, Joe Luscombe, Hila May, Jo McGrath, Kiran Moodley, Julia and David Newman, Sarah Newman, Alex O'Connell, Anja Popp, Jo Potts, Alice Rawsthorn, Emma Staples, Jane Taylor, Ruth Taylor, Rob Thomson, Maaiysa Valli, Roland Watson, Emily Wilson and Leigh Wilson. Thanks as always to my ITN colleagues, especially my editor Ben De Pear; his deputy Nevine Mabro; the *Channel 4 News* director Martin Collett; my co-presenters Jon Snow, Krishnan Guru-Murthy, Matt Frei, Jackie Long and Fatima Manji; our director of communications Hayley Barlow; and Dorothy Byrne, Ian Katz and Alex Mahon at Channel 4.

A big thanks to my broadcast agents Helen Purvis and Sue Ayton at Knight Ayton Management; my literary agent Antony Topping at Greene & Heaton; my fantastic editor Arabella Pike; Marigold Atkey and everyone at HarperCollins; and Kate Johnson for her face-savingly forensic proofing of the manuscript.

Above all, thanks to my husband John for love and support and to our daughters Scarlett and Molly for being so patient and understanding.

Selected Bibliography

Abbott, Mary, *Power Couples* (Longman, 2003)

Allen, Paul, *Idea Man: A Memoir by the Co-Founder of Microsoft* (Penguin, 2011)

Baez, Joan, *And a Voice to Sing With* (Simon & Schuster, 1987)

Brown, Craig, *Hello Goodbye Hello* (Simon & Schuster, 2011)

Burton, Sarah, *A Double Life: A Biography of Charles and Mary Lamb* (Viking, 2003)

Caldwell, Gail, *Let's Take the Long Way Home* (Random House, 2010)

Chadwick, Whitney, and de Courtivron, Isabelle (eds), *Significant Others: Creativity and Intimate Partnership* (Thames & Hudson, 1993)

Clinton, Hillary, *Living History* (Headline, 2003)

Coleridge-Taylor, Jessie, *Memory Sketch: Genius and Musician* (Crowther, 1943)

Craft, Ellen, and William, *Running a Thousand Miles for Freedom* (1860; LSU, 1999)

Doyle, Tom, *Man on the Run: Paul McCartney in the 1970s* (Polygon, 2014)

Dunn, Jane, *A Very Close Conspiracy: Virginia Woolf and Vanessa Bell* (Cape, 1990)

Dylan, Bob, *Chronicles* (Simon & Schuster, 2004)

Eger, Elizabeth (ed.), *Bluestockings Displayed* (Cambridge University Press, 2013)

Ellis, Clive, *Fabulous Fanny Cradock: TV's Outrageous Queen of Cuisine* (History Press, 2011)

Fenby, Eric, *Delius As I Knew Him* (Quality Press, 1948)

Figes, Kate, *Couples: How We Make Love Last* (Virago, 2010)

Gates, Melinda, *The Moment of Lift: How Empowering Women Changes the World* (Pan Macmillan, 2019)

Green, Jeffrey, *Black Edwardians* (Frank Cass, 1998)

Harvell, Drew, *Sea of Glass: Searching for the Blaschkas' Fragile Legacy in an Ocean at Risk* (University of California Press, 2016)

Hawksley, Lucinda, *Lizzie Siddal: The Tragedy of a Pre-Raphaelite Supermodel* (André Deutsch, 2004)

John-Steiner, Vera, *Creative Collaboration* (Oxford University Press, 2000)

McKenna, Neil, *Fanny and Stella* (Faber, 2013)

Mavor, Elizabeth, *The Ladies of Llangollen: A Study in Romantic Friendship* (Penguin, 1971)

Mitchell, Leslie, *Bulwer Lytton: The Rise and Fall of a Victorian Man of Letters* (Bloomsbury, 2003)

Moore, Gerald, *Am I Too Loud? – Memoirs of an Accompanist* (Macmillan, 1962)

Morris, Jan, *Conundrum* (Faber, 1972)

Newton, Michael, *Savage Girls and Wild Boys: A History of Feral Children* (Faber, 2002)

Powell, Michael, *A Life in Movies* (Mandarin, 1992)

Prose, Francine, *The Lives of the Muses* (HarperCollins, 2002)

Radice, Giles, *Odd Couples* (I. B. Tauris, 2015)

Rees, Goronwy, *St Michael: A History of Marks & Spencer* (Weidenfeld & Nicolson, 1969)

Rose, Phyllis, *Parallel Lives: Five Victorian Marriages* (Vintage, 1984)

Silberman, Steve, *NeuroTribes* (Allen & Unwin, 2015)

Simmel, Georg, *The Sociology of Georg Simmel* (Simon & Schuster, 1950)

Smartt Bell, Madison, *Lavoisier in the Year One* (W. W. Norton, 2010)

Smee, Sebastian, *The Art of Rivalry* (Profile, 2017)

Souhami, Diana, *Greta and Cecil* (1994; Orion, 2000)

Stone, Lawrence, *Uncertain Unions and Broken Lives: Separation and Divorce in England 1660–1857* (Oxford University Press, 1993)

Trott, Laura, and Kenny, Jason, *The Inside Track* (Michael O'Mara, 2016)

Vickers, Hugo, *Loving Garbo: The Story of Greta Garbo, Cecil Beaton and Mercedes de Acosta* (Pimlico, 1995)

Wiseman, Richard, *Whatever Happened to Simon Dee? The Story of a Sixties Star* (Aurum, 2006)

Wright, Lawrence, *Twins: Genes, Environment and the Mystery of Identity* (Weidenfeld & Nicolson, 1997)

Notes

Introduction

1 Daniel Weinbren, *The Open University: A History* (Manchester University Press, 2015), ebook.
2 Ian McEwan, *Atonement* (Cape, 2001), p. 4.
3 Stanley Wasserman and Katherine Faust, *Social Network Analysis: Methods and Applications* (Cambridge University Press, 1994), ebook.
4 Quoted in Jan Lin and Christopher Mele (eds), *The Urban Sociology Reader* (Routledge, 2013), p. 31.
5 Georg Simmel, *The Sociology of Georg Simmel* (Simon & Schuster, 1950), p. 123.
6 Simmel, *Sociology*, p. 124.
7 Simmel, *Sociology*, p. 134.
8 Gwyn Macfarlane, *Howard Florey: The Making of a Great Scientist* (Oxford University Press, 1979).
9 Macfarlane, *Howard Florey*.
10 Quoted in Eric Lax, *The Mould in Dr Florey's Coat* (Little, Brown, 2005).
11 Quoted in Lax, *Mould in Dr Florey's Coat*.
12 Gerald Moore, *Am I Too Loud? – Memoirs of an Accompanist* (Macmillan, 1962).
13 Gerald Moore, speaking on his 1955 album *The Unashamed Accompanist*.
14 Steve Morgan, 'Microsoft Co-Founder Bill Gates Was Caught 45 Years Ago', *Forbes*, 18 February 2016.
15 Paul Allen, *Idea Man: A Memoir by the Co-Founder of Microsoft* (Penguin, 2011), ebook.
16 Allen, *Idea Man*, ebook.
17 Allen, *Idea Man*, ebook.
18 Allen, *Idea Man*, ebook.

19 Walter Isaacson, *Steve Jobs* (Simon & Schuster, 2011), ebook.

20 'Mission statement', *The Economist*, (2 June 2009).

21 Cory Stieg, 'Steve Wozniak: When Apple got "big money" Steve Jobs' personality "changed"', CNBC.com, 6 February 2020.

22 Thomas Carlyle, *On Heroes, Hero-worship and the Heroic in History* (1840; Chapman & Hall, 1869), pp. 3–4.

23 Frank McDonough, 'The Role of the Individual in History', *History Today*, 24 March 1996.

24 Ralph C. Epstein, 'Industrial Invention: Heroic, or Systematic?', *Quarterly Journal of Economics* (Oxford University Press, February 1926).

25 Georgi Plekhanov, *On the Role of the Individual in History* (1898; English translation, Lawrence & Wishart, 1961).

26 Alfred Russel Wallace, *My Life: A Record of Events and Opinions*, Vol. 1 (Dodd, Mead, 1906), p. 361.

27 Robin McKie, 'How Darwin won the evolution race', *Observer*, 22 June 2008.

28 Janet Browne, 'Wallace and Darwin', *Current Biology*, Vol. 23, Issue 24; 16 December 2013, pp. R1070–R1072.

29 Browne, 'Wallace and Darwin'.

30 Virginia Woolf, *Moments of Being* (1972; Delphi Classics, 2017), ebook.

31 Jane Dunn, *A Very Close Conspiracy: Vanessa Bell and Virginia Woolf* (Cape, 1990), p. vii.

32 Woolf, *Moments of Being*, ebook.

33 Dunn, *Very Close Conspiracy*.

34 Quoted in Viviane Forrester, *Virginia Woolf: A Portrait* (Columbia University Press, 2015), p. 126.

35 Quoted in Quentin Bell, *Virginia Woolf*, Vol. 2 (Hogarth Press, 1972), p. 18.

36 Quoted in Dunn, *Very Close Conspiracy*.

37 Quoted in Francine Prose, *The Lives of the Muses* (HarperCollins, 2002).

38 Alastair Macauley, '50 Years Ago, Modernism Was Given a Name: "Agon"', *New York Times*, 25 November 2007.

39 Alicia C. Shepard, 'How an unlikely pair – Woodward and Bernstein – broke Watergate,' *Editor & Publisher*, 17 June 2007.

40 Shepard, 'How an unlikely pair . . . broke Watergate.'

41 Vera John-Steiner, *Creative Collaboration* (Oxford University Press, 2000), p. 6.

42 Matt Apuzzo and David D. Kirkpatrick, 'Covid-19 Changed How the World Does Science, Together', *New York Times*, 1 April 2020.

43 Theresa May, 'Nationalism is no ally in this battle without borders', *The Times*, 6 May 2020.

44 Kate Figes, *Couples: How We Make Love Last* (Virago, 2010), ebook.

Chapter 1 Commitment

1 Stephen Taylor, *The Remarkable Lushington Family: Reformers, Pre-Raphaelites and the Bloomsbury Group* (Rowman & Littlefield, 2020), p. 46.
2 https://www.getsurrey.co.uk/news/surrey-news/ockham-unveils-tribute-escaped-slaves-15138622
3 Ellen and William Craft, *Running a Thousand Miles for Freedom* (1860; LSU, 1999), p. 6.
4 Craft, *Running a Thousand Miles*, p. 16.
5 Craft, *Running a Thousand Miles*, p. 19.
6 Craft, *Running a Thousand Miles*, p. 24.
7 Craft, *Running a Thousand Miles*, p. 25.
8 Craft, *Running a Thousand Miles*, p. 42.
9 Quoted in *Anti-Slavery Advocate*, December 1852.
10 Laura Kipnis, *Against Love: A Polemic* (Pantheon, 2003), p. 73.
11 Kipnis, *Against Love*, p. 75.
12 Quoted in Fiona Brideoake, *The Ladies of Llangollen: Desire, Indeterminacy, and the Legacies of Criticism* (Bucknell University Press, 2017), p. 5.
13 Elizabeth Mavor, *The Ladies of Llangollen: A Study in Romantic Friendship* (Penguin, 1973).
14 Quoted in Olga Kenyon, *800 Years of Women's Letters* (The History Press, 2011), p. 51.
15 Mavor, *Ladies of Llangollen*.
16 Quoted in Eleanor Butler, *Life with the Ladies of Llangollen*, edited by Elizabeth Mayor (Viking, 1984), p. 118.
17 Quoted in Butler, *Life with the Ladies of Llangollen*, p. 90.
18 Mavor, *Ladies of Llangollen*.
19 Quoted in Brideoake, *The Ladies of Llangollen*, p. 28.
20 R. Brimley Johnson (ed.), *The Letters of Lady Louisa Stuart* (Bodley Head, 1926), p. 190.
21 Mavor, *Ladies of Llangollen*, p. xvii.
22 Mavor, *Ladies of Llangollen*.
23 Michel de Montaigne, *Complete Essays* (Allen Lane, 1991), p. 210.
24 Mary Pilkington, *Memoirs of Celebrated Female Characters* (Albion Press, 1804), p. 64.
25 Lisa Moore, 'Something More Tender Still than Friendship: Romantic Friendship in Early-Nineteenth-Century England', *Feminist Studies*, Vol. 18, No. 3; autumn 1992, p. 501.
26 Naomi Shragai, 'Untangling the emotional knots in family businesses', *Financial Times*, 14 December 2016.
27 Shragai, 'Untangling the emotional knots . . .'.
28 'Redstone blasts daughter', *Forbes*, 20 July 2007.

29 Darryn King, 'Giles Martin on his father: "Take a sad song and make it better is what he did"', *Guardian*, 13 July 2016.

30 Quoted in Drew Harvell, *Sea of Glass: Searching for the Blaschkas' Fragile Legacy in an Ocean at Risk* (University of California Press, 2016), p. 49.

31 Harvell, *Sea of Glass*, p. 8.

32 Harvell, *Sea of Glass*, p. 127.

33 Letter to Walter Deane, 23 October 1895, Biodiversity Heritage Library https://www.biodiversitylibrary.org/item/158899#page/2/mode/1up

34 Dr Ursula M. Wilder, 'The Psychology of Espionage', *CIA/Studies in Intelligence*, Vol. 61, No. 2.

35 Wilder, 'The Psychology of Espionage', p. 29.

36 Harry Houghton, *Operation Portland* (Hart-Davis, 1972), p. 112.

37 Shaun Walker, 'The day we discovered our parents were Russian spies', *Guardian*, 7 May 2016.

38 Shaun Walker, 'The Russian spy who posed as a Canadian for more than 20 years', *Guardian*, 23 August 2019.

39 Toby Harnden, 'Meet the real life Mr & Mrs Spy', *Sunday Times*, 24 January 2016.

40 Harnden, 'Meet the real life Mr & Mrs Spy'.

Chapter 2   Communication

1 Oliver Sacks, 'Henry Cavendish: An early case of Asperger's syndrome?', *Neurology*, 9 October 2001.

2 Quoted in Amanda Foreman, *Georgiana, Duchess of Devonshire* (HarperCollins, 1998), p. 293.

3 Russell McCommach, *The Personality of Henry Cavendish* (Springer, 2014), p. 13.

4 Quoted in Jenny Uglow, *The Lunar Men: The Inventors of the Modern World 1730–1810* (Faber, 2011), p. 619.

5 George Wilson, *The Life of Henry Cavendish* (1851; Arno Press, 1975), p. 131.

6 'In what equated to something akin to a "super-sauna", Blagden and his co-experimenters (including a dog) subjected themselves to enormously hot temperatures. Beginning at a modest 100 degrees Fahrenheit (38 degrees Celsius), by the 1775 session they progressed to temperatures upward of a whopping 260 degrees Fahrenheit (127 degrees Celsius). Not surprisingly the air was at times quite literally scorching, and a full cladding of clothing was mostly worn to protect their skin, though Blagden did experiment one time being in the room naked from the waist up with only a suspended cloth protecting him from the rays of

the hot irons.' From https://publicdomainreview.org/collection/experiments-and-observations-in-a-heated-room-1774

7 Steve Silberman, *NeuroTribes* (Allen & Unwin, 2015), ebook.

8 Sir John Barrow, *Sketches of the Royal Society, and Royal Society Club* (John Murray, 1849), p. 5.

9 'Sir Charles Blagden FRS', *Osiris*, Vol. 3 (1937), pp. 69–87.

10 Foreman, *Georgiana, Duchess of Devonshire*, p. 292

11 Wilson, *Life of Henry*.

12 Quoted in Christa Jungnickel and Russell K. McCormmach, *Cavendish: The Experimental Life* (American Philosophical Society, 1996), p. 215.

13 Quoted in James Riddick Partington, *History of Chemistry* (Macmillan, 2016), p. 441.

14 Quoted in Madison Smartt Bell, *Lavoisier in the Year One* (W. W. Norton, 2010), p. 24.

15 Quoted in Louise Grinstein, Rose K. Rose et al, *Women in Chemistry and Physics: A Bibliographic Sourcebook* (Greenwood, 1993), p. 316.

16 Eric Fenby, *Delius As I Knew Him* (Quality Press, 1948), p. 8.

17 Eric Fenby, *Fenby on Delius: Collected Writings on Delius to Mark Eric Fenby's 90th Birthday* (Thames, 1996), p. 30.

18 Fenby, *Delius As I Knew Him*, p. 33.

19 Eric Fenby, *Fenby on Delius*, p. 24.

20 Fenby, *Fenby on Delius*, p. 24.

21 Eric Fenby, *Delius* (Crowell, 1972), p. 84.

22 Fenby, *Delius*, p. 83.

23 Fenby, *Delius As I Knew Him*, p. 52.

24 Prose, *Lives of the Muses*, p. 9.

25 Quoted in Elizabeth Eger (ed.), *Bluestockings Displayed* (Cambridge University Press, 2013), p. 194.

26 Eger (ed.), *Bluestockings Displayed*, p. 198.

27 Quoted in Kate Chisholm, *Wits and Wives: Dr Johnson in the Company of Women* (Random House, 2012), p. 142.

28 Hester Lynch Piozzi, *Autobiography* (Longman, 1861), p. 24.

29 Quoted in Chisholm, *Wits and Wives*, p. 139.

30 Quoted in John Wilson Croker (ed.), *Johnsoniana: Or, Supplement to Boswell: Being Anecdotes and Sayings of Dr Johnson* (Carey and Hart, 1842), p. 108.

31 Hester Lynch Piozzi, *Anecdotes of Samuel Johnson* (1786; Cambridge University Press, 1932), p. 83.

32 Quoted in Chisholm, *Wits and Wives*, p. 147.

33 Quoted in Prose, *Lives of the Muses*.

34 http://www.thrale.com/anecdotes_late_samuel_johnson_hester_lynch_thrale_part_7

35 Hester Thrale, 1 May 1780, http://www.thrale.com/henry_thrales_death

36 Hester Thrale, the Project Gutenberg eBook of Autobiography, Letters and Literary Remains of Mrs. Piozzi (Thrale), 2nd ed., https://www.gutenberg.org/files/15045/15045-h/15045-h.htm

37 Fanny Burney, *Diary and Letters of Madame D'Arblay*, Vol. 2 (Philadelphia: Carey and Hart, 1842), p. 9.

38 Quoted in Noël Riley Fitch, 'The Literate Passion of Anaïs Nin & Henry Miller', in Whitney Chadwick and Isabelle de Courtivron (eds), *Significant Others: Creativity and Intimate Partnership* (Thames & Hudson, 1993), ebook.

39 Anaïs Nin, quoted by Riley Fitch, 'The Literate Passion of Anaïs Nin & Henry Miller'.

40 Henry Miller, letter to Anaïs Nin 07 March 1933, quoted Anaïs Nin, quoted by Fitch, 'The Literate Passion of Anaïs Nin & Henry Miller', in Chadwick and de Courtivron (eds), *Significant Others*.

41 Forms appendix to F. Scott Fitzgerald, *The Beautiful and Damned* (1922; Simon & Schuster, 2020), p. 443.

42 Quoted in A. Hook, *F. Scott Fitzgerald: A Literary Life* (Palgrave Macmillan, 2002), p. 147.

43 Quoted by Lucinda Hawksley, *Lizzie Siddal: The Tragedy of a Pre-Raphaelite Supermodel* (André Deutsch, 2004).

44 Jan Marsh, 'Imagining Elizabeth Siddal', *History Workshop Journal*, Vol. 25, Issue 1, SPRING 1988, p. 64.

45 William Holman Hunt, *Pre-Raphaelitism and the Pre-Raphaelite Brotherhood*, Vol. I (1905).

46 Hawksley, *Lizzie Siddal*, p. 29.

47 Marsh, 'Imagining Elizabeth Siddal', p. 70.

48 John Ruskin, The Works of John Ruskin, XXXVI: pp. 203-4, quoted by Margaret Berg, 'The Artistic Relationship Between John Ruskin and Dante Gabriel Rossetti', PhD thesis 25 July 1979, Linacre College, University of Oxford, p. 109.

49 Alison Flood, 'Elizabeth Siddall: pre-Raphaelites' muse finally gets her own voice, 150 years after death', *Guardian*, 5 September 2018.

Chapter 3   Competitiveness

1 Bob Dylan, *Chronicles* (Simon & Schuster, 2004), p. 254.

2 Dylan, *Chronicles*.

3 Dylan, *Chronicles*.

4 Ian MacDonald, *The People's Music* (Pimlico, 2003), p. 17.

5 Dylan, *Chronicles*, p. 254.

6 Joan Baez, *And a Voice to Sing With* (Simon & Schuster, 1987), p. 91.

7   Quoted in Shelton, *Bob Dylan*, ebook.

8   Baez, *And a Voice*, p. 85.

9   Baez, *And a Voice*, p. 92.

10 Baez, *And a Voice*, p. 97.

11 Baez, *And a Voice*, p. 98.

12 Quoted in Shelton, *Bob Dylan*.

13 Shelton, *Bob Dylan*.

14 Bob Dylan, quoted in documentary, *Joan Baez: How Sweet the Sound*, PBS, 2009.

15 Quoted in Mark Bonner, *Media and Gender Equality* (Scientific e-resources, 2019), p. 235.

16 Martha Gellhorn, *The Face of War* (Grove/Atlantic, 2014), ebook.

17 Quoted in Caroline Moorehead, *Gellhorn: A Twentieth Century Life* (Holt, 2007), ebook.

18 'Venus plays down victory', BBC Sport website (6 July 2000).

19 Cassandra Jardine, 'Margaret Drabble: "It's sad but our feud is beyond repair"', *Daily Telegraph*, 13 July 2011.

20 Jardine, 'Margaret Drabble'.

21 Jardine, 'Margaret Drabble'.

22 Jardine, 'Margaret Drabble'.

23 Joan Fontaine, *No Bed of Roses* (Morrow, 1978), p. 71.

24 Fontaine, *No Bed of Roses*, p. 135.

25 'De Havilland breaks silence on Fontaine feud', *USA Today*, 1 July 2016.

26 Sebastian Smee, *The Art of Rivalry* (Profile, 2017), ebook.

27 'Archive: the story of Lucian Freud's stolen portrait of Francis Bacon', *Daily Telegraph*, 3 January 2011.

28 Quoted in Smee, *Art of Rivalry*.

29 Bruce Bernard and David Dawson, *Freud at Work* (Cape, 2006), p. 15.

30 Bernard and Dawson, *Freud at Work*, p. 17.

31 Smee, *Art of Rivalry*.

32 Quoted in Smee, *Art of Rivalry*.

33 Quoted in Smee, *Art of Rivalry*.

34 Smee, *Art of Rivalry*.

35 Quoted in Pascal Bonafoux, *Van Gogh: The Passionate Eye* (Harry N. Abrams, 1992), p. 142.

36 Quoted in Marjan Sterckx, 'The Invisible "Sculpteuse": Sculptures by Women in the Nineteenth-Century Urban Public Space – London, Paris, Brussels', *Nineteenth Century Art Worldwide*, Vol. 7, Issue 2, autumn 2008.

37 Odile Ayral-Clause, *Camille Claudel: A Life* (Abrams, 2002), p. 71.

38 Quoted in Ayral-Clause, *Camille Claudel: A Life* (Plunkett Lake Press, 2019), ebook.

39 Quoted in Ayral-Clause, *Camille Claudel*.

40 Quoted in *Woman's Art Journal* (Volumes 4–6, 1983).

41 Quoted in Ayral-Clause, *Camille Claudel*.

42 Quoted in Smee, *Art of Rivalry*.

43 Quoted in Francis Frascina, *Pollock and After: The Critical Debate* (Psychology Press, 2000), p. 329.

44 Quoted in Frascina, *Pollock and After*, p. 339.

45 Quoted in Frascina, *Pollock and After*, p. 334.

46 Quoted in Whitney Chadwick and Isabelle de Courtivron (eds), *Significant Others: Creativity and Intimate Partnership* (Thames & Hudson, 1993), ebook.

47 Quoted in Frascina, *Pollock and After*, p. 342.

48 Anne M. Wagner, 'Fictions: Krasner's Presence, Pollack's Absence', in Chadwick and de Courtivron (eds), *Significant Others*.

49 Quoted in Jackson Pollock, *Jackson Pollock: Interviews, Articles and Reviews* (MOMA, 1999), p. 265.

50 Quoted in Frascina, *Pollock and After*, p. 334.

51 Ellen G. Landau, 'Lee Krasner: A Catalogue Raisonné', *Woman's Art Journal*, Vol. 18, No. 2, 1997.

52 Quoted in Sophie Gilbert, 'The Irrepressible Emotion of Lee Krasner', *The Atlantic*, 13 June 2019.

53 Quoted in Mary Gabriel, *Ninth Street Women: Lee Krasner, Elaine de Kooning, Grace Hartigan, Joan Mitchell, and Helen Frankenthaler: Five Painters and the Movement That Changed Modern Art* (Little, Brown, 2018), ebook.

54 Quoted in Sara James, *Making a Living, Making a Life: Work, Meaning and Self-Identity* (Routledge, 2017), ebook.

55 Laura Trott and Jason Kenny, *The Inside Track* (Michael O'Mara, 2016), ebook.

56 Louise Carpenter, 'Laura Trott and Jason Kenny: what it takes to be the golden couple of sport', *The Times*, 12 November 2016.

57 Jonathan McEvoy, 'Decathlon icons! Daley and Hingsen recall an Olympic rivalry that shook the world . . .', *Daily Mail*, 24 July 2012.

Chapter 4   Tension

1 Quoted in Diana Souhami, *Greta and Cecil* (1994; Orion, 2000), ebook.

2 Souhami, *Greta and Cecil*.

3 Quoted in Souhami, *Greta and Cecil*.

4 Clive James, *Somewhere Becoming Rain* (Picador, 2019), p. ix.

5   Cecil Beaton, *Self Portrait with Friends: The Selected Diaries of Cecil Beaton, 1926–1974* (Times Books, 1979), p. 34.

6   Quoted in Souhami, *Greta and Cecil*.

7   Hugo Vickers, *Loving Garbo: The Story of Greta Garbo, Cecil Beaton and Mercedes de Acosta* (Pimlico, 1995), ebook

8   Quoted in Vickers, *Loving Garbo*.

9   Quoted in Vickers, *Loving Garbo*.

10   Souhami, *Greta and Cecil*.

11   Souhami, *Greta and Cecil*.

12   Souhami, *Greta and Cecil*.

13   Quoted in Vickers, *Loving Garbo*.

14   Souhami, *Greta and Cecil*.

15   Souhami, *Greta and Cecil*.

16   Quoted in Souhami, *Greta and Cecil*.

17   Virginia Blain, 'Rosina Bulwer Lytton and the Rage of the Unheard', *Huntington Library Quarterly*, 53.3 (1990), pp. 210–36.

18   Blain, 'Rosina Bulwer Lytton and the Rage of the Unheard'.

19   Blain, 'Rosina Bulwer Lytton and the Rage of the Unheard'.

20   Edward Bulwer Lytton, *The Life, Letters and Literary Remains of Edward Bulwer, Lord Lytton* (1883; Cambridge University Press, 2012), p. 39.

21   Quoted in Leslie Mitchell, *Bulwer Lytton: The Rise and Fall of a Victorian Man of Letters* (Bloomsbury, 2003), p. 29.

22   Bulwer Lytton, *Life, Letters and Literary Remains*.

23   Quoted in Mitchell, *Bulwer Lytton*, p. 24.

24   Quoted in Mitchell, *Bulwer Lytton*, p. 27.

25   Quoted in Mitchell, *Bulwer Lytton*, p. 27.

26   Quoted in Sarah Wise, *Inconvenient People: Lunacy, Liberty, and the Mad-Doctors in Victorian England* (Bodley Head, 2012), ebook.

27   Mitchell, *Bulwer Lytton*, p. 36.

28   Quoted in Mitchell, *Bulwer Lytton*, p. 34.

29   Quoted in Mitchell, *Bulwer Lytton*, p. 38.

30   Quoted in Mitchell, *Bulwer Lytton*, p. 37.

31   Quoted in Mitchell, *Bulwer Lytton*, p. 59.

32   Quoted in Wise, *Inconvenient People*.

33   Quoted in Wise, *Inconvenient People*.

34   Quoted in Mitchell, *Bulwer Lytton*, p. 61.

35   Quoted in Wise, *Inconvenient People*.

36   Quoted in Wise, *Inconvenient People*.

37   Quoted in Mitchell, *Bulwer Lytton*, p. 64.

38   Rosina Bulwer Lytton, *Chevelry: Or, The Man of Honour* (E. Bull, 1839), p. viii.

39   Charlie Higson, 'Half glitzy, half dowdy', *TLS*, 19 February 2019.

40 Clive Ellis, *Fabulous Fanny Cradock: TV's Outrageous Queen of Cuisine* (History Press, 2011), ebook.

41 Ellis, *Fabulous Fanny Cradock*.

42 Ellis, *Fabulous Fanny Cradock*.

43 Ellis, *Fabulous Fanny Cradock*.

44 Ellis, *Fabulous Fanny Cradock*.

45 Ellis, *Fabulous Fanny Cradock*.

46 Quoted in Ellis, *Fabulous Fanny Cradock*.

47 Ellis, *Fabulous Fanny Cradock*.

48 Quoted in Ellis, *Fabulous Fanny Cradock*.

49 Quoted in Ellis, *Fabulous Fanny Cradock*.

50 Quoted in Ellis, *Fabulous Fanny Cradock*.

51 Phyllis Rose, *Parallel Lives: Five Victorian Marriages* (Vintage, 1984).

52 Rose, *Parallel Lives*.

53 Souhami, *Greta and Cecil*.

54 Fred Kaplan, *Thomas Carlyle: A Biography* (Cornell University Press, 1983).

55 Thomas Carlyle, *Reminiscences* (1881; Cambridge University Press, 2012), p. 76.

56 Rose, *Parallel Lives* (Vintage, 1984).

57 Quoted in Simon Heffer, *Moral Desperado: A Life of Thomas Carlyle* (Faber, 2012), ebook.

58 Kenneth Fielding, David Sorensen (eds), *Jane Carlyle: Newly Selected Letters* (Routledge, 2017), ebook.

59 Jane Carlyle, *New Letters and Memorials of Jane Welsh Carlyle* (AMS, 1983), pixxxv.

60 Jane Carlyle, *Newly Selected Letters* (Ashgate, 2004), ebook.

61 Jean Wasko, 'Angel in the Envelope: Letters of Jane Welsh Carlyle', *Modern Language Studies*, Vol. 27, No 3/4, autumn/winter 1997, pp. 3–18.

62 Carlyle, *Newly Selected Letters*.

63 Carlyle, *Newly Selected Letters*.

64 Carlyle, *Newly Selected Letters*.

65 Carlyle, *Newly Selected Letters*.

66 Rose, *Parallel Lives*.

67 Carlyle, *Newly Selected Letters*.

68 Jane Carlyle, *New Letters and Memorials of Jane Welsh Carlyle* (AMS, 1983), p. ix.

69 Quoted in Fred Kaplan, *Thomas Carlyle: A Biography* (Open Road, 2013), ebook.

70 Jane Carlyle, *I Too Am Here: Selections from the Letters of Jane Welsh Carlyle* (Cambridge University Press, 1977), p. 237.

71 Rose, *Parallel Lives*.

72 Quoted in James Anthony Froude, *Thomas Carlyle: A History of His Life in London*, 1834–1881 (1884; Cambridge University Press, 2011), ebook.

73 Carlyle, *Reminiscences*, p. 71.

74 Carlyle, *Reminiscences*, p. 82.

75 Rose, *Parallel Lives*.

76 Quoted in Lawrence Stone, *Broken Lives: Separation and Divorce in England 1660–1857* (Oxford University Press, 1993), p. 120.

77 Lawrence Stone, *Uncertain Unions and Broken Lives: Separation and Divorce in England 1660-1857* (Oxford University Press, 1993), p. 391.

78 Stone, *Broken Lives*, p. 126.

79 Quoted in Stone, *Broken Lives*, p. 126.

80 Stone, *Broken Lives*, p. 131.

81 Stone, *Broken Lives*, p. 132.

82 Stone, *Broken Lives*, p. 133.

Chapter 5   Serendipity

1   Craig Brown, *Hello Goodbye Hello* (Simon & Schuster, 2011), p. xxi.

2   William Boyd, *Armadillo* (Penguin, 1998), ebook.

3   Richard Wiseman, *Whatever Happened to Simon Dee? The Story of a Sixties Star* (Aurum, 2006), p. 95.

4   Wiseman, *Whatever Happened to Simon Dee?*, p. 109.

5   Wiseman, *Whatever Happened to Simon Dee?*, p. 155.

6   'Obituary: Simon Dee', *Guardian*, 30 August 2009.

7   Susanna Reid, 'Piers and me? Those fights aren't just for the cameras', *Daily Mail*, 3 June 2020.

8   Reid, 'Piers and me?'.

9   Simon Hattenstone, 'Stacey Dooley: "Some people don't understand why I'm on TV. But I deserve to be there"', *Guardian*, 29 July 2019.

10 Adam Sisman, *The World's Most Incredible Stories: The Best of Fortean Times* (Avon, 1992), p. 20.

11 Lawrence Wright, *Twins: Genes, Environment and the Mystery of Identity* (Weidenfeld & Nicolson, 1997), p. 33.

12 Wright, *Twins: Genes, Environment*, p. 33.

13 https://www.bbc.co.uk/news/magazine-30933718

14 Wright, *Twins: Genes, Environment*, p. 106.

15 Reverend J. A. L. Singh, *Wolf-Children and Feral Man* (Harper, 1939).

16 Singh, *Wolf-Children*.

17 Singh, *Wolf-Children*.

18 Singh, *Wolf-Children*.

19 Singh, *Wolf-Children*.

20 Michael Newton, *Savage Girls and Wild Boys: A History of Feral Children* (Faber, 2002), p. 185.

21 https://www.businessinsider.sg/andre-the-giant-director-breaks-down-memorable-scenes-2018-4/

22 Quoted in Valerie Eliot (ed.), *The Letters of T. S. Eliot, Vol. 4: 1928–1929* (Faber, 2013).

23 Quoted in T. S. Eliot, *The Poems of T. S. Eliot, Vol. 1: Collected and Uncollected Poems* (Faber, 2015).

24 Quoted in Christopher Ricks, *T. S. Eliot and Prejudice* (University of California Press, 1988), p. 50.

25 Groucho Marx, *The Groucho Letters: Letters From and To Groucho Marx* (Simon & Schuster, 2007), p. 154.

26 Brown, *Hello Goodbye Hello*, p. 318.

27 Marx, *Groucho Letters*, p. 159.

28 Marx, *Groucho Letters*, p. 159.

29 Marx, *Groucho Letters*, p. 163.

30 Quoted in Karen Karbo, 'Friendship: The Laws of Attraction', *Psychology Today*, November 2006.

31 Helen Hanff, *84 Charing Cross Road* (Grossman, 1970).

32 Hanff, *84 Charing Cross Road*.

33 Alice B. Toklas, *What Is Remembered* (Joseph, 1963).

34 Toklas, *What Is Remembered*.

35 Linda Simon, *The Biography of Alice B. Toklas* (University of Nebraska Press, 1991), p. 63.

36 Quoted in Sarah Gristwood, *Vita & Virginia: The Lives and Loves of Virginia Woolf and Vita Sackville-West* (Pavilion, 2018).

37 Quoted in Gristwood, *Vita & Virginia*.

38 Gail Caldwell, *Let's Take The Long Way Home* (Random House, 2010), p. 15.

39 Caldwell, *Let's Take The Long Way Home*, p. 3.

40 Caroline Knapp, *Drinking: A Love Story* (Dial Press, 1996), p. 106.

41 Caldwell, *Let's Take the Long Way Home*.

42 Caldwell, *Let's Take the Long Way Home*.

43 Andrew Godley, 'Enterprise and Culture: Jewish Immigrants in London and New York, 1880–1914', *Journal of Economic History*, Vol. 54, No. 2; June 1994, pp. 430–32.

44 Quoted in K. K. Tse, *Marks & Spencer: Anatomy of Britain's Most Efficiently Managed Company* (Pergamon, 1985), p. 17.

45 Asa Briggs, *Marks & Spencer 1884–1984: A Centenary History* (Octopus, 1984).

46 Goronwy Rees, *St Michael: A History of Marks & Spencer* (Weidenfeld & Nicolson, 1969), p. 10.

47 Quoted in Rees, *St Michael.*

48 Briggs, *Marks & Spencer*, p. 12.

49 Michael Powell, *A Life in Movies* (Mandarin, 1992), p. 302.

50 Powell, *A Life in Movies*, p. 303.

51 Powell, *A Life in Movies.*

52 Powell, *A Life in Movies.*

53 Powell, *A Life in Movies.*

54 Quoted in James Howard, *Michael Powell* (Batsford, 1996), p. 40.

55 Michael Bracewell, *England is Mine: Pop Life in Albion from Wilde to Goldie* (Flamingo, 1997).

56 Quoted in Howard, *Michael Powell*, p. 80.

57 Gerald Moore, *Am I Too Loud?* (Macmillan, 1962).

58 William S. Mann, quoted in 'Obituary: Gerald Moore', *New York Times*, 17 March 1987.

59 Moore, *Am I Too Loud?*

Chapter 6 Love

1 Emily Brontë, *Wuthering Heights* (1847).

2 '8 Love Lessons You Can Learn From Celebrity Crack-ups!', *Glamour*, 6 October 2008.

3 Roy Pickard, *The Hollywood Studios* (Muller, 1978), p. 478.

4 Graydon Carter (ed), *Vanity Fair's Tales of Hollywood: Rebels, Reds, and Graduates and the Wild Stories Behind the Making of 13 Iconic Films* (Penguin, 2008), ebook.

5 Carter (ed), *Vanity Fair's Tales of Hollywood.*

6 Donald Spoto, *A Passion for Life: The Biography of Elizabeth Taylor* (HaperCollins, 1995), p. 213.

7 Carter (ed), *Vanity Fair's Tales of Hollywood.*

8 Kitty Kelley, *Elizabeth Taylor: The Last Star* (Simon & Schuster, 1981), p. 177.

9 Kelley, *Elizabeth Taylor*, p. 177.

10 Carter (ed), *Vanity Fair's Tales of Hollywood.*

11 Kelley, *Elizabeth Taylor*, p. 179.

12 Carter (ed), *Vanity Fair's Tales of Hollywood.*

13 Mary Abbott, *Power Couples* (Longman/Pearson, 2003), p. 206

14 Jeffrey Kluger, *The Sibling Effect: What the Bonds Among Brothers and Sisters Reveal About Us* (Penguin, 2011), ebook.

15 Quoted in Alethea Hayter, *Opium and the Romantic Imagination* (University of California Press, 1968), p. 77.

16 Charles Lamb, *The Works of Charles Lamb* (Moxon, 1848).

17 Quoted in Sarah Burton, *A Double Life: A Biography of Charles and Mary Lamb* (Viking, 2003).

18 Quoted in Burton, *A Double Life*, p. 191.

19 Quoted in Burton, *A Double Life*.

20 Quoted in Burton, *A Double Life*.

21 Burton, *A Double Life*, p. 225.

22 Charles and Mary Lamb, *Tales From Shakespeare* (1807; Penguin, 2007), ebook.

23 Wayne McKenna, *Charles Lamb and the Theatre* (Smythe, 1978), p. 98.

24 Lamb, *Tales From Shakespeare*, ebook.

25 Valerie Sanders, *The Brother–Sister Culture in Nineteenth-Century Literature* (Springer, 2001).

26 Jane Fryer, 'Did Wordsworth find forbidden love in the Lakes?', *Daily Mail*, 20 March 2020.

27 Susan M. Levin, *Dorothy Wordsworth and Romanticism* (McFarland, 2009), p. 25.

28 Jules B. Farber, *James Baldwin: Escape from America, Exile in Provence* (Pelican, 2016), ebook.

29 Farber, *James Baldwin*, ebook.

30 Grant F. Scott (ed.), *Joseph Severn: Letters and Memoirs* (Routledge, 2017), ebook.

31 John Keats, Letter to George and Georgiana Keats, Dec–Jan. 1818–1819.

32 Andrew Motion, *Keats* (Faber, 1997), ebook.

33 John Keats, *So Bright and Delicate: Love Letters and Poems of John Keats to Fanny Brawne* (Penguin Classics, 2009), ebook.

34 Keats, *So Bright and Delicate*.

35 Jeffrey Green, *Black Edwardians* (Frank Cass, 1998).

36 https://www.bl.uk/onlinegallery/features/blackeuro/coleridgehiawatha.html

37 Jessie Coleridge-Taylor, *Memory Sketch: Genius and Musician* (Crowther, 1943), p. 11.

38 Coleridge-Taylor, *Memory Sketch*, p. 11.

39 Coleridge-Taylor, *Memory Sketch*, p. 20.

40 Coleridge-Taylor, *Memory Sketch*, p. 21.

41 Coleridge-Taylor, *Memory Sketch*, p. 23.

42 Coleridge-Taylor, *Memory Sketch*, p. 23.

43 Coleridge-Taylor, *Memory Sketch*, p. 13.

44 Coleridge-Taylor, *Memory Sketch*, p. 13.

45 Avril Coleridge-Taylor, *The Heritage of Samuel Coleridge-Taylor* (Dobson, 1979).

46 Coleridge-Taylor, *Memory Sketch*, p. 37.

47 Coleridge-Taylor, *Memory Sketch*, p. 38.

48 Coleridge-Taylor, *Memory Sketch*, p. 38.

49 https://www.bl.uk/onlinegallery/features/blackeuro/coleridgemusic.html

50 Coleridge-Taylor, *Memory Sketch*.

51 Geoffrey Self, *The Hiawatha Man: Life and Music of Samuel Coleridge-Taylor* (Scholar Press, 1995), p. 100.

52 Coleridge-Taylor, *The Heritage of Samuel Coleridge-Taylor*.

53 Coleridge-Taylor, *Memory Sketch*, p. 60.

54 Press release issued by *Liberty*, 21 September 2005.

55 Lynne Featherstone, *Equal Ever After: The Fight for Same-Sex Marriage – and How I Made it Happen* (Biteback, 2016), ebook.

56 http://www.thedrewittbarlows.com/our-story-so-far/

57 Jan Morris, *Conundrum* (Faber, 1972), ebook.

58 Morris, *Conundrum*.

59 Morris, *Conundrum*.

60 Morris, *Conundrum*.

61 Morris, *Conundrum*.

62 Morris, *Conundrum*.

63 https://www.telegraph.co.uk/news/uknews/2070830/Sex-change-author-Jan-Morris-remarries-wife-she-wed-as-a-man.html

Chapter 7   Power

1 Mary Abbott, *Power Couples* (Longman, 2003), p. 1.

2 F. Scott Fitzgerald, 'What a Handsome Pair!', http://www.gutenberg.net.au/fsf/WHAT-A-HANDSOME-PAIR.html

3 Quoted in Shelley Cobb and Neil Ewen (eds), *First Comes Love* (Bloomsbury, 2015), ebook.

4 Dee L. Clayman, *Berenice II and the Golden Age of Ptolemaic Egypt* (Oxford University Press, 2014), p. 121.

5 Robert P. Watson, *The Presidents' Wives: Reassessing the Office of First Lady* (Lynne Rienner, 2000), p. 97.

6 https://www.masshist.org/digitaladams/archive/doc?id=L17760331aa

7 https://www.telegraph.co.uk/news/2017/05/09/theresa-philip-may-one-show-sweet-screamingly-dull/

8 'Clarke Gayford: realities of being partner to Jacinda Ardern', *New Zealand Herald*, 13 March 2020.

9 Charlotte Lydia Riley, 'How Westminster killed the political wife', *Prospect*, 11 December 2019.

10 https://abcnews.go.com/Politics/jacqueline-kennedys-victorian-views-shocked-grandchildren/story?id=14519045

11 Christopher Andersen, *Those Few Precious Days: The Final Year of Jack with Jackie* (Gallery, 2013), p. 34.

12 Andersen, *Those Few Precious Days*, p. 37.

13 Eleanor Roosevelt, *The Autobiography of Eleanor Roosevelt* (Zed Books, 2018).

14 Roosevelt, *The Autobiography of Eleanor Roosevelt*.

15 Quoted in David Emblidge (ed.), *My Day: The Best of Eleanor Roosevelt's Acclaimed Newspaper Columns 1936–1962* (Da Capo Press, 2001).

16 Hillary Clinton, *Living History* (Headline, 2003), ebook.

17 Clinton, *Living History*.

18 Clinton, *Living History*.

19 William H. Chafe, *Bill and Hillary: The Politics of the Personal* (Farrar, Straus and Giroux, 2012).

20 https://www.theguardian.com/us-news/2019/oct/01/hillary-clinton-gutsiest-thing-shes-ever-done-was-to-stay-in-her-marriage

21 Philip Sherwell, 'Bill and Hillary Clinton: America's Power Couple', *Daily Telegraph*, 9 August 2009.

22 Alexis Petridis, 'The Carters: Everything Is Love review', *Guardian*, 17 June 2018.

23 Oneka LaBennett, '"Beyoncé and Her Husband": Representing Infidelity and Kinship in a Black Marriage', *differences* (Duke University Press, 2018) 29 (2), pp. 154–88.

24 LaBennett, '"Beyoncé and Her Husband"'.

25 Jann Wenner, *Lennon Remembers: The Rolling Stone Interviews* (Penguin, 1971).

26 Quoted in Tom Doyle, *Man on the Run: Paul McCartney in the 1970s* (Polygon, 2014), p. 5.

27 Quoted in Doyle, *Man on the Run*, p. 57.

28 https://www.davidbowie.com/2007/2007/05/18/tonights-high-line-david-bowie-recommends

29 Quoted in Sarah Howgate and Dawn Ades, *Gillian Wearing and Claude Cahun: Behind the Mask, Another Mask* (Princeton University Press, 2017), p. 99.

30 Gavin James Bower, *Claude Cahun: The Soldier With No Name* (Zero Books, 2013).

31 Dora Russell, *The Tamarisk Tree, Vol 2: My School and the Years of War* (Virago, 1980), p. 211.

32 Deborah Gorham, 'Dora and Bertrand Russell and Beacon Hill School', in *Russell: The Journal of Bertrand Russell Studies*, summer 2005, p. 43.

33 Gorham, 'Dora and Bertrand Russell and Beacon Hill School', p. 43.

34 Quoted in Deborah Epstein Nord, *The Apprenticeship of Beatrice Webb* (Springer, 1985), p. 108.

35 Quoted in Richard Overy, *The Morbid Age: Britain Between the Wars* (Allen Lane, 2009), p. 54.

36 Overy, *The Morbid Age*, p. 55.

37 Robert Mackay, *The Test of War: Inside Britain 1939–1945* (Routledge, 2003), p. 54.

38 Quoted in Matthew Parris, *Scorn: The Wittiest and Wickedest Insults in Human History* (Profile, 2016).

39 Simon Schama, *A History of Britain: The Fate of Empire 1776–2000* (2002; Bodley Head, 2009), p. 408.

40 Quoted in Leo McKinstry, *Attlee and Churchill: Allies in War, Adversaries in Peace* (Atlantic, 2019), ebook.

41 Quoted in Peter Stansky, *Churchill: A Profile* (Macmillan, 1973), p. 203.

42 https://winstonchurchill.hillsdale.edu/clement-attlee-part-2/

43 https://winstonchurchill.hillsdale.edu/clement-attlee-part-2/

44 Giles Radice, *Odd Couples* (IB Tauris, 2015), p. 239.

45 Radice, *Odd Couples*, p. 240.

46 Devon Maloney, 'Priscilla Chan and Mark Zuckerberg's 99% pledge is born with strings attached', *Guardian*, 2 December 2015.

47 https://www.theatlantic.com/technology/archive/2018/06/against-philanthropy/563834/

48 Francie Ostrower, *Why the Wealthy Give: The Culture of Elite Philanthropy* (Princeton University Press, 1997), p. 76.

49 Ostrower, *Why the Wealthy Give*, p. 71.

50 Melinda Gates, *The Moment of Lift: How Empowering Women Changes the World* (Pan Macmillan, 2019), p. 50.

51 Gates, *The Moment of Lift*, p. 119.

52 Joseph Nye, *The Future of Power* (Public Affairs, 2011), p. 81.

53 Matthew Sweet, *Inventing the Victorians* (Faber, 2001), p. 197.

54 Sweet, *Inventing the Victorians*, p. 197.

55 Neil McKenna, *Fanny and Stella* (Faber, 2013), p. 4.

56 McKenna, *Fanny and Stella*, p. 7.

57 'Fanny and Stella: The young men who shocked Victorian England', *Daily Express*, February 1, 2013.

58 https://www.anothermag.com/fashion-beauty/8742/celebrating-ernest-stella-boulton-victorian-drag-pioneer

Epilogue

1   Agatha Christie, *The Mysterious Affair at Styles* (1920; HarperCollins, 2020), ebook.

2   Quoted in Andrew Norman, *Agatha Christie: The Disappearing Novelist* (Fonthill, 2017), ebook.

3   Laura Thompson, *Agatha Christie: An English Mystery* (Headline Review, 2007), p. 220.

4   Harold Bloom, *How To Read and Why* (Fourth Estate, 2001), p. 19.

Image Credits

Plate Section 1

Page 1:

Bill Gates and Paul Allen: by Ann E. Yow-Dyson / Getty Images

Virginia Woolf and Vanessa Bell: Archive PL / Alamy Stock Photo

George Balanchine and Igor Stravinsky: Everett Collection Inc / Alamy Stock Photo

Page 2:

William and Ellen Craft: Alpha Stock / Alamy Stock Photo

Lady Eleanor Butler and Miss Ponsonby: Chronicle / Alamy Stock Photo

Glass model of *Chrysaora isosceles*: The Natural History Museum / Alamy Stock Photo

Page 3:

Helen and Peter Kroger: Popperfoto / Contributor / Getty Images

Henry Cavendish: Science History Images / Alamy Stock Photo

Antoine-Laurent Lavoisier: FineArt / Alamy Stock Photo

Page 4:

Ken Russell's *Song of Summer* feat. Christopher Gable as Eric Fenby and Max Adrian as Frederick Delius: Everett Collection Inc / Alamy Stock Photo

Dr Samuel Johnson and Hester Thrale: Engraved by Barlow from a drawing by Cruikshanks, 1791; Mary Evans Picture Library

Page 5:

Dante Gabriel Rossetti's *Beata Beatrix*: Photo 12 / Alamy Stock Photo

Elizabeth Siddal drawing Rossetti, 1853: the Print Collector / Alamy Stock Photo

Page 6:

Joan Baez and Bob Dylan: USIA / Alamy Stock Photo

Martha Gellhorn and Ernest Hemingway: Bettmann / Contributor at Getty Images

Page 7:

The Painter of Sunflowers by Gauguin: Art Library / Alamy Stock Photo

Man in a Red Beret by Vincent van Gogh: Fine Art Images / Heritage Images / Getty Images

Page 8:

Lee Krasner and Jackson Pollock: by Martha Holmes / The LIFE Picture Collection via Getty Images

Laura Trott and Jason Kenny: © Action Plus Sports / Alamy Live

Plate Section 2

Page 1:

Greta Garbo and Cecil Beaton: by George W. Hales / Fox Photos / Hulton Archive / Getty Image

Laurel and Hardy: Allstar Picture Library Ltd. / Alamy Stock Photo

Page 2:

Simon Dee and George Lazenby: ITV / Rex Features

James Lewis and James Spring: Ira Berger / Alamy Stock Photo

Marks & Spencer stall: Heritage Image Partnership Ltd / Alamy Stock Photo

Page 3:

Gertrude Stein and Alice B. Toklas: Granger Historical Picture Archive / Alamy Stock Photo

Moira Shearer in Powell & Pressberger's *Red Shoes*: Photo 12 / Alamy Stock Photo

Page 4:

Elizabeth Taylor and Richard Burton in *Antony & Cleopatra*: AA Film Archive / Alamy Stock Photo

Page 5:

Samuel Coleridge-Taylor with his wife Jessie and daughters Hiawatha and Gwendolyn: Royal School of Music / ArenaPAL

Ruth Williams and Seretse Khama: by Margaret Bourke-White / The LIFE Picture Collection via Getty Images

Page 6:

John F. Kennedy and Jacqueline Bouvier: Bettmann / Contributor / Getty Images

Paul and Linda McCartney: United Archives GmbH / Alamy Stock Photo

Page 7:

Jay-Z and Beyoncé: by Kevin Mazur / Getty Images for Parkwood Entertainment

Page 8:

Frederick Park and Eric Bolton (Fanny and Stella): by Fred Spalding, c.1870 (D/F 269/1/3712), reproduced by courtesy of the Essex Record Office

Claude Cahun and Marcel Moore: unknown photographer, Courtesy of the Jersey Heritage Collections

Index